D0916840

The Man Who Sold the Milky Way

David H. Levy

*

The Man Who Sold the Milky Way
A *Biography of Bart Bok*

The University of Arizona Press
Tucson & London

The University of Arizona Press
Copyright © 1993
Arizona Board of Regents
All Rights Reserved

⊗ This book is printed on acid-free, archival-quality paper.
Manufactured in the United States of America

98 97 96 95 94 93   6 5 4 3 2 1

Library of Congress Cataloging-in-Publication Data

Levy, David H., 1948–
    The man who sold the Milky Way : a biography of Bart Bok / David H. Levy.
        p.   cm.
    Includes bibliographical references and index.
    ISBN 0-8165-1149-7 (alk. paper)
    1. Bok, Bart Jan, 1906–   . 2. Astronomers—United States—Biography.
    I. Title.
    QB36.B63L48   1993   93-4039
    520'.92—dc20   CIP
    [B]

British Library Cataloguing-in-Publication Data
A catalogue record for this book is available from the British Library.

166108

BELMONT UNIVERSITY LIBRARY

QB
36
. B63
L48
1993

AAX-9336

To my mother
Edith Pailet Levy
who encouraged me during this
project's difficult beginnings
and whose patience and love for my father
during his last years
helped me to understand
what Bart and Priscilla must have lived through

Contents

Acknowledgments

This project really began in the fall of 1979 when Peter Jedicke asked me to interview Bart Bok. More than a year later I wrote a piece for *Astronomy* magazine about Bok's seventy-fifth birthday. Richard Berry, former editor of *Astronomy*, was very helpful during the preparation of that article which gave me the idea to do this biography. Judy Stowell encouraged me at the time to start the biography project. She was present at many of the interviews I had with Bart, and later transcribed the interviews and assisted with the bibliography.

During the last eighteen months Mark J. Coco, Arthur A. Hoag, Elizabeth J. Maggio, and Sandy Sheehy have provided painstaking criticism of each chapter of the manuscript. I also wish to thank Leo Enright and an anonymous reviewer for their suggestions, and the University of Arizona Press for their advice over a long period of time. Richard Allen did an exceptional job editing the manuscript for University of Arizona Press. Also, Becky Hume transcribed some of the interview tapes, and Roger Myers of the University of Arizona Library helped with my research in their special collection on Bok.

At various stages of the project's evolution, these people sent helpful correspondence: Tony Buckley, Ignace P. Debono, John Glaspey, John Graham, Keith H. Johnson, W. Noel Keyes, Zdenek Kopal, Beverly T. Lynds, Aden Meinel, Freeman D. Miller, Clifford and Arlene Newman, Richard Price, Constance Sawyer, Ray Weymann, and June Jedicke Zehr.

Myron Cohen, David Crawford, Mary Crawford, Tom Gehrels, Owen Gingerich, Leo Goldberg, Mildred Shapley Matthews, Peter Millman,

Donald McCarthy, Carolyn Cordwell McCarthy, Scott McKinzie, Campbell Wade, Fred Whipple, Ray White, and Frances Wright all provided useful insights through interviews or conversations.

The following people provided helpful suggestions: Jeanine Cockrell, Barbara Colón, Donna Donovan-O'Meara, Elizabeth Doucette, Steve Edberg, Paula Eppstein, David Hartsel, Clifford Holmes, Tim Hunter, Edith Levy, Rick Levy, Gil McLaughlin, Matthew Meier, Jean Mueller, Stephen James O'Meara, Denise Sabatini, James V. Scotti, Eugene Shoemaker, Carolyn Shoemaker, Sabrina Sicuro, Duncan Steel, Robby Stein, and Roy Stowell. I also thank Spencer Weart and the American Institute of Physics for access to David H. DeVorkin's 1978–79 interviews of Bok.

Finally, Bart Bok devoted much time in his last years to the many hours of interviews we had as well as to giving me access to much of his correspondence. I thoroughly enjoyed meeting John Bok and his family, and Joyce Bok Ambruster and her family. They provided me with rare insights into their father's life and were always very supportive.

Preface

IN THE BEGINNING, THERE WAS NO BOK. And the Milky Way was without form, and void. But darkness no longer is upon the face of the deep, for Bart J. Bok has helped explain our galaxy to us.[1]

In the fall of 1979 I was taking my friend Peter Jedicke to the airport when he gave me a piece of paper with a phone number on it. "Your mission," he commanded, "is to telephone Bart Bok and interview him for me." The thought of meeting the great astronomer was terrifying, no less so when I telephoned for an appointment. "This is Bok," he declared. "Be quick!" I arrived with a list of several questions, and asked him the first: "Twenty years ago you began your book *The Astronomer's Universe* with these five words: 'Astronomy is on the move.' How would you react to these words after two decades?"

I never got to ask another question. After an hour I had to rush outside to get an extra tape so that Bart Bok could fill that one as well with his incisive comments on the development of astrophysical research, the refinement of telescope technology, and the role of the amateur astronomer. I had pressed the right button; Bart Bok always loved to talk about astronomy's big picture. In his lifetime of commitment to the Milky Way, Bart J. Bok had seen that picture evolve.

Bok's professional experience began at the University of Leiden and as an assistant in Astronomy at Groningen in the Netherlands. At an IAU meeting he met Harlow Shapley and his career blossomed. In 1929 he became Wilson Fellow in astronomy at Harvard, and he was promoted in 1933 to assistant professor of astronomy at Harvard. In 1946 he became Associate Director of Harvard College Observatory. By 1957 he was Professor of Astronomy at Australian National University, and Director of

Mount Stromlo Observatory. In 1966, he became Head of the Department of Astronomy and Director of Steward Observatory, University of Arizona.

But this is not really Bart Bok—not as I knew him, and certainly not why I have written this book. His research was a major part of his life, but there was much more to him than that. There is a big difference between a scientist like Bok and one who devotes his or her professional life to research and teaching without leaving the public with a feeling for the benefits of that research. For example, at a time when astrology was considered very much an off-limits subject for reputable scientists, Bok helped persuade the scientific community to take a stand against it. The public, he felt, had the right and the responsibility to know the difference between the art and science of the universe and the charlatan practices of the astrologers.

Bart Bok was as enthusiastic about informing people about the Milky Way as he was about his own research concerning it. "Scientists have a role in public education that cannot be filled by planetarium people," he maintained. "The astronomer is involved every day with his own research, and he knows its developments intimately. The public ought to be able to share in this." Bart and I discussed this point at length. He explained that astronomy educators have a role that is generalized. Their job, to alert people to appreciate the presence of a universe out there, must be augmented by the astronomer who paints the details, using all the excitement of firsthand acquaintance. In support of this, Bart Bok had an extensive public lecture program. While he was director of Australia's Mt. Stromlo Observatory, he lectured to schools and the public about astronomy. He was in great demand. Later in Arizona, he lectured extensively to diverse groups, including prisoners. These lectures he took as seriously as his professional work.

Bart had a silly side. As mail frequently arrived addressed to "Bart J. Bok, A. A., O. A. P." the postman wanted to know what the initials stand for. "After all, you are a great astronomer, and these letters must refer to some major honor you have received."

"Yes, yes," joked Bok, "the A. A. (for Alcoholics Anonymous) means that I enjoy my sherry, and the O. A. P. means that since I've retired I am an old age pensioner with no income worth speaking of!"

This book has been in preparation for a decade. At first Bart opposed the idea of a biography. But the notion intrigued him: "If I ever change my mind," he allowed, "you would be the one I would want to write it." I prepared a proposal detailing the conditions under which the biography would be written and how the interviews would proceed.

Between October 1982 and August 1983, I interviewed Bart over fifty times. "This is your book," he told me, "and you should be as nasty as you wish." We were both aware that biographies gain by showing a person's full spectrum, not just a narrow band. Nasty, perhaps, but that side of Bok, properly told, presents a fuller picture of an enigmatic personality. The long delay since Bart's death in 1983 has allowed me to complete this project with a more detached eye. However, although I have tried to be objective in portraying Bok's adventures and ideas, I state at the outset that I developed a great admiration and respect for my subject. It is my hope that through this narrative, readers will enjoy and understand what it was like to be an astronomer in the complex time of Bart J. Bok.

1

*

Beginnings

Imagine a group of boy scout patrol leaders camping by fireside in Holland under a dark, moonless night. Their supervisor is testing their knowledge of the constellations, and while their level of awareness varies, it is obvious that one twelve-year-old patrol leader knows much less than anyone else. His name is Bart Jan Bok, and he blushes as his supervisor teases him:

"Now look at Patrol Leader Bok, with his patrol at night as they sit around the campfire, and it's a beautiful night out and the Milky Way is out and all the stars are there. And one of the little boys says, 'Patrol Leader Bok, what is that star?' Well, Patrol Leader Bok can't answer; so he takes a log and puts it into the boy's mouth, and shuts him up for a while. What a picture! At the end of the evening, when everybody should be learning about the stars, Patrol Leader Bok has eight little boy scouts sitting around the fire with logs in their mouths."

The twelve-year-old was so humiliated by his superior's teasing that he immediately set about to learn the constellations. That fireside scolding would lead to a lifelong romance with the night sky, and a career of observing, studying, and selling the Milky Way.

Just as the Earth revolves about the Sun in one year, it also whirls around the center of our galaxy in 220 million years. Thus in the town of Hoorn in North Holland, on the Zuider Zee's western shore, Bartholomeus Jan Bok was born on April 28, 1906, four ten-millionths of a galactic year ago. Bok's long first name, a variation on Bartholemew, lasted until he became a U.S. citizen in 1938, when it legally changed to Bart.

"I was a nice pretty baby," he insists his mother assured him, "and I behaved myself and didn't make a spectacle."

The family lived in Hoorn for only nine months before his father, Jan Bok, a Sergeant Major in the Dutch army, was transferred to military quarters in Haarlem, a town near Amsterdam and less than five miles from the shore of the North Sea. The capital of North Holland, Haarlem was a quiet place of winding streets and old Gothic buildings that disguised its past memories of a Spanish siege in 1572 which ended with a massacre of many of its citizens.

One of Bart's earliest memories was that of a large parade to celebrate the tulip season in spring. To give Bart and his younger brother a good view of the parade which would pass through a tunnel underneath Haarlem's railroad station, his mother ingeniously bought a railway ticket that allowed them on the platform, ostensibly to await the next train. "We could sit down at the railway station, while parade viewers elsewhere along the route had to stand up. No one else was at the railroad station. No one else had thought of that." Each time Bart returned to his birthplace in later years he returned to the same bench to relive that fond early memory.

As a young child Bart was cared for by a maid he called Sister Droste. "She was my heroine," Bart remembered. "I loved her dearly. I remember sitting on her bike and feeling on top of the heap, like a three-year-old would." A small story illustrates both his respect for her and his early stubbornness. When she chided Bart one day for not washing his eyes, he was so impressed that he went to the sink and washed them continuously. "Sister Droste told me to wash them, and I will," he asserted when his mother tried to get him to stop.

Around 1911 the Boks moved to an apartment in Haarlem, not far from the River Spaarne, living near an old mill in this beautiful region until the end of the war in 1919.

Bart went to Nassau Laan, a small primary school in Haarlem. "I was a teacher's pet type of student who looked smart and felt proud," Bart reminisced about those elementary school years. Nassau Laan emphasized academics over recreation. Languages did not receive much emphasis, with French, starting in fourth grade, being the only foreign language Bart learned. Though the school offered almost no athletics—Bart got his exercise from the Boy Scouts—he loved the academic challenge. "They worked us hard, but I didn't mind. I think I profited from it because I wanted to learn and there always was competent leadership." Although the school had an accelerated program for its best students, it did not offer it to Bart, who it felt was a somewhat overconfident child. As he remembered it, the school did not want him "to move too fast for his own good."

Bart Bok was as excited as anyone by the end of the "war to end all wars" in 1918. But the coming of peace meant another move for Bart's family just as he was starting high school. After just one year at City High School in Haarlem, where he started courses in English and German, his father was transferred to The Hague. Still Sergeant Major, he was now one of the early presidents of the Dutch labor union, a somewhat incongruous achievement for a military man.

His new school, Waldeck-Pyrmont Kade, had first-rate mathematicians and physicists, some of whom had doctorates; one even left later to assume an Oxford professorship. Grading and exams at this school could be tough and intimidating. Bok never forgot the harsh grading system of his physics teacher, Dr. Mulders, who impressed on the youngsters that he would grade from 0 to 10. However, he warned: "No one is worth a 10. No one is worth a 9. Only I am worth an 8. You boys and girls start at 7." When Bok returned to Groningen almost sixty years later to give a colloquium, a much older but still robust Mulders appeared in the audience and accosted Bok afterwards: "Good colloquium, Bart—7 plus!"

The final exams consisted of rigorous half-hour conversations between the student and the teacher, and the meeting was often overseen by a university professor. For one exam the student was expected to come prepared to discuss some twenty literary pieces in each language studied. Bok recalls how they were careful to test whether the books had been read in their original languages or in Dutch translation. For example, a literal translation into Dutch of the title of Baroness Orczy's *The Scarlet Pimpernel*, Bart's favorite tale of a band of Englishmen trying to rescue victims of the French Revolution's reign of terror, would be "The Red Pimpernel." It was an easy giveaway that the student had not read the original.

It was in The Hague that Bok, at age twelve, joined the Boy Scouts and his interest in astronomy got its start. Among his earliest books was a German version of Simon Newcomb's *Astronomy*, a classic which he received from his uncle when he first entered high school. It contained a section that introduced Bok to the work of Harlow Shapley, a famous American astronomer.

As he undertook to learn the constellations, Bart's maternal grand-mother told him stories about his late grandfather's interest in the stars, and a trip to the attic uncovered some introductory books. An attaché in the Dutch army, Bart's inventive grandfather had commanded a small torpedo boat, and had even made a hand grenade which Bart prized and kept throughout his life as a souvenir. Bart's grandfather had been curious enough about astronomy to make several visits to the observatory in Leiden University and get to know its chief mechanic, a friendship Bart would appreciate when he later became a student there. Some of Bart's earliest astronomical reading came from the books his grandfather owned. Gustav Kirchhoff, who around 1859 had established the basic principles of spectroscopy, was virtually a hero to Bart's grandfather.[1]

Although Bart's father had an amateur astronomer friend or two, he did not specifically encourage Bart's interest in science: "No one in his right wits," he stressed, "would select astronomy as his career. It might be beautiful as a hobby, but not as a career, because you will never be able to earn a living."[2] But a prominent astronomy magazine named *Hemel en Dampkring* (Heaven and Atmosphere) had a much greater impact on Bart's future than his father's words did. Since he could not afford a subscription, he arranged to write a column for the local news-paper *Bloemen nen Boomen* about astronomical events in return for a sub-scription.

In his high school's healthy intellectual environment Bart quickly ad-vanced to a course in cosmography, the study of the form of the universe. But it was through the famous astronomer Jacobus Cornelius Kapteyn's articles in *Hemel en Dampkring* that Bart first learned about our place in the galaxy in which we live. Kapteyn was convinced we were near the center of our galaxy, and he ridiculed the arguments of the young American astronomer Harlow Shapley, who suggested that we live at its out-skirts. Bok was enthralled by this debate, which provided considerable grist for his column as his high school years ended and his time at Leiden University approached.

Bart never forgot the richness of his high school years. Years later he even wondered whether, had he stayed in the Netherlands, he might have become a high school teacher or principal instead of an astronomer. His father would have wanted that for his son; he thought that being a high school principal in The Hague was a higher honor than a full professorship at Harvard. But Bart's success at high school earned him a City of The Hague thousand guilder-a-year university fellowship.

The city took care of its brightest students; as part of the program each student was assigned a prominent citizen as an advisor. Bart had a mentor named Cornelius Lely, now well known as the father of the Zuider Zee's Ijsselmeer Dam project, which by its completion in 1932 built a dike across the mouth of the Zuider Zee and provided vast amounts of new land.[3] Bok visited this important man every two months with a progress report on his own young career. Blessed with good health, a lively intellect, and the encouragement of his family, teachers, and advisor, Bart ended his high school years strongly prepared to launch a career in astronomy.[4]

2 ✳

Leiden University

When Bok began his freshman year in 1924, the University at Leiden, centerpiece of an ancient city in Western Holland, was an exhilarating place. It had been founded by William of Orange in 1575, allegedly to reward the citizens of Leiden for their brave defense of the city against Spain. Offered the choice of major tax exemptions or the beginning of a new university, the story goes, the citizens chose a university. By this century it was one of the great universities in Europe, including among its visiting scientists the physicists Erwin Schrödinger, Werner Heisenberg, and James Franck, the university offered its students a fertile environment for learning in the sciences. The director of the astronomy department, Willem de Sitter, was an eminent cosmologist whose work led to the modern concept of a Big Bang universe that expands without end.

But a great university can be overwhelming to a new student on his first day. Trying to make sense of what Leiden had to offer, Bok looked around to see if there were clubs or groups of students who shared his interests. The Bok family was not rich enough to allow him membership in the university fraternity frequented by the wealthier students. Exclusion from this social circle, however, led Bok to an early encounter with another to-be-famous astronomer with whom he would have a long, complex, and competitive friendship. Before classes began at Leiden, with the other students busy with fraternity activities and having idle time to fill, Bok explored the physics reading room. There he encountered a tall young man fingering through the catalogue in search of astronomy books. The man was Gerard P. Kuiper, also starting his first-year studies. Bok was surprised and happy to meet Kuiper, for he had thought he was the only new student admitted into astronomy that year. To admit more than one new student at a time was unusual for Leiden's astronomy department, which typically enrolled only one new astronomy student every three years.

Bok began to talk excitedly about his interest in the Milky Way Galaxy. Looking back at him quizzically, in a ploy that would characterize their relationship in later years, Kuiper one-upped him: "Oh, that's a very interesting *minor* field. My interests are much broader!" Kuiper then went on to rave about his pursuits in the solar system.

Later on that semester, Bok and Kuiper found out about an informal society called the Huygens group that met several times each month during the school year. Consisting of people from the university's astronomy and physics communities, its purpose was to share recent astronomical news and ideas through short presentations given by staff and students. "I sat in the first chair," Bok says, "and wanted to tell all the boys how important the Shapley work is."

More than any other person, Harlow Shapley was the reason Bok was going into astronomy. This man Shapley, Bok would explain, was redrawing our notions of where we are: no longer enjoying squatter's rights in the center of the galaxy, the Earth and Sun were now outcasts at the galaxy's edge. Shapley arrived at this conclusion by observing the huge swarms of distant suns we know as globular clusters. Using the Cepheid variable stars that are in these clusters, and a distance-luminosity relationship he devised with Henrietta Leavitt, Shapley could determine how far these clusters were from the Sun. Ranging from 22,000 to 185,000 light years, these clusters surround the galaxy almost as a halo, allowing Shapley to outline the shape of the galaxy as well our place far from its center.

From professors like Jan Oort, Willem de Sitter, and Ejnar Hertzsprung, Leiden provided Bok with an excellent education both in the classroom and in more informal exchanges. All the new students were assigned physicist Jan Woltjier as their instructor; although he was a genius in many areas of theoretical physics, his special interests at the end of 1924 were Cepheid variables and the work of Sir Arthur Eddington on the interiors of the stars. It was Woltjier who first introduced Bok to Eddington's ideas on what elements are found inside stars.

Bok remembered Woltjier as brilliant, "always thinking hard, working hard, doing, talking with you about it but never writing it down. The result is that people don't know now that Woltjier ever existed."

In 1926, Arthur Stanley Eddington published *The Internal Constitution of the Stars*, a book that turned astronomy inside out.[1] Opening up the field of modern stellar physics, Eddington's book turned the stars into real places by revealing their secrets. "It was Eddington who brought it all to life," wrote E. A. Milne, "infusing it with his sense of real physics and endowing it with aspects of splendid beauty."[2] After some speculation as to who would be given the honor of writing a review of this book for the prestigious British journal *Observatory*, Bok was delighted that it came to his own professor Woltjier. This brought Eddington's work directly to Leiden, introducing Bok to it in a personal way that would grow over time. Although Bok would actually meet Eddington in 1928, his first insightful impression of the great physicist would not occur until several years later during a conversation in Harlow Shapley's drawing room that included Ernst Opik, an astronomer with a broad interest in many aspects of the science. Opik had proposed that the universe, instead of expanding forever, as de Sitter had suggested, was alternately expanding and contracting, a proposal far ahead of its time. This night's conversation, however, was far from universes, and much closer to home. Opik was suggesting that the orbits of some meteoroids, tiny objects that occasionally enter Earth's atmosphere as meteors, could bring them from outside the solar system. He based this unusual conclusion, that their orbits were in fact hyperbolic, on an extensive series of observations of meteor velocities.

"Eddington sat," Bok remembered fondly, "in one of those big chairs in Shapley's drawing room and puffed a pipe. Opik came forth and everybody asked questions. Finally, Harlow Shapley got annoyed, looked at Eddington, and said: 'Arthur, you have sat all night in that chair, puffed your damn pipe and said nothing. Why don't you make a comment?' Eddington took the pipe hesitatingly out of his mouth; looked to the left, looked to the right, took one more little puff, and said, 'I would rather believe in ghosts than in hyperbolic meteors.' That was the end, the only comment the great Sir Arthur Eddington made that night."[3]

From the start of his university days in 1924, Bok had a friend and mentor in Paul Ehrenfest, a professor in theoretical physics. A difficult man to know, this Vienna-born physicist had been appointed to Leiden fourteen years before Bok's arrival. Ehrenfest had a considerable impact on the young Bok, although Bok never actually took a course from the great quantum physicist. Ehrenfest delighted in challenging his best students during forums known as "Ehrenfest colloquia" in which animated exchanges were encouraged among students who had been asked to present papers. When Bok was in his junior year, Ehrenfest assigned him to lead a colloquium on the famous Eddington book. Since its German edition was still several months away from publication, Bok would have to use the English version, a language with which he was not yet comfortable.

When the evening came for the colloquium, Bok learned that a distinguished physicist, Hendrik A. Kramers, as well as an English speaking visitor, were in the audience.[4] In fact most of the audience would be physicists, not astronomers. Worse, Ehrenfest wished to know if Bok would be good enough to give the entire colloquium in English for the benefit of that lone English-speaking guest!

No sooner had Bok begun than Kramers attacked, but not on questions relating directly to Eddington! Why, he demanded of the nineteen-year-old undergraduate, should stars be hot inside, rather than cold? "If Mr. Bok knows a single reason why stars should be hot," Bok recalls Kramers's words, "will he please explain it to me?" As if that were not enough, another physicist interrupted Bok's later discussion of magnitudes: why does a star get a larger number, he wanted to know, when it gets fainter? (The centuries-old system of magnitudes is set up so that a star of magnitude 2 is 2.5 times fainter than a star of magnitude 1, and so on.) Bok was being initiated. Although the magnitude system seems reversed when first introduced, even children get used to it quickly. "They had a fine time razzing a young little boy who was boosted by Ehrenfest," Bok felt.[5]

By this time, Woltjier and Oort had introduced the undergraduate students to a type of star that moves as fast as 130 kilometers per second relative to the Sun, more than four times the velocity of typical stars. Virtually all of these fast-moving stars appear to move in the direction from Auriga to the Carina and Sagittarius and Scorpius regions. These stars were important, Woltjier thought, because they could provide a clue to the galaxy's behavior as it rotates. Many of these stars—some 600 are known today—are RR Lyrae-type variable stars, present in a somewhat flattened cloud relatively close to the galactic center. Just as the large outer planets in our solar system, especially Jupiter and Saturn, are flattened instead of spherical because of their rapid rotations, the flattening of the cloud of high velocity RR Lyrae stars suggested that the entire galaxy might rotate in a similar manner.

In 1924 Bok and his fellow first-year students were sitting in Jan Oort's class as the great professor worked out a new theory to explain the rotation of the galaxy. One of the course lectures dealt with the concept of the rotation of our galaxy about its center. The one accepted theory at the time was that of Bertil Lindblad, who stated that the high velocity stars were arranged in somewhat independent groups, each with its own velocity around the center of the galaxy. Our Sun, along with the large number of stars with velocities less than 30 kilometers per second relative to it, actually revolves around the galactic center the fastest, while stars like the RR Lyrae group move more slowly.[6]

It was during this course that Oort was trying to understand Lindblad's theory, but found that he was unsuccessful. He would try to lecture on Lindblad's work, then would stop, claiming that he was "bogged down" and not fully comfortable with it.

Finally Oort worked it out. The galaxy could not be thought of as a solid pinwheel. Just as the innermost planets revolve more quickly around the Sun than do the outer ones, stars closer to the galactic center revolve around it more quickly than do the stars near the edge.[7] Some now think that our Sun, at about 8,500 parsecs from the center of the galaxy,[8] revolves around it at about 220 kilometers per second.[9] Oort, who died in 1992, is now recognized with Lindblad as having established the fact that our galaxy does rotate.

Bok became entranced with Oort's ideas, preferring his work on high-velocity stars and galactic rotation over the lectures of Ejnar Hertzsprung, under whom the other students were quite happy.[10] Bok admitted to being somewhat "scared" of Hertzsprung because of what he saw as Hertzsprung's total preoccupation with having his students scan photographic plates in hopes of discovering variable stars. "He'll give each of these young upstarts," Bok recalled thinking at the time, "a pile of one hundred photographs." (By scanning photographic plates of the same region taken at different times, students could detect stars that had changed in brightness.) Not interested in what he thought was tedious work, Bok chose to stay with Oort and his work on galactic rotation.[11] (Years later, Bok's own students would make similar comments about his predilection for having them make endless counts of stars to determine how stars are distributed in the galaxy.)

Eclipse of the Sun

Bok's first comprehensive examination, the Candidaat, occurred at the end of his third year, in 1927. He had already completed his difficult courses in math, physics, and astronomy, and after a less strenuous year with easier courses, had then prepared for the all-inclusive Candidaat. This exam was intended to follow three years of intense course work, a series of tentative exams, and a fourth year devoted to preparation for it. Both Kuiper and Bok thought that this fourth year was unnecessary. "We thought we were really damn fools to waste that year. We wanted to get onto some big research project." After only six weeks they approached the dean for permission to take the exam early. Both men were quite confident that they would do just fine in every subject, with the possible exception of mathematics, and since, as a rule, students did not fail these exams, they were confident of their plan's success.

But Bok almost failed. He took the exam first and did well in astronomy and physics but poorly in algebra, tripping up on the rarely used concept of semi-convergent series in which one begins with the first of an infinite series of terms, takes the sum of the series, then goes to the second and retakes the sum, and so on. The more totals that are taken, the closer they approximate a definite mathematical limit.

After an anxious wait he heard his dean's words. "Well, my dear Bok," the dean said, "I'll pass you. But when another astronomer comes as poorly prepared in algebra as you are I am going to flunk him." This was fine for Bok, of course; he would pass. "But two weeks later," Bok went on, "Kuiper came and flunked."

Third-year examinations taken care of, Kuiper (who had by now also passed after retaking the exam), Bok, and a third student named Gorter (later to become director of Leiden's low-temperature lab) decided to bicycle to Norway to see an eclipse of the Sun. The trip took place in the middle of an especially important time of life, right after a major examination and before graduate school choices would have to be made. Besides having little money, the three were expected to enlist in the Dutch army for three months that same summer. However, Bok's academic success won him an exemption from military service for one summer so that he could travel to see the eclipse. Kuiper had not started his service; according to Bok he objected to it on moral grounds, and in any event both men felt that with the end of the war there would soon not be a soldier left in Europe.

After adding a fourth member, geologist Carl van Rijsinge, the quartet set out on their adventure with tents, cookery, and sundries all packed on their bicycles, and with no hotel reservations. Their bicycles carried them on a extensive journey. From Holland they entered Germany, where they visited Bremen and Hamburg before heading through Denmark and past Hamlet's castle at Elsinore. They crossed into Sweden to see Copenhagen and the Böhr Institute, and then went on through Göteborg and into Norway. From Oslo they pedaled to the northwest over mountain passes and finally, by the end of June, arrived at the Hallingdal River in time for the eclipse.

Those who have been in the path of a total eclipse are moved by the spectacle whether it is cloudy or not. The effect of the Moon's onrushing shadow causes such dramatic changes in the sky and the landscape that even moderately thick clouds cannot ruin its impact. Especially for someone viewing an eclipse for the first time, these effects clearly give the impression of the observer's being an active participant in the precise alignment of Sun, Earth, and Moon. To prepare for this eclipse, Kuiper and Bok designed a simple experiment to determine the true color of the Sun's tenuous outer atmosphere or corona by shining lights on disks of different colors and comparing the results with their visual observations of the corona. The test was to have been set up so that the lights pointed away from the observers in order not to disrupt their observing of the corona, and they did find some power source to illuminate the disks with a dim, flat, neutral light. (Three decades later, Kuiper would use this technique again for visual estimates of surface colors on Mars.)

Although thick clouds prevented the group from seeing the eclipse and trying their experiment, the trio observed the rapidly darkening sky as the valley plunged into the Moon's shadow. "The shadow of the Moon came very quickly over and we saw the darkness quickly approaching across the snow on the mountains. That was the most glorious sight."

After this extraordinary event the quartet continued across the mountains to some fjords. By the time they arrived at Bergen, on Norway's west coast, they were so exhausted that they loaded their bicycles onto the famous Bergen-Oslo train and enjoyed the spectacular mountain scenery from a more relaxed perspective. In the trip's final phase they continued by ferry back to the German island of Rügen, and then by bike back to Holland.

Groningen and Graduate Work

By the end of that summer of 1927, it had become clear that Bok's military service would be delayed indefinitely. On his return from Hallingdal he found a letter from Pieter van Rhijn, one of the country's best-known astronomers, at the Kapteyn Lab at Groningen University. Inside was an invitation to complete his graduate studies in Groningen under the Kapteyn Assistantship, a major honor named to commemorate the great astronomer Jacobus Cornelius Kapteyn (1851–1922) who believed that the Earth and the solar system were in the center of the galaxy (see chapter 1). Not only was the Kapteyn the most distinguished assistantship available to an astronomy student in Holland, but it was also the most highly remunerative. Three such awards were made, valued at eighteen hundred guilders each, two at Leiden and one with van Rhijn at Groningen. However, at Leiden de Sitter had split the two awards into three, each worth twelve hundred guilders. Thus van Rhijn's single recipient was the most fortunate in all Holland. "I felt like a real big shot for the first time in my life," Bok recalled.

But before accepting this assistantship, Bok had to visit his old advisor Lely, who was administering his City of The Hague scholarship. Although this fellowship, which was putting him through Leiden, was still active, Bok wished to end it, explaining to Lely that he could not pass up the opportunity to work with van Rhijn. Lely countered that if Bok stayed at Leiden with his five-year scholarship from the City of The Hague, he would be completely free to pursue his own line of research and to begin work on his doctorate. As an assistant, Lely continued, he would be under someone else's direction.

His mind made up as usual, Bok could not be persuaded to stay. Lely gave him his blessing, adding that he had wanted to make sure that Bok was serious about his intentions. In the fall of 1927 he moved to Groningen to begin his graduate studies under van Rhijn.

At Groningen, Bok joined in van Rhijn's work on the structure of the galaxy. It was part of a procession of galactic research; in the late eighteenth century, William Herschel's simple but vital counts of stars in regions of the sky were an effective beginning to understanding how stars are distributed. Then in 1904 Kapteyn discovered that stars do not move randomly through space.[12] Van Rhijn's and Bok's work at Groningen studied how stars are distributed from the point of view of luminosity function, a value that considers the numbers of stars of different absolute magnitudes in a given volume of space.[13]

As part of a team of eight led by van Rhijn, Bok spent the 1927–28 academic season working on a vast survey of stars, of eighteenth magnitude or brighter, in the Sun's neighborhood in order to determine the graphic curve of the luminosity function. In beginning this work Kapteyn had suspected that the result would be a simple Gaussian distribution, a bell-shaped curve. Van Rhijn's investigation showed that the spread was not Gaussian at all, but far more complex.

From the outset Bok's major responsibility was to take charge of the six assistants handling the computations. He spent most of his time in science and administration, managing what he called a "big human computer organization." Soon van Rhijn and Bok published significant results of this survey, especially for the more luminous stars. Bok's paper discussed the effects of the rotation of the galaxy on the observed proper motions of distant stars.[14] The Groningen effort was Bok's first serious taste of applying a statistical approach to the question of the structure of our galaxy, a field in which he would soon become expert.

As part of his work on the star count for van Rhijn, Bok published a study of spectra in the early class O and B stars. This first professional publication led to a lifelong friendship with Otto Struve. Not yet a well-known astronomer, Struve was studying the absorption lines of calcium in the spectra of stars.[15] These absorption lines seemed to oscillate for a double star, while they did not for a single star. To explain this discrepancy, Struve proposed the existence of large calcium clouds around these double stars. Then he suggested a "motor boat effect," a rippling through the dark matter surrounding the double star. "It seems probable," Struve wrote, "that whirls of calcium dust will be produced in the vicinity of a rapidly revolving double star, similar to the whirls of water caused by the rotation of the propeller of a rapidly moving boat."[16]

Bok thought this to be a baseless interpretation, and said so in his first published paper. Hotly disputing Struve's motorboat proposal, Bok contended that the cause was instead a simple "blending of a stationary Ca [calcium] line of the interstellar cloud with an oscillating line of the binary itself."[17] Fully expecting either no reaction or a hostile one from Struve, Bok was pleasantly surprised to receive a long letter from Struve that praised Bok's ideas and invited him to come to meet Struve at Yerkes.

The IAU and Priscilla Fairfield

The winter of 1927–28 was an exciting one, for the third triennial congress of the International Astronomical Union would take place in Leiden from July 5 to 13, 1928.[18] For a 22-year-old student planning a career in astronomy, the thought of attending such an event was electrifying. Most of the world's astronomers would be at this gathering, especially the ones from America, where, van Rhijn had told Bok, the best openings for positions were. While teaching posts might be available in Europe after a several-year wait, in the United States one could hope for an immediate opening for a position that would allow time for research. Bok hoped to make his first contacts for such an opening at the IAU in Leiden, where he planned to ask Harlow Shapley if he could come to Harvard. This IAU assembly would completely change Bok's life in a way he could hardly have expected.

Another young IAU delegate was Priscilla Fairfield, an associate professor of astronomy at Smith College in Northampton, Massachusetts. The daughter of the Unitarian Rev. O. J. Fairfield, Priscilla was from a family that had moved to Littleton, near Boston. As there were no funds to send her to college, she worked her way through Boston University, where she developed an interest in solar observing and research. At the time, that university's solar observatory was closed on Sundays, but she found a way to come in and observe the Sun anyway: she bribed the watchman to let her walk up to the roof.[19]

After Priscilla graduated from Boston University, she applied for a position at the General Electric Company. Her employment interview went well, the representative considering her well qualified for the job until he asked her what she wanted to do as a long-term career. When she answered truthfully that she eventually wanted to be an astronomer, the recruitment officer promptly rejected her. "If you want to have a job in astronomy," Priscilla was told, "you would be able to get one. But it is up to you to find one, and not up to me to tell you how to do it. The only thing I can do is to say, 'No job offer from here.'"

Fairfield went home, got her copy of *The American Ephemeris and*

Nautical Almanac, and wrote to some of the observatories listed therein. She had no trouble getting offers at Lick and the University of California at Berkeley, but instead went to Smith College where she advanced to associate professor. Subsequently she began working at Harvard on weekends for Shapley and Lindblad, computing absolute magnitudes for some RR Lyrae variables. It was at this time in her life, at age 32, that Priscilla traveled to Leiden to the IAU meeting and met Bart J. Bok, ten years her junior.

Their encounter, at least as Bok remembered it with a smile, could have been a scene from an old black-and-white movie in which two would-be lovers meet for the first time in a crowded train station, for that is where Bart first saw Priscilla. He and two former Leiden fellow students, Kuiper and Oosterof, had been assigned to the IAU welcoming committee that greeted and assisted delegates as they stepped off the arriving trains. "I was on the reception committee," Bok reminisced, "and I received Priscilla as she came off the train. Received her so well that a year later we were married and another year later we had our son. And three years later a daughter to match."

Although Bart proposed to Priscilla at the end of that IAU meeting, she thought at first that things were being rushed too much, especially since the following year their relationship would mature only through correspondence. Decades later, Jan Oort wrote about the start of Bart's romance with Priscilla: "My wife and I saw this love grow from a tiny spark at their first meeting at the IAU assembly . . . to a wonderful relationship like a sublime crystal."[20]

Bok's preoccupation with Priscilla at the IAU assembly did not overshadow his conversations with Shapley, whom he successfully pushed for an invitation to Harvard. Shapley told him about the Agassiz Research Fellowship for eleven hundred dollars per annum that was intended for a bright student who had not yet finished a doctorate. It appeared that Bok would be well qualified for this fellowship.

As is typical at most universities, at Groningen a student wouldn't even begin a thesis until the final pre-doctoral orals were completed. But Bok was on his way to Harvard. He remained at Groningen for another year, and he would return for four months in 1932 to finish writing his thesis. Bok completed his pre-doctoral examinations only three days before leaving for the United States in the late summer of 1929 for his new life as an astronomer.

3

Harlow Shapley
A *Right* Good Captain Too

*There have been no major changes in the staff during the past year,
except that . . . Mr. Bart J. Bok, of Groningen, Holland, who
has been Agassiz Research Fellow during the past year, has been
appointed Robert W. Wilson Teaching Fellow and will have charge
of the lectures in the introductory course in astronomy in Harvard
throughout the coming academic year.*
— H. Shapley, Report of the Director, 1931

From early high school on, Bok emulated the ideas and career of Harlow
Shapley. Although he longed to meet Harvard's eloquent young director,
he missed his first opportunity because he was away on a boat cruise when
Shapley unexpectedly visited Leiden in 1926. When Bok returned, his
fellow student Gerard Kuiper reported that Shapley used the "horrible
language" of America, and had not spoken the English with which Eu-
ropeans were familiar. Kuiper, in effect, could not understand him since
"he didn't speak English; he spoke American."

Harlow Shapley began his career in Joplin, Missouri, as a young newspaper reporter covering brawls and shootings. By the time he entered the
University of Missouri he was serious about journalism as a career. However, he was dissatisfied with the journalistic lifestyle, not the least of
which was a sense of having to exaggerate his stories—"fanning the
breeze," as he put it.[1] He decided to consider other fields. Reading through
the university's catalog of courses in alphabetical order, he rejected ar-
chaeology on the grounds that he couldn't pronounce it. Astronomy was
next; he could pronounce that and thus he became an astronomer.[2]

With such an austere beginning, Shapley was considered by some older astronomers, particularly J. C. Kapteyn, to be an upstart. But at Princeton he wrote a classic thesis under Henry Norris Russell on eclipsing binaries, and then got his first big break when George Ellery Hale and Frederick Seares invited him in the spring of 1914 to come to Mt. Wilson Observatory in southern California, where a great new chapter in astronomy was opening. Work on what would be the world's largest telescope, the 100-inch Hooker reflector, was rapidly approaching its completion. In the meantime, Mt. Wilson's superb 60-inch telescope was a proven instrument for Shapley's work on globular clusters. Both geographically and astronomically, Mt. Wilson was a frontier institution and a very exciting place.[3]

By this time Shapley had become very interested in the variable stars in globular star clusters. Solon Bailey, acting director of Harvard Observatory before Shapley arrived there and definitely one of Shapley's early mentors, knew that the Mt. Wilson telescopes would offer Shapley a chance to make a significant contribution.

Thus Shapley left Princeton after receiving his Ph.D. in 1913, traveled to Kansas City to marry Martha Betz, and set out for Mt. Wilson. Years later Bok would imagine the two newlyweds, sitting on the front seat of a covered wagon, traveling across the land "to conquer the new frontier." In fact, they traveled somewhat less dramatically by the Santa Fe Super Chief train, studying light curves most of the time.[4]

Shapley had taken Bailey's advice seriously. As soon as he arrived at Mt. Wilson, he began working on the strange stars known as Cepheid variables. "Our goal was to do things we had not done before," Shapley wrote, "to be leaders in scientific research, and to live up to Hale's dream of Mount Wilson as a research institution."[5]

A variable star is simply a star that is not constant in brightness. Depending on a star's type, its period of variation could be as short as a few hours or as long as several years in rare cases.[6] While there are several causes for this variation, the Cepheid variables change brightness as they expand and contract on a regular basis; as they expand they fade, and as they contract they brighten.

It was the Cepheids that caused the most excitement for astronomers trying to learn about the size of the galaxy. Harvard's Solon Bailey had noted large numbers of them in the globular clusters, and Henrietta Leavitt, also of Harvard, had studied some twenty-five Cepheids in the Small Magellanic Cloud, now known as one of the closest galaxies to us. In

1912 Leavitt found that the brighter their average magnitudes were, the longer were their periods of variation. Since all the stars in the distant Magellanic Cloud are about the same distance from us, Shapley later concluded that the stars display a correlation between their periods of variation and their average magnitudes. For two Cepheid variables with the same period of variation, the one with the brighter mean apparent magnitude is closer to us. Thus, Shapley turned this relationship into an astronomical yardstick for measuring distances.[7]

Shapley based his work at Mt. Wilson on this new yardstick, although it was not initially accepted by his colleagues. Kapteyn, especially, was reluctant to accept Shapley's work, preferring instead to rely on his classic determinations of the actual proper motions of particular stars.[8] In the end, however, Shapley's research led to the understanding that our Milky Way Galaxy was much larger than previously thought, and—Kapteyn definitely missed the boat on this one—that our Sun is far from its center.

As we noted in the first chapter, Bok first learned about Shapley in high school from articles in the magazine *Hemel en Dampkring* (Heaven and Atmosphere); the magazine reported news on amateur and professional astronomy much as *Sky and Telescope* does today. Through newspaper accounts Bok also learned about the conflict between Shapley's and Kapteyn's approaches to measuring distance; while Kapteyn relied on the motions of nearby stars, Shapley used the behavior of the Cepheids themselves to divulge their distances.

Bok thought that Kapteyn had a personal objection to Shapley's work: that Shapley did not have the mathematical background to be an astronomer, and that he had to reach his conclusions through the techniques of observation. "All he had done," Bok stressed, "was to rack up sufficient observations of (Cepheid) variable stars, and Kapteyn thought it to be an undignified approach to astronomy."

Although he had met neither Kapteyn nor Shapley (he would never meet Kapteyn), as a young student at Leiden Bok became even more entranced with Shapley and his work. Bok thought that Shapley was unfolding "a new universe for us." Shapley accomplished much at Mt. Wilson despite his dislike of actual observing: "Even though Harlow Shapley was an excellent observer," Bok emphasized, "the amazing thing about it was that he *did not like* observing. I love observing, but Shapley, through his whole life, hated it. He thought it was necessary but he also thought that it was an unbelievable bore and a dull thing to do."

Shapley's daughter Mildred Shapley Matthews offers a different version of this story. According to her Bok had bragged, shortly after he had arrived at Harvard, that he had done a lot of good astronomy without having done a single night of observing. At that point Shapley immediately assigned him to observe; "no astronomer," Shapley had explained, "should be able to boast about not having done observing."[9]

In April 1921 Shapley arrived at Harvard as director of the Observatory. At the young age of 36, the appointment was bound to touch off some jealousies among his colleagues, including his old mentor Solon Bailey, who was now somewhat uncomfortable with the young director. Shapley suggested that Bailey work on a history of Harvard, and his enthusiastic support of Bailey's project quickly soothed ruffled feathers. He tried to make people feel at home. "If he saw some way to make people work better in actual science," says Matthews, "rather than just nominal things, away he went with it."[10] Bailey completed his history and the observatory published it in 1931.[11]

Bringing out the talent in a young person was one of Shapley's most laudable traits. He looked for such talent anywhere he could find it, and in 1928 at the IAU assembly in Leiden he "discovered" Bok's potential. Bok wanted to work with Shapley. Had Shapley stayed at Mt. Wilson Observatory in California, Bok might have gone there too; his interest in Shapley's work was that profound.

Coming to America

When Bart Bok arrived in the United States in the fall of 1929, his first priority was to meet Priscilla's family. Naturally he wanted to make the best possible impression. Preparing for bed at a New York hotel the night before their meeting, Bok was troubled; would he make a good impression? After all, his clothes were not the most suave. But at least, he thought, his shoes would be nicely shined. Following the custom of European hotels, Bok left his shoes outside his room door so that the following morning they would be returned, freshly shined and dignified.

At sunrise Bok opened his door, and there were no shoes!

Facing the embarrassing prospect of crossing town shoeless to meet Priscilla's family, he quickly found out that it was this hotel's custom that anything left outside a room was to be tossed out. After a frantic search by the hotel staff, the shoes were found and returned. Bok met the Fairfields, not with the best clothes, and not with the shiniest shoes, but at least not in stocking feet.[12]

Bart and Priscilla were married in a quiet ceremony at her parents' home in Troy, N. Y., on September 9, 1929.

"I suppose you fell in love with her great mind?" a reporter later asked Bok.

"No!" he shot back, his Dutch accent making it even more emphatic but hinting at a bit of exaggeration. "She had blond hair. She had mesh stockings, and she wore short skirts!"

They quickly left for a honeymoon in the Berkshires. Although the trip had been planned to last two weeks, after only five days both Bart and Priscilla wanted to return home to start their new lives together. They left their hotel early—to the end of his life he never forgot that the hotel never refunded their money—and soon afterwards they found themselves in a small apartment on Shaler Lane in Cambridge. Due perhaps to Shapley's feeling that Bart and Priscilla had married too hastily, the first meeting between Bok and Shapley at Harvard was tense. Could Bart have married just to get a fast trip to the U.S. and an easy visa? Would Bart divorce Priscilla within a year of his arriving? Bok believed that Shapley had consented to Bok's growing interest in coming to Harvard with some doubt, and he thought that Shapley did not trust him at first. Priscilla was Shapley's favorite; she was a scientist in whom he had great confidence, and a person he doted on like a protective father.

Bok had been awarded the second George Russell Agassiz Fellowship, its sum of eleven hundred dollars for one year being one of the highest in the country at the time. Bok was anxious to make a good impression on Shapley. The director took charge of that first evening's conversation. At first it was an unlikely chat about the houses on Buckingham Street, and who might live in them. Since Bok didn't even know of the existence of Buckingham Street, let alone its residences, he had little to say, especially in his then-uncertain English. Then there was an even more curious twist—Shapley switched the conversation to unusual breeds of dogs. Again Bok could only nod and mutter. Finally the evening ended. At the front door Shapley took Priscilla aside and said: "Bart looks like a nice fellow and a handsome boy, but he hasn't got much to say for himself!"

It was a rough evening, and Bok left angry and dejected. "It was a little unkind of him," Bok noted, "to talk about who lives on Buckingham

Street and the names of breeds of dogs. That's not the way you introduce new people and make them feel welcome." Probably Bok was overreacting; Shapley would not purposefully have hurt Bok's feelings. "My father," Mildred Shapley insists, "did not deliberately start out with a person that way."

The *Pinafore*

For a few weeks Bok and Shapley did not see much of each other, and Bok wondered if the two would continue along separate paths. However, two apparently unrelated things soon conspired to enhance the Shapley-Bok relationship. The first was that Shapley liked Bok's idea for a dissertation on spectra of the Eta Carinae region. The second—and perhaps more important—was the *Harvard Observatory Pinafore*, an amateur play produced at the observatory.

Both occurrences came to a head during the winter meeting of the American Astronomical Society held over the New Year holiday—December 30, 1929, to January 2, 1930—in Cambridge. It was for that same meeting that Shapley wanted to present the *Harvard Observatory Pinafore* at the meeting's New Year's party at his residence.

Shortly after Bok arrived at Harvard, Shapley had uncovered a dusty libretto, written some thirty years earlier during four days of summer rain in Vermont in 1879 by Harvard astronomer Winslow Upton.[13] (Obviously a very creative person, Upton later produced a famous star atlas for amateur astronomers.)[14] A spoof on Gilbert and Sullivan's 1878 *H.M.S. Pinafore*, the light opera poked fun at the Harvard Observatory then under the direction of Edward Charles Pickering. Apparently the work had never been performed.[15] Shapley decided that this play would be perfect for the American Astronomical Society meeting. It would lighten the meeting's atmosphere, and provide a lot of fun for the observatory's graduate students and faculty. Besides, Shapley intended to direct it personally.

The libretto tells the story of a competent but inexperienced young Harvard assistant named Josephine, "the fairest flower that ever blossomed on scientific timber," who is offered a comfortable job at Seagrave Observatory, a fine old institution near Providence, Rhode Island. Bok played the role of Leonard Waldo (a real Pickering-era assistant), leader of the "influential men of Providence." Waldo tempts Josephine with promises of fine carpets and other amenities at Seagrave, hoping that she would sacrifice her position at Harvard's mighty 15-inch refractor and move to Providence. But Josephine hopes to stay at Harvard and, with one of the professors, devises a strategy to impress Director Pickering. Josephine's idea is to repair the prisms of Photometer P, the latest of several Harvard Observatory photometers acquired by Pickering, who had identified each by a letter of the alphabet. The real Photometer P had notoriously bad prisms, and was noted for yielding poor results. Once the photometer was reinstalled, Josephine would produce such impressive results with it that Pickering, unaware of the repair, would appreciate her value to the observatory and insist that she stay at Harvard. Late one night she and her mentor, William Rogers (another real assistant), stealthily remove the optics of Photometer P.

Josephine is to take the photometer's two prisms to Alvan Clark, the best known of the nineteenth-century telescope makers, for refiguring, and then return them secretly. But Pickering is tipped off and catches Josephine in her act. Startled, she drops the prisms. He demands an explanation and is told about the plan to refigure them. Thrilled that Josephine would go to such lengths to perfect Photometer P, Pickering forgives all, Josephine rejects the Seagrave offer for Harvard, and everyone lives happily ever after.[16]

The "Dick Dead-Eye" character who tattles on Josephine is the observer assigned Photometer P. In his opening song he rejoices in his endless work with the various photometers:

In the cool night air with S and P
I wearied my eyes on photometree.
Bright stars with H, faint stars with I,
Blue doubles reserved for a cloudy sky.
So many close doubles were measured by me
That now I am observing with Photometer P.

Another verse is a tale of observing disasters that will warm the heart of anyone who has tried to work a recalcitrant observatory dome and moving chair:

I turned the dome with so grand a shock
That I broke two windows and the Elliott clock;
I burst the gas pipe rolling the chair,
And created a blaze for the winter's scare.

For my worthy zeal they requested me
To try my strength on Photometer P.[17]

The most complete surviving account of the 1929 performance of the *Pinafore* appears in the March 1930 issue of *Popular Astronomy*. In that delightful summary, Josephine decides to forego Seagrave because she finds that she cannot tear herself away from the telescope's meridian circle, which is to her "an object of passionate love." And Waldo's disappointment seems completely assuaged by the unexpected offer of one of the fair assistants to go with him and hover about him "in his years of declination."

"Those who struggle with photometers," the *Popular Astronomy* account of the play noted, "sympathized with Pickering in his lament: 'all my magnitudes are at sixes and sevens and now my prisms all rebel,' and appreciative applause was given by the astronomer who did not need to be told that

His knees should bend and his neck should curl,
His back should twist and his face should scowl,
One eye should squint and the other protrude,
And this should be his customary attitude."[18]

The cast of the *Pinafore* reads almost like an imaginary *Who's Who* in astronomy around 1930. Besides Shapley and Bok, there were several very bright students who later would leave their marks in astronomy. Peter Millman and Helen Sawyer would become two of Canada's foremost astronomers. Adelaide Ames would assist Shapley with the first comprehensive catalog of galaxies. Henrietta Swope and Cecilia Payne were Harvard astronomy students facing notable careers with variable stars. ("Alas," Cecilia Payne-Gaposchkin wrote later, "it is a soprano part, and I was a contralto. No matter, it had to be done, with the result that I have never been able to sing since.")[19] Peter Millman organized much of the activity. Cecilia Payne, who played Josephine, sang some beautiful arias as she fell in love with the meridian circle. Finally, Mildred Shapley, who would follow a career with the University of Arizona, was also in the cast. Conspicuous by her absence was Priscilla Bok, who was pregnant with her first child, John.

The *Harvard Observatory Pinafore* completely erased the tension that Bok perceived existed between him and Shapley. Having been asked by the director to play the influential man of Providence, Bok took to his role with relish, and during the extensive rehearsals he and Shapley really got to know one another.[20] "He is a really nice boy when you get to know him," Shapley told Priscilla. "I know," she answered playfully. "You started him off on the wrong foot with Buckingham Street and strange breeds of dogs that first night." By now Shapley was probably starting to recognize the depth of Bok's admiration for him, and he made more of an effort to cultivate their friendship. With typical aplomb he told Bok, "As a little boy, you always wanted to work with Harlow Shapley, and now, Bok, that you are a grown man, you've got to stick with him!"

Thanks to the *Pinafore*, Bok reminisces with a degree of questionable modesty: "Harlow then realized that I wasn't a cheat and became quite fond of me. We worked very closely ever since. I became—sort of— Shapley's Boy Friday, and I enjoyed that very much." Incidentally, Bok's reputation as a singer was made during the *Pinafore*. With his bellowing deep voice enhanced by his Dutch accent, he was one of the stars.[21] It was a reputation that would last throughout his life. Years later Ricardo Gonzales, then a night assistant and opera buff at the Cerro Tololo Observatory, would try to ward off fatigue: "Professor Bok, would you please start singing?" Soon Bok and Gonzales would be singing at the top of their lungs, their music reverberating around the dome.

There were other good astronomers at Harvard in those early years; one of the finest was Annie Jump Cannon, with whom the Boks became very close. Among the best of "Pickering's girls," Cannon was finishing a decades-long career discovering and following variable stars on the Harvard plates, and compiling the 500,000-star Henry Draper Catalogue. Bok recalled that by the time he arrived, Cannon had become "a sort of elder statesman: Shapley loved her; everybody loved her. She was the most lovable person I have ever met."

The phrase "Pickering's girls" dates back to the directorship of E. C. Pickering, who boasted of the large numbers of hours spent by several women he had hired as research assistants.[22] Shapley coined the phrase "girl hour" to indicate how much calculating work a particular project might take. Commenting on this practice, Supt. Helweg of the U.S. Naval Observatory once added that the largest unit of work at HCO was one "kilogirl hour." Although abysmally sexist by modern standards, the concept was not intended to be demeaning; it allowed women to advance in the heavily male-dominated astronomical world of the time. Under Shapley's regime this system continued, although some of his colleagues resented it: "The kilogirl hour was no joke," Fred Whipple later recalled. "Shapley appallingly underpaid his staff, especially female staff." Some of the women, notably Dorrit Hoffleit, went on to get their doctorates.[23] Far from being sexist, Shapley encouraged bright women like Hoffleit to continue their studies. Unsure whether she should proceed, she turned to Bok for advice. His unequivocal response: "When God tells you to go after a Ph.D., you go for it."[24]

4

"Miscellaneous Nonsense Vaguely Related to Eta Carinae"

With his relationship with Shapley now firmly established following the success of the *Pinafore*, Bok immediately set to work on his own dissertation. Although Bok was interested in the astrophysics of the absorption of light around stars and in nebulae, Shapley had suggested that he study some early spectra of the star Eta Carinae. It was this suggestion that led, in 1930, to Bok's first English-language magazine article, in *Popular Astronomy*.[1] At the same time he was helping Shapley set up the Observatory's graduate school. Before he even set upon a course for his own dissertation, he was already supervising other students' theses. The first was that of Eric Lindsay.

Having arrived only two days after Bok, Lindsay was having difficulty finding the front door of the observatory. As Bok remembers the story, Lindsay rang the doorbell of the observatory residence and met the director, who was in his pajamas. Shapley suggested that the new student could walk through the hall to the back of the house, and keep on walking to the observatory. Not knowing of any other entrances, the following morning Lindsay rang the doorbell and again met Shapley, again in his pajamas. It was not too long before he found a more appropriate entrance: "This," Bok laughed, "is how Eric Lindsay met the director of Harvard Observatory." The thesis that Lindsay later completed under Bok demonstrated the value of star counts in learning about the structure of the galaxy, particularly how stars in the galaxy's high latitudes are not clustered but distributed at random. Together, Lindsay and Bok's work on star clouds and dark nebulae contributed to the picture of the galaxy Bok later portrayed in his first book *The Distribution of the Stars in Space*.[2] Bok remembers Lindsay as a friend and a first-class astronomer who went on to work at Harvard's Boyden Station in South Africa and who later founded Ireland's first planetarium.

Shapley had also brought in the Canadian astronomer Harry Plaskett to help with organizing the graduate school. The son of John Plaskett, discoverer of the very massive star that now bears his name, Harry H. Plaskett was one of the best-known astronomers of the time. His arrival was the beginning of a well-organized graduate program with good courses.[3] However, he and Bok did not get along: "I came there and Harry didn't like me," Bok stressed. Somewhat reminiscent of his earlier argument with Struve, this trouble began during the summer of 1930. Edward Arthur Milne had written what Bok called "a very silly paper," to explain how radiation is transferred through planetary nebulae, but he had not taken into account the absorption of light by the nebula.[4]

Bok had a different idea that he hoped to expand into his dissertation. He introduced it in an early unpublished paper that took advantage of the recent discovery that very hot dwarf stars were at the centers of planetary nebulae. The hot star at the center of a nebula, he thought, releases ultraviolet radiation that ionizes the hydrogen in the cloud, causing it to glow. However, if the cloud is thin enough, some of the UV radiation leaks out through the spherical cloud. At the outer edge of the nebula, the ionized hydrogen begins to lose its ionization to become ordinary hydrogen. The edges of a thin nebula, where the UV is leaking out, might be quite sharp. Bok explained the shells to be the sharp edges of what we now call Strömgren spheres, the H II regions surrounding stars.

After Bok finished this unique paper, he sent it to Harry Plaskett for review. "I was a nice open Dutch boy who said that my good friend, E. Arthur Milne, had done it wrong. Milne seemed to be easily pleased, but Plaskett thought it was awful!" The lack of any objection from Milne made no difference; as far as Plaskett was concerned, Bok had insulted the established professor at Oxford.

Plaskett was livid. He compared Bok to "a general who couldn't capture a big city and so had gone and raped and murdered all the rural peasants." Plaskett would not permit the paper to be published. Bok suspects that Plaskett's real reason was that he wanted to leave Harvard and become "the other professor" at Oxford and wanted to maintain good relations with Milne.

Bok became as furious as Plaskett at a rejection he thought to be unfair.

He complained to Shapley, who reminded Bok that he earlier had suggested a dissertation on Eta Carinae spectra, instead of his current work. "I liked the Eta Carinae region when you gave it to me to study," Bok agreed with Shapley.[5] Bok's paper on planetary nebulae was never published, leaving it to the Danish astronomer Bengt Strömgren to describe these spherical regions of ionized hydrogen which are now known as Strömgren spheres. But this subject could have been Bok's thesis, a study on how light is scattered and the patterns in which it is absorbed in the gaseous shells around stars and in emission nebulae.

This rather ominous beginning to what turned out to be an illustrious career at Harvard was typical in a sense. Bok was never one to negotiate, and his handling of the nebula paper was in the character he had developed by that time and which would continue to evolve. Two years later he would repeat this uncompromising pattern with his thesis director at Groningen, Pieter van Rhijn. Incidentally, it was not uncommon for a doctoral student to finish a thesis under the aegis of one institution and be employed at another.

Now Bok took a more careful look at Shapley's suggestion that he concentrate his studies on Eta Carinae and write his dissertation on that unique star. Eta Carinae first attracted attention in 1677 when Edmond Halley noticed that it had brightened to fourth magnitude, making it easily visible to the naked eye. In 1827 it brightened to first magnitude, making it one of the brightest stars in the sky. A year later it had faded only half a magnitude. In 1843 it shone briefly at magnitude minus 1.5, tied with Sirius for being *the* brightest star in the sky. In this century it has varied between magnitudes 6.5 and 7.9.[6]

Now Bok was returning to Shapley's original suggestion for a thesis, but with a twist. While Shapley's push was toward the star itself, with its pre-outburst narrow-line spectrum and its post-outburst broad-line or "flare" spectrum,[7] Bok was developing a curiosity about the nebulosity surrounding the star, and about the smaller stars in this nebulosity. In considering the nebula, Bok realized that the star itself is only part of the story, and that "the grand sweep of the swirling gases" of the nebula surrounding the star was even more interesting.[8] "Right away, I saw in that region an important part of the Milky Way," Bok thought; here was a good place to begin looking for examples of how young, hot stars are distributed in space.

Thus the dissertation began to take form. From a study of the distribution of stars in the region of Eta Carinae Bok was hoping to shed some light on the structure and rotation of our galaxy. He would later expand his thesis to work with problems involving the stability of clusters, their disintegration, and other problems that arose because of the galaxy's rotation.

For Bok, the thesis was an "end of the beginning." In its last section Bok even included some of his unpublished work on planetary nebulae. Shapley agreed with the basic thrust of Bok's new direction and enjoyed the quality and enthusiasm of his dissertation. But once, for fun, he tried to bring Bok down a notch or two by suggesting that Bok title his work "Miscellaneous Nonsense Vaguely Related to the Eta Carinae Nebula."

Even though Shapley was supporting Bok's scientific theme, the thesis was at least nominally under the direction of van Rhijn back in Holland. It was rare for van Rhijn to have a Ph.D. student, perhaps one or two a decade, and Bok recalls that van Rhijn felt "a little sad" when he departed for Harvard. Thus Bok was not too comfortable about abandoning him and wanted to return to present the thesis to him. This seemed a good idea until Bart, Priscilla, and their two-year-old son John arrived in 1932 to find—shades of Plaskett—van Rhijn objecting to the entire project.

Although van Rhijn accepted the results of Bok's research, he thought that it did not cover a large enough sample of the Milky Way. The concentration of work on the Eta Carinae region, he felt, did not represent a conclusion about its stars that could be generalized throughout the galaxy. "Well, that's nice," Bok looked back on van Rhijn's statement, "now we know this about the Eta Carinae region. Now if you had this for 24 regions varying by 15 degrees in galactic longitude all along the Milky Way, you would have a result." The understated request was that Bok return to Harvard and spend another four years repeating the Carina work on many other fields. To van Rhijn the Eta Carinae region was nothing special, and certainly not the unique region Bok thought it was and which it is now generally accepted to be.

"I knew van Rhijn didn't know what the Eta Carinae region was, which was embarrassing. So I told him politely but firmly he could go to hell, that I would go back to Harvard and get a degree from Shapley, that he was glad to give it to me."

Eventually van Rhijn relented, and on July 6, 1932, Bok defended his thesis successfully.[9] Bok did get his degree from Holland, but not without further problems from bruised egos. While it was customary in Holland for the thesis supervisor to award the degree with such words as "it gives me pleasure . . . ," van Rhijn said coldly "I herewith award you the degree." However, as time passed van Rhijn's feelings were assuaged. As Bok remembered the contents of a note he received from van Rhijn a few months later, van Rhijn wrote: "Bok, I am glad that you got your degree with me. It was nice of you to have stayed through all the troubles. Sincerely yours, Piet."

"At the end," Bok said, "there was a cheerful dinner, and everybody loved everybody, but I didn't love van Rhijn, and he didn't love me."

To an impatient doctoral candidate, getting a degree often is seen as a process designed to stand in the way of "real" research. On the surface it could appear that Bok might have been impatient, that he could have compromised and repeated the study on a different region at least as a control. Bok chose Eta Carinae because it was possibly the most unusual region then known in the entire galaxy.

All this time Bok's reputation in the community and his stature with Shapley were increasing steadily. "I sort of fell upstairs," he noted, "by lack of gravity." His thesis was published as a *Harvard College Observatory Reprint* in 1932.[10]

With the infectious enthusiasm of its director, its staff, and its students, the 1930s were Harvard Observatory's golden decade. The students were bright—notwithstanding the one who by the mid-1930s should have known better, who circled a perfectly ordinary galaxy on one of the Harvard plates with a penciled comment on the plate envelope: "Dr. Bok, what is this?"[11]

Carl Seyfert was one of Professor Bok's best students. He started out as a young amateur astronomer in Cleveland; Bok met him one evening while lecturing there, and learned later that he would be coming to Harvard. Seyfert enrolled in Bok's introductory astronomy course, and he and Bok quickly developed a rapport. At graduation Seyfert was asked to present the Ivy Oration, a sort of valedictory. Fortunately Seyfert showed Bok the speech in advance, for it included a thought that Copernicus did not die in vain at the stake. "It was Bruno who did not die in vain at the stake," says Bok; "Copernicus died peacefully in bed with his new book (*De Revolutionibus*, in 1543) in front of him. He must have felt good," Bok added, using one of his favorite expressions, "to pop off like that!"

Seyfert turned out to be a highly enthusiastic astronomer. Later at Mt. Wilson he listened to Rudolf Minkowski say that "I think I have a couple of spectra of galaxies that do funny things." He would go no further than that; Seyfert was on his own to examine these galaxies characterized by bright, almost starlike cores. After some two years at Mt. Wilson he went to Vanderbilt University in Nashville, where he built up the now-prominent Arthur Dyer Observatory. In the late 1950s a local radio station asked him to become their late afternoon weatherman. Seyfert accepted, and soon he was popular both as a weatherman and as an astronomer. "He always did too much," Bok stressed. "He would work at the observatory and then race over to the radio station." In June 1960, on his way to the station, Seyfert was killed in a car accident.

At the time of Seyfert's death the strange galaxies with bright, starlike cores had not reached the level of attention we understand today; they are now seen as intermediate between normal galaxies and galaxies with quasars in them. In fact, the obituary in *Sky and Telescope* evaluated his rich career without specifically mentioning the Seyfert Galaxies.[12] It was not until later that decade, when Bok became director of Steward Observatory, that a symposium on these galaxies took place. "It turned out to be a very important symposium that gave the Seyfert Galaxies a sort of send-off," Bok noted.

During one symposium session Bok formally suggested that the galaxy class be named both for Seyfert and for Minkowski. "Rudolf," proposed Bok, "it is about time the world knows that your name ought to be associated with these galaxies. They ought to be called the Minkowski-Seyfert galaxies or something like that."

Minkowski looked completely blank; so Bok repeated: "It was you who supervised Seyfert's work when he was a young fellow at Mt. Wilson." Again, Minkowski looked blankly at Bok, who added, "so your name ought to be . . ."

Then, in front of the whole audience, Minkowski announced, "I don't remember a thing about this." Thus, these fascinating systems are called Seyfert Galaxies, even though Bok is convinced that "Minkowski had the real vision and did the basic work." Had Seyfert lived, he likely would have insisted that some of the credit go to Minkowski.

Partly because of enthusiastic astronomers like Bok, the atmosphere at Harvard was very conducive to bringing out the best in its bright students. However by 1935 director Shapley's research effort had been reduced. Although he had been reluctant to give public talks in his younger days, Shapley was spending more and more time on the lecture circuit, to the detriment of his research. "He had this exciting way of lecturing," his daughter Mildred says, "that people just sat on the edge of their seats, including me. He was fun to listen to and his enthusiasm was infectious."[13]

From the time he arrived in 1921, Harlow Shapley was an active "directing director," as Bok put it, who influenced Harvard astronomy enormously. While even he joked about his vanity—he apparently enjoyed impersonating Napoleon at parties[14]—by the later 1930s the thrusts of Shapley's lectures began to change from astronomy to politics. His pride got him into trouble, "pushing him," as Bok underscored, "to the places where the loudest applause was." Shapley was now lecturing about the role of the scientist in society; one such lecture was to a crowd of three thousand people at New York's Waldorf-Astoria. Considering the deteriorating world picture of the time—the economy was in depression, and Germany was preparing for war—Shapley's espousal of liberal and social issues was not a bad idea; other astronomers and physicists, including Einstein, were also politically active. These lectures covered topics far removed from astronomy. In 1967 several of them were published in his book of philosophical commentary *Beyond the Observatory.* His discussion is pointed and thoughtful, particularly when he describes God's painful questioning of Job: "This is no elementary quiz. I would call it a swift-moving doctoral oral."[15]

Shapley's politics as well as his science helped to create the legend that he became. Shapley's efforts were not limited to speechmaking. During these years he began actively to rescue Jewish scientists from Europe. During the late 1930s Shapley's time was devoted to a large extent to these humanitarian concerns, to finding jobs and housing for European Jewish scientists. Richard Prager was one Jewish astronomer whom Shapley brought from the Berlin Observatory to Harvard: he told Bok "quietly and seriously that every night at least a thousand Jewish scientists must say a prayer of thanks for Harlow Shapley's humanitarian efforts to help save them and their families."[16] Bok worked closely with Shapley on these matters all during this period. "We saw each other very, very regularly during those days."

Even during the depression, Shapley had a way of getting money for Harvard. He raised the money for the new Building "D" by 1930, during one of the worst economic times in American history. He got the funds for Bok's first position as R. W. Wilson Fellow in 1929, and then he got more funds for Bok's promotion to assistant professor in 1933. He also hired two new young astronomers, Fred Whipple from Berkeley, and Donald Menzel from Lick Observatory. And any major (or minor) observatory success—the funding for Building "D" being a case in point—provided a fine excuse for a party.

Held usually at the director's residence three or four times each year—almost every night during *Pinafore* rehearsals—the Shapley parties could become quite elaborate. "They were a heap of fun," Mildred recalls. "My father wanted people to have fun; he felt they'd work better." At the Christmas parties Bok was famous for his rendition of "We Three Kings." Arthur Hoag, then a student, remembered Bok "as one of the three kings, or all of them, which he did with a great deal of gusto and mirth."[17] Some were informal student gatherings with pizza.[18]

A special guest was often an excuse for a fancier party. One Russian astronomer was so delighted he clicked his heels, approached Mrs. Shapley, and kissed her hand. The Shapley residence was large and accommodating, with a huge living room entered through a hallway that could be used as a stage. The director's residence was sometimes lavishly decorated, including each post in the living room. There was dancing and plenty of refreshments, and card tables were set up so that the guests could play bridge if they wished. People wishing to converse could go to one of several smaller rooms set aside for this purpose.

These parties were definitely not typical staff-student mixers. The dining room was often converted to a gambling saloon, although not for money. These games were popular, and even the Boks took part. "At first there was just Dr. Bok," astronomer Francis Wright remembered. "Then at one party he and Priscilla came in and sat on the sofa together, holding hands like young sweethearts instead of a married couple. At the time it was braver than what most people did. He would hold her hand if he felt like it. Could you imagine him restraining himself? And Priscilla looked as if she enjoyed it. She never would have initiated it herself, but she enjoyed it."

In later years concerts were held at the Shapley residence with observatory astronomers participating. Frances Wright and Cecilia Payne-Gaposchkin directed what became known as the Observatory Philharmonic. Fred Whipple was concertmaster, Uco van Wijk, a Dutch student who arrived in 1941, played triangle, and Bok reluctantly played mandolin.[19] Different types of music were performed, including pieces written by William Herschel, the famous eighteenth-century British astronomer and musician. Apparently these concerts were very much family events, organized at the observatory for the benefit of the astronomical family.

Bok had obtained the mandolin in a trade from Shapley. Bok had wanted the instrument badly but really did not have the funds for it. At the time, Bok's two-year-old daughter Joyce had outgrown her crib. Shapley thought he could use an extra one for his grandchildren, and offered to trade something for it. "I love that mandolin," Bok smiled; so in exchange for the crib he got the mandolin. Each evening he described the day's events at the observatory to Priscilla, and then played the mandolin. John and Joyce would leave ("they didn't have the slightest appreciation of their dad's great achievements"), and Bart would serenade Priscilla with folk songs in several languages, including German, Norwegian, and naturally Dutch. "We had a wonderful arrangement, for Priscilla loved the mandolin. I stopped playing it when Priscilla died."[20]

While Bart enjoyed playing quietly for his wife, he certainly did not enjoy playing in public, and Francis Wright remembers him tense and unhappy before an Observatory Philharmonic performance. He did it because Shapley wanted him to do it. Bok would do almost anything for Shapley, for by now they had become very good friends. One afternoon at Harvard's observatory at Oak Ridge, Bok had climbed high up in a tree near the observatory, perhaps to repair a children's swing. His children were arguing, and Bok wanted them inside. "Get in the house!" he ordered. "Get in the house!" Meanwhile, Shapley was walking nearby through the wooded parklike area around the observatory. As he told his family later, it sounded like God shouting from heaven in a deep booming voice "Get in the house!"

"My father," Mildred reminisces, "always hoped that Bart would follow him as director. He wanted him very, very much to be director. He thought that Bok could handle people better than any of the others." The closeness between the two scientists lasted until Shapley's death in 1972. But Bok would never become director of the observatory at Harvard.

"One requirement of the National Academy of Sciences," Bok noted, "is to arrange for a biographical memoir about a member who has died. I wanted so much to do the one of Shapley." In the memoir he wrote, Bok exulted in Shapley's clear writing: "I wish that every scientist could have a chance to read the Shapley papers in the *Mount Wilson Contributions*. They make for remarkably easy reading. Every one of them is simple and straightforward, and the papers can be read with ease by any student in a beginning course on astronomy, including those without any knowledge of calculus or of modern physics." Bok saw his colleague and friend as a man of great intellectual strength and as one who, as director of Harvard College Observatory, offered much freedom for the researches of his staff. Bok even forgave one of Shapley's shortcomings: he describes Shapley's "volume of informal reminiscences entitled *Through Rugged Ways to the Stars:* it is not the very best of autobiographies but it does show the true Harlow Shapley with all his wonderful ideals, his vanity, his compassion, and his greatness."[21]

5

★

Astronomy and Astropolitics

Of studie took he moost cure and most heede.
Noght o word spak he moore than was neede,
And that was sayd in forme and reverence,
And short and quyk and full of hy sentence;
Sownynge in moral vertu was his speche,
And gladly wolde he lerne, and gladly teche.
—Chaucer, *Canterbury Tales*

By the mid-1930s Bok was deeply involved in several aspects of astronomy at Harvard—he was teaching, he was observing and doing research, and he was getting involved in the political issues of the observatory. These were good years. With his thesis out of the way, his reputation as a scientist grew rapidly. Moreover, having won his battles with Plaskett and with van Rhijn, he had become very self-confident. So pleased was he with this period that he later asked that his biographer portray him as the cleric from Oxford in the *Canterbury Tales* who was scrupulous and ethical, and who loved teaching as well as research.

Not all Bok's colleagues would have agreed with the cleric's insistence that everything that he said was "formal and reverent" to them!

Considering Bok's assertive and sometimes uncooperative personality, it was not surprising that he would be involved in matters best called "astropolitics." Questions of who got credit for what might be in this category, like the naming of the Seyfert galaxies discussed in chapter 4. Possibly his first major encounter with astropolitics took place shortly after his arrival at Harvard. The question came up of who actually did the original work for what is now known as the Hertzsprung-Russell diagram. One of the most important tools in our understanding of the evolution of stars, the H-R diagram connects theory and observation to reveal the relation between the absolute magnitude or luminosity and the spectral type for a particular group of stars.[1] In 1911, Ejnar Hertzsprung plotted the colors of a large series of stars in star clusters against their apparent magnitudes and had produced a diagram detailing the result. Although it would be a seminal piece of research, Hertzsprung's work was not widely noted. Two years later Henry Norris Russell independently did something similar, but he restricted his work to stars in the neighborhood of the Sun, so that he could utilize a star's absolute, or intrinsic, magnitude instead of the apparent magnitude that depends on its distance. As Bok interpreted Hertzsprung's complaint, "Russell took a big brass drum and beat it very hard and made a terrific impression. Then it became the Russell diagram."

Bok liked to describe Hertzsprung's story as the "Umm, by the way, *I* did it but was afraid to announce it" type: "Always write your most important discovery in a place where no one else can see it, then when someone else comes up with the same thing you can dig it up and claim credit." It is true that the original Hertzsprung work was not widely known, and it is also true that Russell made some significant changes in the diagram based on his work with eclipsing variables. He also turned the diagram's axes by ninety degrees to give it its now-familiar appearance with absolute magnitude on the Y axis and spectral class on the X axis.

When Bok arrived at Harvard, to his surprise he found that astronomers were getting pretty comfortable calling this the "Russell Diagram." With his friends Otto Struve and William Morgan (who later would become prominent in Milky Way research; see chapter 9) he suggested that Hertzsprung's name should be added, that it should be called the Russell-Hertzsprung diagram. But they did more than propose; they politicized the issue and built a constituency in favor of the change. But as they planned to spread the new name around, they realized that Hertzsprung really was the first to figure it out, having completed his work at least two years before Russell announced his results in 1913. Thus, just before astronomers became too comfortable with just Russell or even Russell-Hertzsprung, Bok and his colleagues talked up the Hertzsprung-Russell idea, and that is how the diagram is known to this day. Bok reflected that Russell generously did not mind sharing the credit in this manner.[2]

Bok's developing skills in "astropolitics" were honed by his mentor Shapley, who had his own ambition to be the undisputed ruler of the extragalactic universe field. But his dream was being thwarted by Edwin Hubble, a highly respected astronomer from Mt. Wilson. From both personality and science, Shapley and Hubble were in conflict: "They disliked each other very thoroughly," Bok recollected. Shapley even resented Hubble's accent, once confiding in Bok that "I was not like Edwin Hubble, who went to Oxford to put a hot potato in his mouth, and developed an accent which was impeccable."[3] Shapley's daughter Mildred Matthews mentions that the Missouri-born Hubble's accent, which the Shapleys thought was fabricated, was especially difficult for her mother Martha Betz to accept.

Perhaps the coup de grace was Hubble's publication in 1936 of a popular book called *The Realm of the Nebulae*, in which he summarized everything then known about galaxies.[4] Naturally it was written from Hubble's point of view, complete with Hubble's conviction that the galaxies, on the scale of the universe, were distributed evenly in space. But it was very well written, certain to be a best seller. "Shapley got it in the late afternoon," Bok remembered, "spent the whole night reading the book, and returned feeling very upset the next morning." Shapley's own popular book *Galaxies* did not appear until 1943.[5] Neither Bok nor Shapley agreed with Hubble about how the galaxies were distributed in space. In fact, in his *Harvard Bulletin* no. 895 (1934), Bok noted that the distant galaxies were apparently clustered, a view definitely not held by Hubble but hinted at by Shapley in 1932.[6] Some evidence for clustering certainly was apparent in the survey that had been completed earlier by Shapley and Adelaide Ames using the massive collection of survey plates in Harvard's collection, and which formed the basis for the *Shapley-Ames Catalogue of Galaxies.*[7]

At about the same time that the finishing touches were being put on *Realm of the Nebulae*, another sky survey was being done by Clyde Tombaugh, an amateur astronomer turned planet hunter whose work at Lowell Observatory in Flagstaff, Arizona, had led to the discovery of Pluto in 1930. Although the primary purpose of that search was to discover new planets, Tombaugh noted several examples of large clusterings of galaxies, especially a huge supercluster in Perseus and Andromeda.[8] He had read Hubble's book too, and on the basis of his own observations Tombaugh knew Hubble was wrong in his idea of an even distribution of clusters of galaxies in the universe. He later tried to argue the point with Hubble, who apparently was not interested in discussing it.[9] Tombaugh felt that his not having a Ph.D. in astronomy led to that unhappy result, and he did not learn for almost fifty years that Hubble had had the same argument with both Shapley and Bok.[10] Although Hubble was aware of the earlier argument, he never told Tombaugh about it; so violent was the animosity between Hubble and Shapley that in Bok's presence, Hubble tossed a copy of the *Shapley-Ames Catalogue* into a wastebasket. Bok recalled that Hubble's reaction to his *Harvard Bulletin* on galaxy clustering was so icy that Hubble avoided Bok for two years.

"Hubble wasn't playing fair," Mildred recollected her father saying. *Shapley-Ames* was a seminal publication; its 75 pages of catalogue and commentary, covering 1249 objects brighter than 13th magnitude, laid a foundation for the larger catalogues to come.[11] It was not until 1954 that George Abell, using the 935 plates of the mighty Palomar Observatory Sky Survey, showed conclusively that the distribution of galaxy clusters in the universe we see is indeed highly uneven.

But Bok's assessment of Shapley and Hubble was about to change. Within a few years of the appearance of the *Shapley-Ames Catalogue* in 1932, Bok was thinking that Shapley's work had become somewhat "shoddy" and less thorough than that of Hubble; he got the impression that Shapley measured progress in the study of galaxies by the "girl-hour"—how much work his assistants had put in—rather than through refereed publications. Bok believed also that Shapley was being a bit too careless with the photographic plates his observers were taking and calibrating, especially those from the Bruce telescope in South Africa. "Hubble in the 1930s ran way ahead of Shapley, a thought that clearly bothered Shapley." Had Shapley known that the great Space Telescope would be named after Hubble, he would have been even more upset, though probably not surprised.

These criticisms of Shapley's work in the late 1930s should not reflect on Bok's high opinion of his earlier work at Harvard, particularly that involving *Shapley-Ames*. The catalogue is still in print, still popular and heavily referenced in modern publications.

Adelaide Ames was Shapley's associate on the work on the *Catalogue*. Bok remembered her as a somewhat aristocratic but delightful woman who was on her way to becoming one of the observatory's best astronomers. Examining the old plates in the Harvard stacks was a massive job, involving many hours in the dimly lit archives. By 1932 her role in the project was largely completed. Early that summer, Ames and a friend went canoeing on a New Hampshire pond. The canoe overturned and Ames drowned.

The observatory family was numbed when Shapley announced this tragedy. It was a horrible jolt, even more so because the group had become so closely knit. "Adelaide was a beautiful person," Bok reminisced. Astronomer Cecilia Payne, her closest friend, was devastated: "For me," she later wrote, "it was a tragedy so great that I can hardly write of it, and even now I cannot bear to speak of it. In my first year at Harvard we had been inseparable; they used to call us 'the Heavenly Twins.' "[12]

First Book

By 1933 Bok had become interested in the dynamics of open star clusters, the groupings of hundreds of stars like the Pleiades in the constellation of Taurus. He was asking how such aggregations of stars evolve, how long they last, and what process makes them fall apart.[13] Shapley had already classified the open clusters according to a scheme that measured their concentration, from the very loosely held-together clusters to the very tight and highly concentrated ones. Bok's interest was in the clusters at the loose end of Shapley's scale, the ones that might disintegrate more quickly as the forces of the rotating galaxy tear the clusters apart. On the galactic time scale of several billion years, these clusters' lifespans are almost fleeting. Our Sun, in fact, might once have been a member of an open cluster which has long since dissociated, its members now spread out all over the galaxy.

In the brief history of these clusters might lie a clue to our understanding of our whole galaxy and of how it rotates over a certain period of time. As the galaxy rotates, Bok reasoned, its gravity would produce massive tidal disruptions that could cause the loose open clusters to fall apart. At almost the same time the young Soviet astronomer Viktor Ambartsumian, a student at the Institute for Theoretical Astronomy in Leningrad, had thought of the same problem but from a different angle.[14] Bok first met Ambartsumian at the IAU Assembly at Stockholm, where, he recalls, "he and I were both among the rising little shots who were about to become bigger shots as time went on." Their friendship matured over many years and they remained in touch until Bok's death. Ambartsumian later identified several loose groupings of stars he called associations. One such association consists of stars in the Orion nebula. It now appears likely that the stars in that nebula were formed by some cataclysm that took place only 2.5 million years ago, and that the stars are rapidly moving apart.[15]

As Bok's interest in the distribution of stars and the structure of the galaxy continued to grow, in the summer of 1936 he gave a series of lectures at Yerkes Observatory about his research. In the audience was his friend Otto Struve of Yerkes. As an editor of the *Astronomical Monographs*, Struve suggested that Bok write the series' opening book about this subject.

The idea was enticing. Bok was well prepared for the task; he had a summary of each lecture he had given, and had even taken the trouble to photograph the notes he had written on the blackboard. Since Struve wanted this book to be short, Bok was confident, as most authors are at the start of their work, that it would not take too long to write.

By early 1937 Bok had begun work on *The Distribution of the Stars in Space*, and the first draft went quickly.[16] By the Memorial Day weekend of 1937, Bok was completing the final stages of *Distribution* from his home in Lexington. But this work would be interrupted by a disease whose first symptom appeared on that pleasant Memorial Day as Bok took a few hours off from his work to clip the garden hedge. With his hand-operated clippers the job took several hours, and, even though he was tiring, he ignored his wife's repeated entreaties to rest. Finally an exasperated Priscilla pleaded with him to stop. "*You fool!*" Bart recalls her warning, "you damn, stubborn Dutchman, stop and finish it tomorrow!"

"No, look. Here I am now, four-fifths done!" Bart toiled until late in the day. When he lay down in bed that night, his legs and back were stiff, but because he didn't want another lecture from Priscilla he said nothing to her. The next day he had a fever. Thinking that he might be catching a cold, he moved to the spare bedroom and rested there. As his discomfort grew intense, he blamed the bed: "This is the damndest bed that any young couple has had. I feel more crampy now than before!" When his temperature started to rise they called their family physician. Bok rested for some time, but as he began to recover he noticed that his right arm was so painful he could hardly hold it to drive his car, and his thumb hurt so much he could not write. "I didn't want to let Priscilla see how difficult it all was," Bok reminisced on his stoic approach to those difficult days.

Several weeks later Bok attended a party at the Oak Ridge Observatory at which his doctor was present as a friend of the Shapleys'. "Bart," he asked, "when are you coming down to see me to treat your polio?"

"What?"

"Look at your hand. That's polio! Didn't you know? This is now the time to start exercises."

"*Polio?*" Bok had not the slightest idea of that diagnosis. When Bok arrived home that evening he broke the news to Priscilla. "Oh my God!" she exclaimed, almost in shock. Bok always wondered why their physician had never told him earlier. The pain eventually left, but his right thumb remained a bit disfigured.

As Bok recovered over the ensuing weeks, he completed his revisions to *The Distribution of Stars in Space*. This careful work marked the emergence of Bok as a major scientific expository writer. Divided logically into sections on Methods of Analysis, The Data of Observation, and The Problems of Galactic Structure, the arrangement of this book is a forecast of the basic plan of his later opus *The Milky Way*, which he would write with Priscilla. Bok's former thesis advisor Pieter van Rhijn liked Bok's new book, although he inveighed against Bok's interest in the dark clouds of gas called nebulae: "They are no good," Bok recalls van Rhijn intoning, "and only a damn fool would be bothered by such a thing. A sensible person does not get involved with the dark nebulae but steers to the clear parts in between." Van Rhijn was wrong. The importance of the huge quantities of obscuring matter that are the dark nebulae would increase dramatically as astronomers understood them better, and Bok would play a strong research role on them.

The *Distribution* had a considerable impact at the time since it did more than just summarize past research; it predicted where things were going by mentioning names and research in progress: "Miller's star counts," Bok wrote prophetically about the work of calculating the numbers of stars in specific regions of the sky, "will be continued along the rift through Aquila and Scutum," and future surveys would produce new discoveries of dark nebulae in "intermediate latitudes" at a distance from the plane of the Milky Way.[17] "We live in a time in which the general outlines of the structure are known with a fair degree of certainty," Bok correctly observed in that book, "but we have, as yet, no positive information about any of the finer structural details."[18]

In 1930 Bok thought that the Milky Way Galaxy might be a giant spiral galaxy; by the time *The Distribution of The Stars in Space* was completed in 1937 Bok was almost convinced of it. Techniques to trace the galaxy's spiral shape, however, were still more than a decade away. But the ever-more-important dark matter, which would provide a big clue to spiral structure, and the question of how starlight is absorbed by dark matter, were slowly becoming better understood.

When Bok completed the 124-page *Distribution* in 1937, he was only 31 years old. It is a remarkable book, written with a prescience and understanding of the subject not shared by most of his peers.[19]

If *Distribution* gave Bok a major academic boost, then a major university-wide celebration opened a door for him to become a spokesman for astronomy. When Harvard College was founded in 1636, no one could foresee how vital and important it would become over three centuries. In 1936 Harvard celebrated its tercentennial anniversary with a series of public lectures, honorary degree awards, and other events. Several nationally known science writers were to cover the events, with the help of an instructor in each department advising the writers of important papers coming up. Bok was the chosen liaison from Harvard College Observatory, and each day he met with these renowned writers. It was a wonderful exercise in public relations. Not only did Bok have to use his judgment on which forthcoming lectures would be the most interesting, but he would also have to comment on them—for the record—up to a full day before the lectures were even presented. While Bok learned much about how science is explained to nonscientists during this time, his role with the press fueled his own enthusiasm for public lecturing. Unlike scientists who felt more comfortable holding a test tube than a microphone, Bok thoroughly enjoyed talking about his work. Bart and Priscilla were becoming so well known that a *Boston Globe* reporter called them "salesmen of the Milky Way." It is a sobriquet that lasted throughout Bok's life.[20]

Hale, Gale, and Frost

From 1912 to 1933 the *Astrophysical Journal* (*Ap. J.* as it is popularly known) was edited by a team of three—George E. Hale, Edwin B. Frost, and Henry G. Gale—"the three meteorologists," Bok noted. The flagship publication of the American Astronomical Society, *Ap. J.* is still the journal of record for the most important papers in astrophysics. Around 1920 *Ap. J.* received a paper by a physical chemist from India named Megh Nad Saha (1894–1956) that had, through a new theory of ionization in stellar atmospheres, offered a whole new approach to the interpretation of the spectra of stars. Whether a spectral line appears depended, Saha noted, on the temperature and pressure in the star's atmosphere.[21] But as Saha was relatively unknown and the subject seemed inappropriate for a journal that focused on pure astronomy, the editors rejected the paper. Disappointed, Saha published this paper in *Philosophical Magazine.*[22] Bok cited this as a fine example of how non-peer reviewed journals can be scientifically important: the paper turned out to be a seminal one which helped make Saha one of India's most respected physical chemists.

In 1933 Otto Struve was added to the journal's list of editors. Not wanting to make the same mistake his predecessors made, Struve appointed Bok to referee an unusual paper by another unknown science researcher. This time the subject was radio astronomy, and the author was Grote Reber, an amateur astronomer who had built a radio telescope near his home in Wheaton, Illinois, and had used to it produce a map of the Milky Way in radio wavelengths. The paper's most controversial suggestion was that radio radiation is coming from the direction of the Milky Way.

So novel was Reber's submission that Struve suggested that he and Bok visit Reber's radio telescope and evaluate his data. Bok did not enter this task in an entirely objective mood. Earlier that decade he and Priscilla had attended a lecture on radio astronomy by Karl Jansky, now regarded as the founder of radio astronomy, and both were doubtful as to the possibilities of that field of observing. During this visit, while Struve spoke with Reber, Bok talked to Reber's mother who complained that the huge unwieldy telescope, towering high above their house and visible throughout the neighborhood, was "an awful nuisance that interfered with hanging up the washing."

On the return trip the discussion turned serious. "I wish I was smarter and really knew how good this is," Bok began. "It is a completely new direction in astronomy." Then he reminded Struve of the Saha mistake of a decade earlier. There was no way of evaluating the results, and yet, if Reber's data were confirmed later on, this paper would be crucial. "If the paper is one of the great failures," Bok opined, "everybody will forget about it in no time. But if it is a great success, the *Astrophysical Journal* will forever have the credit of having published it. Don't do what Hale, Gale, and Frost did," concluded Bok, "don't turn him down. I'll stick my neck out—publish it by all means." Reber's investigation was published as a note entitled "Cosmic Static" in 1940, and included a large picture of his "antenna system" dwarfing his family home in Wheaton.[23]

Bok felt that the idea of observing in this wavelength showed tremendous promise. His main fear was that Reber's result—a radio map of the entire northern Milky Way—was possibly too good to be true, too simple to be real. Bok need not have feared.

Bok's experience with Reber and his radio telescope would pay him back a hundredfold when, by the 1950s, he became one of the prime movers of the radio astronomy field. Years later, Bok lectured on radio astronomy at the University of Tasmania. He was introduced as the man who had done more than anyone else for radio astronomy, the man who brought radio and optical astronomy together.

Had this been a typical university audience Bok would have simply said thank you and proceeded with his lecture. But this was hardly typical; Grote Reber sat somewhat stiffly in the front row. In a set of humorous remarks designed to make a serious point about how slow astronomers are to embrace new fields, Bok began his tongue-in-cheek introduction: "Under the circumstances, I think I should confess just how great a radio astronomer I really am." Immediately Reber started to laugh. Bok went on to say how Karl Jansky addressed the American Astronomical Society in the early 1930s, with Bart and Priscilla murmuring in the audience, "Do you believe all this?" "I don't know. I don't follow it." He continued that this first reaction of the great supportive Bok was to forget the whole thing and stay with optical astronomy. The next great reaction, he went on, was the *Astrophysical Journal* incident when all he said to Otto Struve was "what have you got to lose?"

Bok's train of thought continued; after the war, when radio astronomy was beginning to develop, did Bok assist? "No, nothing at all. I went on studying the galactic centers, studying colors of young stars, getting absorptions of dark nebulae, all the usual things." By this time Reber was laughing hard, thoroughly enjoying the point Bok was trying to make. Bok went on: "Finally the 21 cm line was discovered at Harvard. Was I involved in that? No, Purcell and Ewen found that line using a small antenna." Of course, as Bok continued and everyone laughed, he strongly understated his strong supporting role in building Harvard's first radio telescope, for 21 cm research, in the 1950s. (The 21 cm line reveals the existence of neutral hydrogen atoms, which are essentially the basic building blocks of our galaxy. This discovery was crucial in determining the galaxy's shape as a spiral; see chapter 9.)

Bok harked back to how he had listened to Karl Jansky in 1932, and only in 1950 was the field finally coming to its own. Although Bok would be a latecomer on the radio astronomy bandwagon, once aboard he enthusiastically supported it.

All that changed with the discovery of the 21 cm line. The development of radio astronomy at Harvard made the observatory a unique place where one could study at both optical and radio wavelengths. Around 1970 the telescope's original 60-foot-diameter dish was expanded to 85 feet. And through the efforts of Harvard astronomer Paul Horowitz and his colleagues, the telescope was also used for the first formally funded search for extraterrestrial intelligence, beginning around 1984. It was an intriguing and adventurous journey for a field of endeavor that dawned with a homemade metal dish in a suburban back yard.

6

Waves of War

By 1937 Bok had become a well-known astronomer, and with good reason. Anyone reading his *Distribution of the Stars in Space* and other writings would have been impressed by the thoroughness of his scholarship. But by the end of World War II Bok had become much more; because of his political activities he was now a major *public* figure. The demands of the war had forced many scientists, including those at Harvard College Observatory, to turn away from their research. Bok faced the coming of war with real concern: while many astronomers were turning the applications of science to war, Bok was attending to the plight of science in wartime.

In the late 1930s a group of prominent physicists, chemists, and biologists started the American Association of Scientific Workers, abbreviated AAScW, with the intention of solidifying the relationship between science and American democracy, particularly by increasing public awareness of science.[1] Bok was one of the group's founding members, and at one point early in its lifetime was even its vice-president.[2] But the AAScW was not his only area of political activism; in 1938 he also helped launch the International Council of Scientific Unions' Committee on Science and its Social Relations. Bok's intention with this committee was to publish a report "dealing with the various aspects of the relations between science and society," and to encourage astronomers worldwide to become active with community projects emphasizing schools, museums and planetaria, and amateur astronomy societies.[3] A similar report appeared in *Popular Astronomy*.[4] In 1940 it was translated into Chinese and presented to Bok during his visit to China.

By 1939 Bok had prepared a long article detailing specific areas where astronomers could improve their public communication. One promising new area Bok considered was radio broadcasting. "Very few astronomers," Bok wrote, "have acquired the correct technique of broadcasting. There is a wide open field for scientific broadcasting, and astronomers would do well to watch such opportunities."[5] Bok clobbered astrology hard, as he would again later through the American Association of Scientific Workers: "The astronomers of the world should take a determined stand against this absurd pseudo-science," Bok argued. "Its evil influence will never be killed if astronomers continue to be evasive on the subject; on the other hand, they would be performing a distinct service to humanity if they could succeed in wiping out astrological superstition among civilized people."[6]

As we shall see in chapter 15, Bok's interest in attacking astrology continued throughout his lifetime. It became part of a dramatic anti-ivory-tower "manifesto" called "Science and the Press."[7] This major AAScW proposal, made during the December 1939 meeting of the American Association for the Advancement of Science (AAAS), was intended to disabuse the American public of pseudoscientific attempts to explain natural phenomena.[8]

At its start the AAScW tried to tackle the single most difficult task of a scientist: to explain the purpose of science to the society of which the science is a part. Although at Harvard a scientist's foremost responsibility was to publish papers in scientific journals, Bok thought that rewriting these papers in a form that would bring the ideas, theories, and discoveries to laypeople was as important a mission.

The emergence of *Sky and Telescope* magazine was part of this calling. It was born in 1941 out of the merger of *The Sky* and *The Telescope*, two popular astronomy periodicals. When Harlan Stetson of Ohio's Perkins Observatory started an informal magazine called *The Telescope* in 1931 his idea was that a popular magazine would benefit both amateur and professional astronomers.[9] In 1936 *The Telescope* moved to Cambridge to be produced by the Bond Astronomical Club and Harvard Observatory, where Harvard staff would contribute regularly to its pages.

In April 1929 New York's Amateur Astronomers Association started *The Amateur Astronomer*, a magazine which was absorbed by *The Sky* in October 1936 under the editorship of Hans Christian Adamson at New York's Hayden Planetarium.[10] By 1941 it made sense to merge these two publications into the new *Sky and Telescope*, with Charles and Helen Federer as editors and publishers.[11] Headquartered at the Harvard College Observatory for its first few years, the magazine benefited from articles from the observatory's faculty.

Although Bok supported the start and early trials of *Sky and Telescope*, his name did not commonly appear in its early issues because his main social interest at the time was more politically directed. Appalled by the perils of European astronomers during the war, including their isolation from the international world of astronomy, he was trying quietly to build up a mail net among scientists on both sides of the Atlantic.

Bok began with an innocuous letter in the January 1941 issue of *Popular Astronomy* calling attention to "the virtual isolation of all astronomers in continental Europe." He echoed an idea first made in a plea to Bok from his mentor Jan Oort, namely that at least one copy of every notable astronomical publication be sent abroad. Bok's idea was that a "circulation manager" be named for each of several countries: Germany, Italy, Holland, France, Belgium, and Scandinavia. At first, eight copies of the major journals would be sent to these countries, but that number increased with time.

The "committee to promote the continued distribution of American astronomical literature abroad" managed to create a network of "safe routes" through which the astronomers of the world could communicate with one another.[12] Some of these routes were as informal as Bok's asking travelers to Europe to take a set of newsletters with them and deliver them to another person who would eventually get them to their destinations. The idea was to keep the lines of communication open just enough so that astronomers would know what was happening worldwide and that research done during these difficult years would not be needlessly duplicated.

In addition to the publications, Bok edited and sent abroad a series of letters that were designed to keep astronomers in enemy countries up to date with news of recent discoveries, theories, meetings, and ideas. Through these courageous newsletters astronomers could share in an informal way the results of work being done all over the world.

On the afternoon of December 7, 1941, the Boks were enjoying a lazy Sunday movie in Boston. As they crossed the bridge to Cambridge after the show, they heard the first radio reports of a massive Japanese attack on the U.S. Pacific Fleet at Pearl Harbor. They continued home, where, totally absorbed by the radio news, they were soon interrupted by a telephone call from someone Bok had never heard of before, a seventeen-year-old Dutch student named Uco van Wijk. He had a profound story. He had just graduated from a high school in Java, Indonesia, the former Dutch East Indies. His parents, he told Bok, were facing incarceration in a Japanese prison camp, but had been able to send him to the United States with instructions to find Bok as quickly as possible. "Professor Bok will look after you," van Wijk's father had said. "You go to Cambridge. Bok will get you to Harvard and everything will work out all right for you."

So desperate was van Wijk's situation that his father did not even have a chance to write to Bok about his plan in advance. The Boks were moved by van Wijk's predicament and decided to help him. "Uco became almost like a member of our family," Bok related. "We sort of adopted him. His father had given him ten thousand dollars so that he could get an education at Harvard and go on into astronomy."

"Using all the push and pull I had," Bok succeeded in getting his new student admitted into Harvard. It turned out to be a wise decision. After two years at Harvard van Wijk was drafted by the Dutch army and sent to do work similar to that of today's Peace Corps. Trained by the army to do judiciary work, he started in New Guinea, but there he got malaria. After this experience he returned to astronomy at Harvard where he graduated *summa cum laude* in 1948. While working on his doctorate he accompanied Bok to Africa, where in 1952 the two were able to show the presence of large amounts of dark matter within 3000 parsecs of the Sun.[13] Married to Harlow Shapley's niece Dora, van Wijk faced a promising career. But his New Guinea illnesses had worn him out, and before he reached middle age he died from heart failure.[14]

The Mexican National Observatory

On the same gloomy December day that Bok spent getting Uco van Wijk into Harvard, he was also preoccupied with a new international project, the Mexican National Observatory in Tonanzintla, not far from Mexico City. This was a sensitive project politically, since relations between the U.S. and Mexico had been strained following the election of Lázaro Cárdenas to Mexico's presidency in 1934. An intensely popular man, Cárdenas settled a strike of Mexican oil workers by appointing an arbitration board which ordered salary increases of one-third. Seventeen American-owned companies refused to honor this arrangement, even after it was upheld by the Mexican Supreme Court, a defiance which led to Cárdenas' fateful decision to nationalize the companies in 1938.[15] With the onset of war in 1941, President Roosevelt was anxious to improve relations with Mexico.

A colorful astronomer named Luis Enrique Erro was working to start the Mexican National Observatory during the tumultuous first years of the Cárdenas administration. He had arranged for a grant directly from the president.[16] As an amateur astronomer and prominent variable star observer, Erro had earlier appealed to Shapley to help get the new observatory project under way, and Shapley in turn had asked Bok to take the project under his wing. The dedication ceremony was about to occur when war broke out, and Bok desperately needed to learn if the United States would still participate. It was Vice President Henry Wallace who confirmed the decision to go ahead with the observatory plans. Wallace had consulted with Roosevelt, who saw the dedication as an opportunity to reaffirm good relations with Mexico, and consequently he insisted that the astronomers go to Mexico.

So on February 17, 1942, with Manuel Camacho now president of Mexico, twenty-seven astronomers and physicists from the United States and Canada braved wartime conditions to attend the dedication. "There were all the big shots and a couple of little shots from the U.S.," Bok recounted the event. The observatory's largest telescope was a 26-inch duplicate of Harvard's Jewett Schmidt camera, completed in only six months by the new firm of Perkin-Elmer and ready in time for the opening.[17] In November 1944 Bok visited Mexico again for three months with his son John, now a teenager.[18]

Bok found Erro a very colorful man with a good sense of humor. For one visit Erro had promised him that even though the observatory buildings were still not all completed, the guest bungalow would be ready for their use. When he arrived, Erro took him immediately to the observatory, where an afternoon tour convinced Bok that work was well advanced. A new dome and office buildings were almost complete. Finally, Erro took Bok to the foundations where the guest house was supposed to be. Erro reassured him: "Now here would have been your bedroom, here would have been your living room, here you would have had your dining room. But for now we go to town and find a rooming house!" Once completed, the observatory produced a generation of good astronomical data.

Bok recalled another example of the Erro's flamboyant style. During a tour of the unfinished Schmidt camera one hot afternoon, a shirtless Erro displayed the 26-inch lens at the front of the telescope by standing on a ladder, removing the lens from its mount, and holding it above his head.

Captain Bok

From his days at Leiden, when he traveled with Gerard Kuiper to see an eclipse and discuss philosophy, Bok had been a pacifist. By the late 1930s, although he was certainly not in favor of appeasing Hitler, neither was he about to join the war effort directly. Priscilla felt just as strongly. "I don't want to lie in bed," she said, "with a husband who, in the middle of the night, says that he has this idea how to kill fifteen more when a bomb falls."

Until 1941 that view was popular—President Roosevelt himself campaigned successfully for President in 1940 on a platform of keeping the United States out of the conflict. All that changed when Japan attacked Pearl Harbor, and within a day the United States was at war. The military buildup that followed was so sudden and massive that virtually everyone, including university scientists, played a role. At Harvard, as everywhere else, pure science gave way to war-related government contracts, and Bok faced the dilemma of living according to his own values in a time when he clearly realized that his adopted country needed him.

Bok admired President Roosevelt, whose frequent fireside chats became events taken quite seriously in the Bok household. "Roosevelt told us to put another log on the fire and listen," Bok noted; "that was a very reassuring thing in that difficult time. Roosevelt was an unbelievable leader." Priscilla insisted literally on "putting another log on the fire" when these chats began. The fireside chat just after Christmas 1941 was one of Roosevelt's most impressive evening talks, explaining why "a nation can have peace with the Nazis only at the price of total surrender."[19] These radio broadcasts were literally chats. Not intended as addresses or lectures, they were designed to be listened to by a relaxed and contemplative audience.

Events were happening that would soon turn Bok's military dilemma into something very positive. Through its newly created Engineer Amphibian Command, the Army had set out to plan the beachhead landings. The first such landing, in 1942 at Casablanca in northwest Africa, ended badly when an off-course troop ship collided with a large French cruiser.

Soon after that Shapley learned from an army colonel that "our people need navigation teaching in a hurry." Shapley replied that he had just the man, and promptly summoned Bok. Bok had never taught navigation, although he had had a little experience navigating boats in Holland. Bok accepted the plan to design and teach a course in navigation to military officers, and suddenly Bart Bok the pacifist became a valued cog in the U.S. military machine. Assisting him was Frances Wright, a young astronomer at Harvard. Across the country a small group of other astronomers, including Clyde Tombaugh of Pluto fame, taught similar navigation courses.[20]

"This was an exceedingly interesting assignment," Bok exulted. In three weeks the officers needed to know enough simple navigation that they could go from one place to another in the Pacific theater. Each course lasted just three weeks for a group of twenty officers, and then a new group would arrive. In all Bok taught a total of 11 groups stretching over 33 weeks. Field practice was held offshore at Cape Cod.

Bok divided each new group into three levels based on ability, typically with his own sense of whimsy: one that could add and subtract, a second that could add but not subtract, and a third that could do neither. Most of the amphibious engineers who took his course found him a highly effective teacher. Bok taught, for example, that the greatest mistake that one can make navigating across water is to try to travel directly from one island to another. Instead, one should head only for the correct latitude of the second island, and then it would be a simple matter to stay at that latitude and travel east or west to one's destination.

One lecture would begin as Bok took a piece of string to demonstrate a great circle; he would simply run the string along a world globe to determine the shortest route from one point to another. A different lecture would end with Bok holding up a large waterproof star chart which was intended for use during emergencies, but, as he explained, was useful for other purposes. As he unfolded it he said, "You can use it for navigation." Holding it high above him he added, "Look how you can make a sail out of it." Then he folded it into a cup: "You can use it to drink water." Finally, he concluded: "Once you are safely home, you can use it to protect the baby's crib!" Bok had a very dramatic way of pointing toward the celestial pole. Thrusting his arm towards the North he gave a loud, piercing whistle that startled his students into never forgetting the importance of knowing where North is.

Bok also wrote a pamphlet called *Navigation in Emergencies*.[21] The tract was soaked in banana oil so that it would be water-resistant and would help you even if, as Bok advertised, you were "Captain Bligh, forty days in an open boat without a compass." The continuing challenge of making navigation easy led to Bok and Wright's 1944 book *Basic Marine Navigation*, written so that a mathematically naive reader could understand navigation without logarithms or trigonometric functions. "The Navy was very upset about this technique," Bok proudly remembered. "They called it an undignified approach to navigation, a book made up by a stupid Harvard professor who was trying to help people along." Frances Wright concentrated on the many exercises and examples while Bok wrote much of the text.

Frances Wright stressed that "we felt we were doing the most important thing in the world, for the world depended on these people knowing their navigation. We felt as though we didn't have a moment to spend doing anything else."

Since neither astronomer knew much about navigation, both Bok and Wright took a summer course in navigation to prepare for their teaching. By the end of the course, which Wright took for actual credit and Bok audited, no one could tell that Bok had not studied navigation all his life. As one student bubbled, "He has such a robust and weathered look, like a sea captain. You can just tell he is a man of the sea."[22]

7

Putting the S in UNESCO

"UNESCO . . . is not a little mental Security Council that comes running with a first aid kit to patch up each threat to the peace. It is the organization that looks into the basic causes for war and suggests remedies for their removal." —Bart Bok, 1949[1]

When the war ended in Europe, Bok's quiet international newsletter effort—to keep communication alive among astronomers in different lands—led naturally into a much bigger project, the founding of the United Nations Educational and Cultural Organization (UNECO). It would be formed as part of the United Nations to help rebuild devastated countries through the transfer of technology and education. During the war years, Bok had worked with the Boston-Cambridge branch of the American Association of Scientific Workers, consisting largely of people at Harvard and MIT, to propose a similar post-war institution to use the world's scientific resources in this way.

Not surprisingly, Bok strongly supported the United Nations idea but insisted that "there should be an 'S' in UNECO." By the end of the war the AAScW had lost much of its effectiveness, each of its various members pursuing separate directions. Besides Bok, chemist Isadore Amdur was the only AAScW member really pushing the UNESCO idea. The two scientists mounted a campaign that included articles and letters. At first their work met a brick wall: one official from the American Association for the Advancement of Science even warned Bok that he was premature in thinking about international relief efforts in the closing months of the war and that the AAAS would not support any such plan. After those heady early days in the late 1930s, it seemed as though the AAScW was dead, and so might be the idea for a postwar international scientific organization.

By the opening day of the April–June 1945 San Francisco conference to draft the United Nations Charter, the title and purpose of UNECO were still in dispute. With some members opposing even the inclusion of the word "education," it looked as though the science angle was doomed. However, at the same time the Science Commission of the Conference of Allied Ministers of Education (CAME) had tendered a tentative suggestion to include "Scientific" in the title of UNECO.

With different ideas coming from an alphabet soup of commissions, Bok decided to go to the public directly. During the summer of 1945 he spoke with Waldemar Kaempffert, science editor of the *New York Times*, about publishing a letter supporting UNESCO. A strong advocate of scientists explaining their work to the people, Kaempffert often had used the *Times* to push for greater social responsibility for scientists, and he considered Bok's effort to be a positive step in using science to help set up the recovery effort. On Thursday, August 30, Bok and Amdur mailed their letter for publication in the following Sunday's edition.

The choice of date could not have been more appropriate. On Sunday, September 2, the *Times* trumpeted a rare all-column headline:

JAPAN SURRENDERS TO ALLIES, SIGNS RIGID TERMS ON WARSHIP; TRUMAN SETS TODAY AS V-J DAY

On this first day of peace, the letter was featured prominently in the *Times*'s editorial page:

> The recently announced plans for a congress to consider the formation of a United Nations cultural and educational organization show that there exists a full realization of the importance of culture and education in the maintenance of world peace. It is, however, noteworthy that the words "science" and "technology" do not occur in the press releases about the agenda for the congress.
>
> There exists a danger that science and technology will be neglected in the initial schemes for the cultural and educational world organization. We wish, therefore, to draw attention to a proposal submitted last April by the American Association of Scientific Workers to the Secretary of State for the formation of an international scientific office.
>
> One of its first tasks should be the re-establishment of contacts among the scientists of the United Nations. To this end, the office should undertake promptly the organization of small but representative congresses for the various sciences, where the leaders in each field can meet to discuss problems of international organization and cooperation.

The office could further international collaboration in many ways. Some of the items that should rank near the top are the giving of aid in the rebuilding and restaffing of scientific institutions in devastated countries, the establishment of adequately equipped research centers in backward nations and the promotion of international exchanges of scientists, young and old.

The office could take action that would lead to the appointment of diplomatic scientific attachés to the legations of the United Nations and it could make available as needed expert assistance and advice in developments of a technological or agricultural nature.

During the war many normal channels of international communication in science and technology have become disrupted. The office could fulfill an important need by promoting the prompt exchange of scientific and technological papers published in various countries.

It is relatively unimportant whether the office is a separate unit, operating under the Economic and Social Council, or that it becomes a part of the Cultural and Educational Organization.

Bart J. Bok, I. Amdur
Cambridge, Mass., Aug. 30, 1945.[2]

The letter pushed the idea for putting the S into UNESCO so eloquently that it produced considerable response, including a positive letter from neurologist Detlev Wulf Bronk, president of the National Academy of Sciences (1950–62). By now the war was over; the United Nations had started, and an enthusiastic conference to start UNECO finally began in London in November 1945. The earlier CAME proposal to include "Science" was discussed, and its logic seemed attractive. The meeting participants agreed that international scientific exchanges had been more capably organized than in any other field.

"The sciences have a place in UNESCO," Bok would write later, "not only because they have a big contribution to make toward the achievement of a better material life, but also because scientists are potentially among the most effective ambassadors of good will."[3] Harlow Shapley attended the meeting in London. Once it began, the British delegation proposed that "scientific" be added to the title, and with strong support by the Americans the proposal was adopted quickly.[4]

Now Bok was under a different kind of pressure. After doing the groundwork to set up the scientific side of UNESCO, would he then drop the ball? "The trouble with some of you scientists," Bok quoted Bronk as saying, "is that you get on your high horse for a cause, but as soon as you have accomplished it you abandon ship and go on to other things."

Charged with nominating a chairman for the AAAS-sponsored Committee on Science in UNESCO, Bronk proposed Bok, who naturally accepted with relish and never regretted his decision. It was unlikely that Bok would abandon this project in the way Bronk had suggested. He always felt this committee was dedicated to preserving the basic principle of UNESCO, which at the time was truly lofty. Archibald MacLeish, then Assistant Secretary of State, had written that "since wars begin in the minds of men, it is in the minds of men that the defenses of peace must be constructed."[5] These words opened the preamble to UNESCO's constitution, and Bok took them literally. "Whenever our committee met, I took a quiet moment, almost a prayer, and said, 'O. K. boys, sit down. We're going to read the preamble so that we will remember what we are.'"

Bok's remarkable efforts during and after the war to keep the lines of communication open among scientists in a divided world are touching and inspiring. On the surface, they might be seen to have little in common with his professional career interest in the galaxy. Governed by physical laws that have little in common with the philosophies of war, the Milky Way actually beckons the kind of cooperative spirit toward which Bok was working. Studying it—like all great mysteries of science—was a task to challenge the minds of scientists all over the world. Bok's roll-up-your-sleeves approach to wartime communication and the founding of UNESCO would continue in other forms and become one of his greatest contributions to the spirit of scientific inquiry. He loved his work with UNESCO. "It was a glorious committee to be chairman of, one of the most difficult of its day," Bok harked back on the group he headed for four years. In March 1947 he attended the first American conference on UNESCO. From the start Bok saw its purpose as threefold: first, to assist in rebuilding lands that had been devastated by the war; second, to build a "program for international understanding, and to work toward better fundamental education." He saw the third purpose as "basically a fight against illiteracy . . . one of the most admirable undertakings of UNESCO."[6]

Even during its optimistic early days, Bok's work with UNESCO had a strong negative side. He was later told by an FBI agent that his "premature interest" in the founding of the United Nations made him suspected of being a communist. At the time he scoffed at the idea, although, as we shall later see, by 1954 the McCarthy era forced him to take these accusations seriously. Bok also knew that the Communist party had become involved in the AAScW. Although the aim of the AAScW was not to propose radical change in political thought, members of the Communist party were active in the Boston-Cambridge branch. Bok later admitted that the AAScW "had about half a dozen good Communist members, who tried to use us for party purposes."[7] The organization's eventual failure, in fact, was partly due to the suspicion that these members caused.[8]

In June 1948 Bok's committee met in Paris, this time to tackle the question of what specific roles scientists could play in "the maintenance of peace." Ideas as specific as teaching South Seas fishermen how to preserve their catch were considered. However, the meeting's main purpose was to establish the general importance of scientists in reconstruction efforts. As Bok saw it, UNESCO would translate scientific work towards the promotion of peace by allowing the nature of the scientific method to foster a spirit of international cooperation. This would benefit the sciences themselves through improving international contacts among their participants.

As the United Nations matured, its original noble aims were bound to suffer some attenuation. Unfortunately, politics has badly harmed UNESCO. By the fortieth anniversary of Bok's letter to the *Times*, the organization was hamstrung and unable to fulfill its mission. In 1984, the Reagan administration decided to pull the United States out, partly because it perceived that the U.S. was paying the lion's share of UNESCO's bills without having a commensurate degree of control over its activities.

The idea that scientists could help make a peaceful world became generally accepted as the war years faded and UNESCO's scientific role became stronger. In 1948 President Truman concluded that "when more of the peoples of the world have learned the ways of thought of the scientist, we shall have better reason to expect lasting peace and a fuller life for all."[9]

8

Darkness and Brightness
in the Milky Way

A book devoted completely to the Milky Way seemed a natural part of
Shapley's new series, The Harvard Books on Astronomy, when it was
launched at the end of the 1930s. Shapley's idea was to take a number of
fields—the Milky Way, galaxies, planets, the Sun—and have the faculty
write a series of explanatory books for general readers. He asked Bok to
became associate editor for the series. As Harvard University Press was
not interested in such general interest books at the time, Bok found a
small Philadelphia publisher called Blakiston, which specialized in medical books. Bok assisted Shapley in editing all the other books in the ep-
ochal series.

Bok's main contribution would be, naturally, a book called *The Milky
Way*. Bringing Priscilla aboard as co-author was an exceptionally interesting idea. With John and Joyce in high school, this seemed an ideal
route for Priscilla to reenter her astronomical work. It was a daunting task
Bok shared on top of his other teaching and research duties, but it gave
him the opportunity to sell the Milky Way almost as a thing of romance.
It was during the writing of *The Milky Way*'s first edition in 1940 that
Priscilla developed her writer's law: "Affix the seat of your pants to the seat
of your chair and leave it there until your work is finished."

In the opening chapter, "Presenting the Milky Way," the Boks sell the
Milky Way as though it were a product: "When Jupiter summoned the
Gods to council to end the frightful condition of things on Earth 'they
obeyed the call, and took the road to the palace of heaven. The road . . .
is called the Milky Way. Along the road stand the palaces of the illustrious
gods; the common people of the skies live apart on either side.'"[1] One can

hear the invitation to join the authors as they lead the reader "on a brief tour along the road to the heaven of the Greeks."[2]

Trying to change "two times four chapters" into a unified eight-chapter book turned out to be quite stressful. Although Bart and Priscilla wrote different sections, the entire book was so well edited that it was impossible to tell who penned what. The years of working together were not always harmonic. With four chapters assigned to Priscilla and four to Bart, the working arrangement seemed ideal, Priscilla working for several uninterrupted hours each day in a small attic room in their Lexington home.

The toughest moment took place one evening as Bart was editing his wife's writing. Bart made, or so he thought, some "very reasonable suggestions," but Priscilla did not find them so prudent. She was so incensed that she stood up and walked to the fireplace, manuscript in hand. "If you say one more word about my four chapters," Priscilla challenged, "I will burn them up." Bart never forgot the image of Priscilla standing lividly by the fire, her chapters a flip of the hand away from incineration. "That was the greatest crisis we had in our whole marriage," Bart noted, adding that Priscilla had become so fond of what she had written that any criticisms would appear "a blemish on her character." Bart caved in completely, but he later teased his wife about her "fine gesture"—*he* knew that she had carbon copies tucked safely away.

The argument was kindled again when Dirk Brouwer's review of the book appeared in the *American Scientist*. As co-editor of The Harvard Books on Astronomy series, Bart was delighted at the review's opening remarks calling "for congratulations to a courageous publishing company and to an enterprising observatory staff."[3] However, the reviewer was far more favorably inclined toward Priscilla's early chapters than he was toward the later ones largely written by her husband:

> The development of the subject occupies about three-quarters of the book; the remaining three chapters deal with current research problems, with a comparison of the Milky Way System with other galaxies and, finally, with the problem of the age of the Milky Way System. Somehow these chapters do not quite measure up to the excellence of the preceding parts of the book. Perhaps because the unity that governed the earlier chapters is lacking, perhaps because the authors attempted to cover too much in too few pages. If the latter is correct, why was it necessary to deal in so much detail with the problems of energy generation in stellar interiors? This subject will certainly find a more fitting place in another volume of the series.[4]

"See," Priscilla gloated, "that shows that I'm the big shot! You're a no-body."

"No it doesn't," Bart said, laughing at her teasing and unable to make a fitting comeback; "all it shows is that Brouwer has no sense for the fitness of things in the galaxy!"

Although by 1940 many astronomers strongly suspected the Milky Way of being a spiral galaxy, the patterns of the arms were far from proven at that time. Without too much scientific evidence, Bok imagined a Milky Way that spiraled out like a monstrous pinwheel. But where the arms might be required a leap of faith that challenged his career as well as his imagination. Bok had suggested the presence of a single arm of the galaxy that stretched from the far southern constellation of Carina all the way through us, and northward through the constellation of Cygnus. The presence of this arm made sense as he stared at the Milky Way during a dark night in 1933. On a shipboard vacation with Priscilla and John, they were passing through the Panama Canal. From that unusual observing site near the Earth's equator, Bok had a magnificent view of both the Milky Way's northern and southern stretches, and he could visualize the sweep of this possible arm. This concept, however, did not survive the rigor of astronomical observation. The Carina-Cygnus idea lasted long enough to appear as the closing words of *Distribution of the Stars in Space:* "The observer in the tropics should not find it difficult to accept as a working model for our Milky Way system one with a distant center in Sagittarius and in which a spiral arm passes from Carina through the sun toward Cygnus."[5] The idea was also considered for the first edition of *The Milky Way,* but the theory hasn't survived. There is probably an arm in Carina (known as the Sagittarius-Carina arm), as there is in Cygnus, but they do not connect through our region of the galaxy.

The Bok Globules

Bright stars are not the only things that make up the Milky Way and other galaxies; strange dark material is also a major component. When John Herschel first observed patches of sky totally devoid of stars, he thought they were windows or gateways to the outside universe and called them "holes in the heavens." In the early 1900s the highly astute observer Edward Emerson Barnard carefully catalogued a great many dark regions. It was apparent to Barnard that rather than being clear windows, these star-poor regions were really huge clouds of dust. Unlit by nearby stars, these dark clouds blocked the light of all the stars behind them.

Bok's interest in this so-called dark matter dates back at least to his doctoral dissertation, in which he reported the existence of a dark nebula perhaps 800 parsecs, or over 2700 light years, away.[6] In *The Distribution of the Stars in Space* he described in detail the numbers, sizes, and studies of all known dark nebulae in the Milky Way.

Around 1947, Edith Reilly had begun working as a technical assistant at the observatory with Shapley and Cecilia Payne-Gaposchkin. One afternoon Reilly asked Bok if she could study dark nebulae with him. With his navigation work over, he was anxious to spend more time on his Milky Way research, and the dark areas were certainly high on his wish list. He had especially hoped to develop a classification scheme and was looking for someone to investigate the nebulae on Harvard's plates. Unfortunately Reilly had multiple sclerosis, and she was not physically strong enough to handle the 8″ by 10″ glass photographic plates.

Bok soon saw a perfect opportunity in Reilly's request. Why not have her examine the old catalogs of several hundred dark nebulae that Barnard had prepared, to determine which of them would be candidates for further study? At first the work was relatively routine. As it progressed, Reilly noted several very small, round, and unusually dense nebulae. His interest aroused, Bok began photographing these dark clouds. Forgetting about their classification project, Reilly concentrated on identifying these nebulae while Bok set out to photograph them using the Jewitt Schmidt telescope at Harvard's Oak Ridge Observatory station. In 1947 a preliminary paper discussed their work on these "small dark nebulae."[7] They were typically roundish, from three to five arc minutes wide (about one-sixth the diameter of the full Moon) and located in regions of the Milky Way with no bright nebulae or unusual stars nearby. "Through a telescope," Bok later described, "you would come to the leading edge of one of these things and suddenly the stars would just disappear. And then you would push the telescope's slow motion button a bit and bloop! the stars come back."

Bok and Reilly found about two hundred of these dark objects within the relatively close distance of some 500 parsecs (somewhat more than 1500 light years) outside the solar system, the best examples being in the constellations Taurus and Ophiuchus. These tiny nebulae were optically extremely thick, with possibly *thirty magnitudes* of extinction; if one could, for example, cover a first magnitude star with one of these clouds, it would become invisible even through today's Hubble Space Telescope.

Bok thought that these nebulae marked the birthplaces of new stars.[8] As their dark gases move about slowly, he reasoned, they begin a slow collapse under their own gravity that intensifies until stellar fusion starts. With evidence of their importance, Bok thought about giving them a simple name. That thought was in his mind one morning as he walked downstairs in his pajamas and bathrobe, opened the front door of his Belmont home, and found bottles of milk delivered fresh from the H. B. Hood Company.

At the time, milk was not homogenized, so at the top of each bottle the cream would separate out. In the cream floated small globules of fat. "My God!" Bok exclaimed, "these things look just like my *globules!*"

The astronomical community was slow to accept the idea that these objects represented a special stage in the evolution of stars. George Herbig, who later concentrated his work on the formation of new stars, felt that these objects might not even be real, but transitory little wisps of material that come and go. "George," Bok challenged, "have you ever *looked* at one in a telescope?" Bok added that they seem "as physically real as a globular cluster." When Herbig did see one, he became a convert, and he asked Bok for a photograph of one of these objects: "I'd like to have one on my wall," he said; "It is a beautiful thing."

One of the strongest early skeptics was Walter Baade from Palomar. "Frankly," he wrote Bok in March 1947, "I cannot convince myself that these objects are in any way peculiar . . . I am afraid you have been misled either by the Lick print of M(essier) 8 on which the objects in question may appear as inky spots on account of some stepping up process [artificially increasing the contrast on the plate] or by some Harvard plates of insufficient scale."[9] Before replying Bok examined as many other plates of Messier 8 as he could find, including one from the large 82-inch telescope at McDonald Observatory. "From the material available to me," he argued, correctly as it turned out, "that there is little doubt about the reality. . . . Edith Reilly and I have examined a number of the objects in Barnard's famous list of dark objects. As examples of objects I would be tempted to classify as globules I list the following. Barnard 34 and Barnard 92 are examples of the somewhat larger variety. They appear to be clearly defined, they are probably all relatively near by and to my mind there can be little doubt that they are really unlit dark nebulae."[10] But Baade was unconvinced. "With Hubble I believe," he wrote, "that they are parts of outlying streamers of Messier 8 which are not hit by the radiation of the exciting star. The whole behavior of the streamer system suggests this interpretation."[11]

In 1956 a search of two prints of the newly completed Palomar Sky Survey revealed seventeen thousand new dark objects, averaging about one minute of arc (about a thirtieth the apparent diameter of the full Moon) in diameter.[12] When radio telescopes began studying these objects around the same time, the nature of these small dark nebulae as star precursors became much more credible. "My biggest boosters have been the radio astronomers," Bok explained, adding that the objects were good hunting grounds for cosmic dust and very cold carbon monoxide at only a few degrees above absolute zero.

As the idea of the globules gradually became accepted, the name "Bok globule" suddenly riveted the popular imagination thanks to a science fiction story called *The Black Cloud* published in 1957 by the noted British astronomer Fred Hoyle. As the story opens, astronomers using Palomar's 18-inch Schmidt telescope discover a terrible black cloud approaching them. "Such globules are not uncommon in the Milky Way," the astronomer says, "but usually they're tiny things. My God, look at this! It's huge, it must be the best part of two and a half degrees across!"[13] Finally a senior astronomer examines the Schmidt plate and pronounces the object "a fine example of a Bok Globule."[14] As the drama unfolds, the globule gets larger and larger as it closes in on the Earth, until one morning the assistant appears in a great panic:

> "It's not there, sir, it's not there!"
> "What isn't there?"
> "The day, sir! There's no Sun!"

People going outside that awful morning saw an eerie sight: "It was pitch black, unrelieved even by starlight, which was unable to penetrate the thick cloud cover. An unreasoning primitive fear seemed to be abroad. The light of the world had gone."[15]

But this was no garden-variety Bok globule. It had intelligence and the ability to communicate with the scientists on Earth, and was very surprised to find that life forms inhabited an actual planet instead of living freely in space. It hung around for several months, and after negotiations had succeeded, the globule finally departed.

The book went into several printings, and Bok was delighted for its "wonderful advertising" of his globules. Partly as a result of Hoyle's novel, they are now generally known as Bok globules. However, Bok modestly suggested that his globules should not really be named for him, that it was really Barnard who photographed them first and called attention to them, and his assistant Reilly whose work helped lead to their discovery. "The only thing that B. J. Bok did was to kick everybody in the pants and say you'd better pay attention to these Barnard objects. . . . In 1947 and 1948, Edith Reilly and I suggested the globules and no one believed that they were real, physical things. No one paid any attention until the radio astronomers came in."

Comet Bappu-Bok-Newkirk

Astronomer Frances Wright was always inspired by the enthusiasm of the Observatory group. When Uco Van Wijk suggested that Wright take some wide-angle pictures near the Sun to search for comets, she spent her entire summer vacation photographing in the evening and morning hours, developing and checking the plates and working herself to exhaustion. Although she did find a known asteroid, she found no new comets.

A new student from India named Vainu Bappu seemed envious of Wright's project. On one occasion, complaining that no Indian astronomers had ever found a comet, he told Wright that "I would give anything to find one." Since he had not had much observing experience at his native home, he asked Bok if he could spend some nights at the observatory's wide field telescope, not to find comets but to learn basic astrophotography at Harvard's Oak Ridge Station.[16]

July 1, 1949, was hot and sticky as Bok and Bappu set up for observing. Bok spent the afternoon and evening hours teaching Bappu how to find stars and to guide the 24-inch Schmidt camera, and later to make actual observations. Bok observed the sky while Bappu observed Bok. Toward morning, Bok chose an area to photograph in Cygnus and decided to let Bappu handle the sixty-minute exposure. "This is your big chance. I am going to let you do the whole works: load the plate, carry it out to the telescope, and find the star. And then I'll let you guide the telescope for one full hour until dawn comes. Vainu, I'll let you make your own mistakes."

Observing with Bok at Agassiz, or anywhere else, was a special experience. One night at this station student Arthur Hoag had observed the entire night: "We turned in to the men's dormitory at the observing station. The following day I was gently wakened out of a stupor by the distinguished professor of astronomy. Dr. Bok was shaking me, gently, and saying, 'Your breakfast is ready, sir.'"

After Bappu and Bok were ready for a hot and humid day's work in a small building near the telescope, Bappu was taught how to process the plate that had been exposed the previous night. After it was dry, they examined it under a binocular microscope in the 24-inch reflector telescope building. "Vainu and I looked at the plate, and the images were perfect. He had focused correctly, done everything right, nothing wrong. It was a beautiful plate."

At this point Gordon Newkirk, an undergraduate student, walked in, looking for his shirt. "Have either of you seen my shirt?" he asked, probably somewhat embarrassed. "I lost my shirt."

Bok said, "No, we haven't seen your shirt. It's not in this building. But you must come and have a look at Vainu's first beautiful plate!"

Newkirk studied the plate briefly. Almost casually he asked, "Hey, what is that fuzzy line there? Is that a flaw on the plate?"

Concerned, Bok sat down and studied the plate carefully. He noted a fuzzy streak with a protrusion off in one direction. Finally he looked up. "Gordon, that is no funny plate defect. That blob there is a bloody comet!"

With mounting excitement the three first checked to see if the trailed image was not an already known comet. They did that by checking the published positions of the several comets known to be in the sky at that time. Then they measured its position accurately, relative to nearby stars, took a second exposure to confirm that it was real and not a photographic artifact, and then found the comet's image on a patrol plate that had been taken a few nights earlier, on June 29. Finally, Bok telephoned Shapley and reported the discovery.

Naming a new comet that had been found on a photograph depends somewhat on the policy of the institution at which the object was discovered. At some observatories the comet would bear only the name of the person who actually found the comet on the plate, no matter who actually took the plate at the telescope. However, according to Frances Wright, the comet was so bright that Vainu Bappu would doubtless have found it himself in the normal course of examining his plate.[17] Thus, Shapley suggested that the comet be named for the three members of the group in alphabetical order, and the name became Bappu-Bok-Newkirk.

Vainu Bappu was delighted to be the first Indian to discover a comet and even wrote his funding agency about it. Their reply was less than rhapsodic: "We awarded you the fellowship to learn astrophysics at Harvard," Bok recalled their words. "We did not offer you the fellowship to discover comets there. Please return to your assigned works. Sincerely yours."

Comet Bappu-Bok-Newkirk was a diffuse object, somewhat condensed in appearance, and about thirteenth magnitude at discovery. It was still several months away from perihelion (closest point to the Sun). By September 2 it had reached its maximum magnitude of about 11.7.[18] It moved out of the constellation of Cygnus and through Lyra, Hercules, and Bootes, sporting a small tail and a large diffuse coma. Then it started to fade. As it moved farther from the Sun, it was last sighted in March 1951.[19]

South Africa

In 1890, Harvard founded a remote southern station near Arequipa, Peru, that, it was hoped, would be ideal for observing objects, particularly variable stars, visible only in the Southern Hemisphere sky. Initially the Peruvian sky had offered promise, but a long period of unsettled weather there persuaded both Shapley and his associate Solon Bailey that the station needed a better location. After some searching, astronomers at Harvard found an entirely new site in South Africa, about six miles outside Bloemfontein. Opened in 1928, it offered good skies and a fine view of the Magellanic Clouds, the two closest galaxies to the Milky Way.

This was a change that the observatory announced with much promise: The Boyden station "will be the largest telescope in operation in the southern hemisphere," Shapley trumpeted in his Director's Report of 1928. Its "Bruce Telescope" had a 24-inch doublet lens made by the famous English telescope maker Andrew Ainsley Common and purchased through a bequest of Catherine Wolfe Bruce.[20] The station would be funded through a Harvard bequest that had been established on the death of Uriah Boyden in 1879.[21]

Boyden was an observatory of considerable stature with good research telescopes. J. S. Paraskevopoulos, the director, ran the Boyden station with a lot of attention to small details but, Bok says, little originality; he was a good administrator. Most of Paraskevopoulos's work focused on patrol photographs of the southern variable stars, collecting invaluable data that would help form the basis for Harvard's prominent reputation in variable star research. He independently discovered comet Whipple-Paraskevopoulos 1940 IV in October 1940, and a year later found comet de Kock-Paraskevopoulos 1941 IV.

"I had always wanted to go to Boyden," Bok noted, "but Shapley rather loved the idea that he was the sole controlling force in the station." Shapley oversaw Boyden as his own kingdom; so he was unenthusiastic when Bok completed his dissertation on Eta Carinae and wanted to go to Boyden to study the region firsthand.

Then suddenly, just before the United States entered World War II, Shapley changed his mind. He also decided that the Bruce telescope would be dismantled and removed from its observatory, and that a new state-of-the-art Baker-Schmidt telescope would be mounted in its place. Designed by James Baker of Lick Observatory, this innovative instrument would be the first of a new type of Schmidt camera. Instead of having the light pass through a correcting lens and then reflect off a larger primary mirror to hit the photographic plate, the Baker design adds another convex mirror to the system that reflects light back toward the primary mirror. The result was a wider field of view than a traditional Schmidt, with the star images still in sharp focus from edge to edge.[22] Hoping to go to South Africa to observe, Bok was delighted with the new plan. The large new telescope would be ideal for studying the rich regions of stars and nebulae of the southern Milky Way.

Not all the astronomers were pleased with the change, however. One staff astronomer assailed Shapley for what he called "the rape of the Bruce." When the war began, plans for the new telescope were put aside, and the new Schmidt telescope was still not in place at the start of 1949. But Bok wouldn't let Shapley forget the plan; "I kept on reminding him I wanted to go for a year with Priscilla to the Boyden station." By 1949 new funding had cleared the way. Bok received a special leave from Harvard, and the entire family prepared to head for Africa. Because of further delays, partly with the new telescope, they did not get out until February 1950.

Before leaving, Bok inspected the nearly completed Baker-Schmidt, still in the shop in the United States, and posed for a picture that would appear on the April 1950 cover of *Sky and Telescope*. Later that year the new Baker-Schmidt telescope, destined for the Boyden station, was completed and scheduled to leave for Africa.

The observatory was some 30 miles outside Bloemfontein, a small city of about 70,000. The Boks were met by Paraskevopoulos, "who half welcomed us and half didn't welcome us," Bok remembered. Paraskevopoulos might have been worried that Bok had come down to take over his job, resulting in his chilly reception. Considering the hoopla that accompanied Bok's trip, including the *Sky and Telescope* cover, it is not surprising that the director did worry.

Before the Boks left for Africa, Shapley treated them to one of his legendary parties. "We left Harvard in great form," Bok noted. "I always kept a bathrobe that the staff gave me at that party, a beautiful one that lasted for over thirty years." Then, as Bart and Priscilla sat in "Bok's seats," the students sang a farewell melody to the tune of "Carolina in the Morning":

Nothing could be fina'
Than to guide on old Carina
   In the morning.
Nothing could be greata'
Than to follow good old Eta
   'Til the dawning.
One of heaven's glories
That's what I go for—
Twinkling little staries
I long to see once more
Nothing could be fina'
Than to guide on old Carina
   In the morning.[23]

Because there were no living quarters at the observatory, the Boks stayed on a large farm about a mile away at the foot of the observatory hill. Since the Baker-Schmidt still was not working properly, the first observing season with the galactic center high overhead was a disappointment. "Those Baker-Schmidts are tricky fellows," wrote Walter Baade from Palomar, "and that is one reason why I never could work up enthusiasm for them. . . . The southern hemisphere is really the place to tackle this job and not our northern latitudes."[24]

They arrived in a country two years into its nationalist movement, and though Bok befriended almost everyone he met there, he feared for their future. "It's an impossible situation," he recalled. "I loved every element of the population. I stayed at an Afrikaaner family's house. I speak their language. I love them each individually. But as a group, they make a hell of a mess of living together."

Bok was concerned but excited about the politics of South Africa as an emerging nation, an opinion some colleagues back at Harvard found na-ive and unsettling. "When I think of South Africa," Bok wrote later in *Harper's Magazine*, "I think of sunshine, of flowers, of wide-open spaces."[25] Maintaining contact with troubled nations was an axiom of Bok's philosophy that never changed throughout his lifetime, and South Africa was no exception: "Increased cultural and economic co-operation between the United States and South Africa will serve a multiple pur-pose," he wrote. "First, there would be direct benefits to the economic and cultural life of both countries. Second, South Africans would see how, on a small scale, we share with them some of the same racial prob-lems and how we are progressing toward finding a solution. And, finally, we in America would obtain an insight into South African problems and with that insight an understanding of South Africa's approach toward their solution."[26] What really surprised Bok's colleagues, especially Fred Whipple, was his opinion, published in *Harper's*, that "the Nationalist program [of which *Apartheid* was the key] is a sincere attempt to find a solution to the Native problem, which will make it possible for white and black to live in peace within the borders of the Union."[27] But in another opinion Bok was prescient: "I am not optimistic about the prospects for the next fifty years."[28]

The Boks had planned to remain in Africa about eighteen months, but since their daughter Joyce wanted to graduate from a U.S. high school, she and Priscilla returned at the end of 1950. John stayed with his father to complete his undergraduate thesis on the origin and development of the Nationalist Party in South Africa. Two graduate students, Uco Van Wijk and Ivan King, visited Boyden while Bok was there.

In March 1951 Paraskevopoulos unexpectedly died, and it was quickly apparent that his wife Dorothy, who had assisted her husband in his work, was determined to take over management of the station. "Nobody wanted that, neither Shapley nor the staff at Boyden. And Shapley asked me to become acting director." It was a busy time. In addition to familiarizing himself with the daily operation of the station, he had to attend to the fine tuning of the new Baker-Schmidt.

Bok's eighteen months in Africa were productive and enjoyable. He worked mostly on his beloved Eta Carinae region, although he spent some time on the galactic center and even a little time observing the Milky Way's nearest neighbor galaxies, the Magellanic Clouds. Doing any research or observations concerning the clouds was inviting trouble, for Shapley was extremely territorial about them. "He told me to stay the hell off his clouds—they're not my department! He wanted me to worry about the Milky Way and leave his clouds alone." Nevertheless Bok did begin a somewhat understated photographic program of the Clouds and quickly became enraptured by them. In September 1951, Bart and John Bok returned to the United States, but by different ships: John went through Venice and bicycled across Europe, imitating a happy trip his father had taken a generation earlier.

But the Boks returned to a Harvard profoundly changed, a Harvard he no longer knew.

9

*

Harvard Twilight

*Had it not been for Senator McCarthy and his goddamned
investigations, I might never have left Harvard.*
                                        —Bart Bok, 1983

When Harlow Shapley wrote a simple letter to a liberal candidate for
Congress named Martha Sharp, he had no idea that it could lead ulti-
mately to the departure of Bart Bok from Harvard. Shapley's letter had
offered money to Sharp's campaign on behalf of the National Council of
the Arts, Sciences, and Professions, a group that raised funds for political
campaigns.[1] The letter came to the attention of a high ranking member
of the House Committee on Un-American Activities, Congressman John
Rankin, and forced Shapley into the front line of the Red Scare.

The "Balance of Terror," as Churchill called it, between the United
States and the Soviet Union began almost immediately after World War
II ended and intensified late in the summer of 1949 when the Soviets
exploded their first atomic bomb. In December 1951 disarmament talks
between Britain, France, the United States, and the Soviet Union ended
without any agreement. In the United States the birth pangs of the cold
war were most noticeable in the loyalty investigations; in January 1950,
Alger Hiss, one of President Roosevelt's senior advisors at the Yalta conference in 1945, was sentenced to five years in prison for having sworn
falsely that he was not a Communist. Three years later Julius and Ethel
Rosenberg were convicted of treason in trading atomic secrets to the Soviets, and executed.

In this period of anti-intellectual hysteria, attacking progressive thinkers became almost the accepted thing to do. Professional and business
people, artists, writers, and actors all were subject to attacks on their loy-

alty to the United States. The most ambitious of the attackers was Wisconsin's Republican Senator Joseph McCarthy, who announced that the State Department was full of Communist sympathizers; he worked to get Secretary of State Dean Acheson to resign. In September 1950 the McCarran Internal Security Act was passed by Congress, vetoed by Truman, and then successfully overridden by Congress. Among other things, it allowed the government to arrest Communist sympathizers in vaguely defined periods of "wartime."

It was in the wake of these events that artists, intellectuals, and other citizens were harassed, forced to inform on each other, blacklisted by their professions, and dismissed from their jobs. It was in this atmosphere that Harlow Shapley was challenged.

Early in November 1946 Rankin served Shapley with a subpoena to appear before the House Committee on Un-American Activities (usually abbreviated as HUAC). From its creation at the end of World War II, HUAC's enthusiastically pursued mission was to ferret out artists and intellectuals it considered subversive, especially if their influence extended beyond university walls. Shapley was spoiling for a fight. Claiming that the committee had no right to investigate the funding of a political campaign, he charged that the subpoena was "an obvious political maneuver to discredit the work of all independent voters."[2]

On November 15, 1946, accompanied by his secretary and an attorney, Shapley entered the HUAC hearing room amidst a burst of flashbulbs. Rankin first demanded that the lawyer leave and somehow managed to get him out of the room. In the few minutes the lawyer was away, possibly talking with reporters, Shapley turned to his secretary and asked her to write down something. Rankin promptly demanded that the secretary "get the hell out of here." When he threatened to call security guards, Shapley asked her to comply. But the observatory director had one more ace up his sleeve; since he knew shorthand he then began to write down everything that was said.

Rankin lost whatever was left of his composure. In a red-faced rage he left his chair, slid over a table, scuffled with Shapley, yanked the notes, and declared that the Harvard director would be cited for contempt of Congress.[3]

After he left the hearing room, Shapley quickly prepared a strong message for reporters: "I stand on my rights as an American citizen and will not submit to the star-chamber methods of the Gestapo used by Rankin.

It is time that this most un-American of all procedures in the country is recognized as the Nazi method and that it be eliminated so that private citizens can be free under our Constitution."[4]

Rankin had a statement too. "I have never seen a witness treat a committee with more contempt," he howled, also asking that charges be prepared to cite Shapley for contempt of Congress.[5]

The following day Shapley told Bok the story "with tears in his eyes." Bok remembered Shapley angry enough to say, "That dirty, no-good son of a bitch had the nerve to tell *me* that I was un-American. I resent that. I have worked much harder for the good of America than he has."

Apparently others agreed. Rankin had to back off his contempt charge. In a face-saving gesture he announced that he would "bring the matter . . . to the full membership" of HUAC.[6]

Bok urged Harvard's faculty and students to support Shapley; the college community responded overwhelmingly. More than a third of the Harvard undergraduate population signed a petition drafted by Bok and others that praised Shapley's courage in standing up to Rankin. In March 1947 Harvard's President James Conant was one of eight college presidents to sign a letter labeling Shapley's treatment "a glaring example of disgraceful procedure. The abuse of power is a disgrace to Congress. There must be no more star-chamber proceedings." Although Rankin was alone, the letter noted that he had acted "with full authority of the House Committee on Un-American activitities, of which he is a member."[7]

The episode unfortunately did not end there. In fact, Shapley's next run-in, though hardly remembered now, was far more damaging to Bart Bok's chances to succeed Shapley as director of Harvard College Observatory. Shapley was approaching his sixty-fifth birthday in the spring of 1950. He actively promoted Bok, who had already left temporarily for South Africa, as his successor. Meanwhile, Senator Joseph McCarthy, busy with his own agenda against the Red Menace, asked Harvard's President Conant why he had not fired Shapley. Conant's reluctant reply: "That isn't the way we do things."[8]

When McCarthy was testifying before a Senate foreign relations subcommittee hearing on March 14, 1950, the fact that Harvard was not an arm of the State Department did not keep him from accusing Shapley of being a Communist closely linked to the State Department. "Keep in mind," the senator said, "[Harlow Shapley] is the man who headed the peace conference which the Secretary [of State] labeled as a sounding board for Russia."[9]

The other senators on the subcommittee acted as though they had no idea who Shapley was. Chairman Tydings asked only whether Shapley was one of the official numbered cases. McCarthy replied that he wasn't; it was just that Shapley was someone the Secretary of State had referred to in a news release.

McCarthy then accused the State Department of having "conveniently omitted" certain "facts" about its relationship with Shapley. One was that State had appointed him to the National Commission for UNESCO, and another was that State had actually paid his transportation expenses and $10 per diem for his trip to London (see chapter 7). "I am at a complete loss to understand how the State Department could seek to avoid responsibility for Dr. Shapley's [UNESCO] appointment . . . in view of these uncontroverted facts," McCarthy thundered.

Then came the list. "Dr. Shapley's active participation in the Soviet Peace Conference is not the last nor only Communist front with which this man has been affiliated. His record with Communist fronts is a long and interesting one."[10] The official account then presented 37 "Communist-front organizations which this individual has belonged to"—including, one might be interested to know, the National Council of Arts, Sciences, and Professions, a teacher's union (where he was a speaker), and, as might be expected, the "Citizens United to Abolish the Wood-Rankin Committee."[11]

Shapley did not appear before the subcommittee, but he did answer McCarthy's accusations in a letter. Although this repulsive episode seemed finally coming to a close, it left a bad taste as far as other observatory senior staff were concerned, especially Donald Menzel and Fred Whipple. "I've always sworn," Bok stressed Menzel's words, "when people asked me, that Shapley is not a communist. I just hope now that I shall not be asked again."

It was bad timing for Bok's future that the Foreign Relations subcommittee hearings took place just as Shapley was urging Bok's appointment to succeed him as director. Harvard's president, James Conant, publicly defended Shapley's views and actions, although he was uncomfortable with the director's outspoken behavior. He did not want to see it continued in the attitudes of whoever succeeded Shapley. "Considering Shapley's relationship with the Harvard administration at the time," Fred

Whipple said, "this was a kiss of death. I don't think Bart Bok was ever considered seriously, simply because of that."[12]

A man with strong anti-Communist views, James Conant was clearly embarrassed by Shapley. The Harvard president was forced to defend Shapley on the basis of academic freedom, but, as Bok put it, "wished the man would drop dead." Whipple added that the administration's dislike for Shapley had grown over decades: "He ran his own store," Whipple noted, "and did not accept advice from the university administration. The McCarthy issue was only the straw that broke the camel's back."

While Senator McCarthy was thorough in his charges against Shapley, he apparently overlooked Bok's own "stained" past, including Bok's *New York Times* letter as well as his extensive history of international contacts (see chapter 7). This was a difficult record to justify in the xenophobic postwar decade.

Shapley Retires

Although Fred Whipple collaborated with Bok on only one paper, about a 1939 nova in the constellation of Monoceros,[13] he and Bok had become very close friends since their early days at Harvard. "He was the only one Priscilla and I used to get drunk with," Bok looked back fondly on their early friendship. Late one evening in 1945, for instance, Whipple joined the Boks on the roof of their home to celebrate the end of the war.

As a graduate student at the University of California at Berkeley in 1930, Whipple helped produce the first orbital calculations of the newly discovered planet Pluto, calculations which were published only three weeks after the announcement of its discovery.[14] Whipple's fascination with orbits grew after he arrived at Harvard, and by the end of the war he was mulling over a profound issue: while studying the orbits of meteors, he realized that they were very much like those of comets. The very short lifetimes of meteors dictated that somehow comets, then thought to be large "flying sandbanks" of dust, must be replenishing this huge supply of solar system debris. Whipple soon became so engrossed in the relationship between comets and meteors that he decided to "leave the Universe to other astronomers" and devote his career to the comets. He soon formulated a new theory that comets were large conglomerates of ices and meteoric particles, now popularly known as "dirty snowballs."[15] Whipple's model has withstood four decades of observations and is the basis of his current reputation as "Mr. Comet."

In September 1951 Fred Whipple published the results of his work in two of the most important papers in the history of comet science.[16] His friend Bok was fresh from Africa with his own first observations of the Eta Carinae region of the Southern Hemisphere sky. Bok was enthusiastic about his work there and wanted to tell Whipple about it, but he felt even happier to be back at Harvard and with Priscilla, from whom he had been apart for the last several months of his trip. "It was a long time," he noted; "Yes, sir, that's a long time to be separated."

Before leaving for Africa, Bok had looked forward to a weekly lunch with Fred Whipple. So the day after he returned to Harvard, Bok sought out his old friend and colleague to resume their midday meetings. But Whipple was in no mood to reminisce about old times, or to discuss South African politics, about which he considered Bok quite unsophisticated. But in any event, Harvard, not Africa or comets, was the main topic of lunch that day. "It was an unpleasant occasion," Bok recollected.

"Fred," Bok recalled saying, "this is my first day back, so I'll want the privilege. I'll pay for your lunch."

"No, Bart, it would be better if each of us pays for his own lunch. There are important things we need to discuss."

"What the hell is going on?"

"You know that Shapley's retirement is coming up. You also should know that you and I and Don [Menzel] are the three principal contenders to succeed him. Who will get it I don't know. But it is not going to be easy to sort it out. It will be a difficult time."

Bok was stunned. "Is Shapley already close to retirement?"

With Harvard as with Africa, Whipple was struck by Bok's disengagement. Was Bok not aware that the director was approaching age sixty-six and that he was staying on an extra year already? "My God, man!" Whipple exclaimed. "Where have you been? You don't even know that?"

"No. I had not considered his age."

It is hard to believe that associate director Bok had not considered that Shapley would soon retire, but Bok has described that lunch in those terms to several different people at different times. Bok admitted later that "Priscilla and I were never great schemers or planners. Otherwise we would have known that Shapley was retiring. It had really not occurred to me that Harlow's time was up."

Intimidated by the McCarthy hearings, powerful Harvard administration people were now seeing Shapley as a liability; that might have been obvious to Bok if he had heard about the Senate hearings while in South Africa. Bok had returned from Africa confident that some day he would become director; he knew he was good and that he had Shapley's vote of confidence. ("Bok would give you his winter overcoat if he thought you were cold," Shapley had said.) What more could Harvard possibly ask for? Bok had apparently never considered that after more than thirty years as director, Shapley had used up his political influence.

Frances Wright, who had worked closely with Bok on navigation and later just as closely with Whipple on his meteor research, underscored that Bok had hoped to fly into the director's chair on the enthusiastic—and quite unanimous—shoulders of his colleagues. Whipple was trying to say only that the observatory had options, that his becoming director was no longer a foregone conclusion. There was a search committee, and there were other candidates. Bok took this as a personal rejection and accused Whipple of being a ringleader. Three decades later, neither Whipple nor Wright could recall, at least at that early stage, any personal design at all. Wright also saw the reticent Whipple contrasting in style with the far more ebullient Bok, who concluded that silence meant conspiracy.

Though Bok was surprised that he had heard of nothing of Shapley's fall from favor or of the search committee during his stay in Africa, he was still optimistic about his future at Harvard. If he was not to get the directorship he would be just as happy with returning to Blomfontein and becoming director of the Boyden station. He still wrote publicly about his support of Shapley, and he was still very active with international relations.

At about the same time as Bok and Whipple were having their fateful lunch, UNESCO published *Freedom and Culture*, a collection of essays by renowned scientists. Psychologist Jean Piaget, for example, wrote of "The Right to Education in the Modern World."[17] Bok's contribution to the volume was a discourse on "Freedom and Science," in which he emphasized a pivotal focus of his thinking: "Scientists are citizens and they want to exercise their rights as free citizens."[18] It was a plea to repudiate any threat to the freedom of scientific inquiry. As illustrations he chose the infamous Lysenko genetics controversy in the Soviet Union and Red-baiting in the United States.

The Soviet case involved Trofim Lysenko and the Lamarckian school of genetics. Based on an experiment using identical twins brought up in vastly different environments, Lysenko claimed that environment played a far greater role in the development of the individual than had been previously thought. Bok's complaint was that although there was once a lively debate about this in the Soviet Union, all the geneticists opposed to Lysenko's view had been muzzled. Only Lysenko's theories agreed with the official Communist Party doctrine of scientific materialism, where all reality must be in observable matter.

Thus, in Stalinist Russia all geneticists had to study and approve of Lysenko's approach. "No scientist," Bok charged, "however friendly he may feel toward the Soviet Union, can ever tolerate this policy. For it is the basis of all true science that the results of experiments are the supreme arbiters in controversies and that political or doctrinaire concepts should have no place in scientific argument. Impartiality and freedom from bias are the very root of scientific inquiry. Science totally loses its bearings if the government can lay down rules with regards to permitted and forbidden directions of scientific thought."[19]

But Bok was not about to let his own country off the hook. He next attacked military-supported research in the United States, a policy of "restrictions imposed upon the discussion of results of scientific research falling under the security regulations set by the Military Establishment."[20] Here Bok argued that in the interest of maintaining the peace, the results of certain scientific research were restricted or classified. Bok objected to the way in which such research was restricted, and proposed that a security officer should have to "demonstrate the need for classification before an impartial board."[21] "Classification," Bok concluded, "is in a way the partial or total hiding of the results of scientific research and there is no denying that classification procedures will generally work against the best interests of science."[22]

Bok then cited the case of his friend Shapley. "The almost inevitable result," he insisted, "is a series of so-called *loyalty investigations* by legal and extra-legal bodies within each country."[23] "The fact that men like Dr. Harlow Shapley and Dr. Edward U. Condon have defended themselves successfully against all attacks, does not however prove that loyalty investigations really do no harm."[24]

Less than a year after the memorable Whipple-Bok lunch, Shapley retired as director of Harvard College Observatory and Donald Howard Menzel, Harvard's solar astronomer, was appointed acting director. One reason often cited for this decision was that Menzel had seniority over Bok. He didn't. Although Menzel first arrived at Harvard in 1921, at the time he was actually only working there as a Princeton University graduate student and did not join the Harvard Observatory staff until 1932, three years after Bok arrived and after he had some experience at Lick Observatory.[25] In any event, although Bok kept his Harvard professorship, he eventually resigned as associate director, and on January 15, 1954, Harvard President Conant announced Menzel's permanent appointment as director. If Shapley was leaving under any cloud at all, he didn't show it; his March 1954 *Sky and Telescope* article was a fine testimonial to his successor's capabilities, and only mentioned Bok once: "The future of that important part of the observatory [the Agassiz station] will include further development of the radio astronomy work which, under the supervision of Dr. Bart J. Bok, has in the past year become highly significant."[26]

Of course, Shapley could afford to be magnanimous, for he was retiring as director. It was his young friend Bok who was facing his career's biggest crisis.

Closing Boyden

During the war a strong alliance developed between individual scientists (at many universities) and the military. As a solar astronomer, Donald Menzel, for example, designed an antiaircraft gunsight that defended against attacks by planes coming out of the sun's glare.[27] Generally the military-scientific collaboration served both parties well, and it remained strong after the war ended. The early years of rocketry at Aberdeen and White Sands Proving Grounds, for instance, provided enormous scientific benefits in studies of the Earth's upper atmosphere. Princeton's great astronomer Henry Norris Russell (of the Hertzsprung-Russell diagram, see chapter 5) developed a camera that traced a missile's ballistic path by comparing it with star images recorded later that night on the same film.

By the mid-1950s Harvard Observatory was getting substantial military funding, an important factor since Harvard was facing a financial crunch—something all too familiar in university life. Having lost the directorship, Bok was already nervous when President Conant asked the Observatory Council, a group of senior staff formed during the Shapley administration, to meet with him in the spring of 1953 about this financial problem. Conant's suggestion was quite specific: Boyden station, he proposed, must be completely liquidated. In view of its financial struggles, the Harvard Corporation had decided that it was not a good policy to own real estate so far from home.

"That pulled the rug out from under me," Bok stressed. "I felt completely stranded without the southern base on which I had counted." He appealed, but Conant seemed so intent on the specific act of closing Boyden that Bok believed the action was intended partly to hurt Shapley, who had been so proud of it. Within the next few years other changes would take place at the Observatory as well; both *Sky and Telescope* and the American Association of Variable Star Observers would be forced to leave Harvard, all in the name of financial difficulties.

One little-known argument for closing Boyden might have been valid. Except for the new Schmidt camera (see chapter 8), the equipment there was in such substandard condition that users had, as then-student Campbell Wade noted, to "fight the telescopes" to get any reasonable data out of them. Under the Menzel administration and the dictates of tight finances, it might have made sense to solar observer Menzel not to argue too strongly in favor of keeping a southern station whose main purpose would be to photograph Bok's southern Milky Way.

As it turned out, Menzel did not destroy Boyden when Conant demanded that it be liquidated; instead he organized an international group of six different observatories to run it.[28] For many years the station was managed by the University of the Orange Free State.

By now Bok was convinced there was a conspiracy that had begun in response to Shapley's outspoken politics and Bok's support of Shapley. "Had it not been for McCarthy and his goddamned investigations, I might never have left Harvard," he said later. That might be correct, but Bok was mistaken about the conspiracy. "Bok thought that Menzel and I were conspiring," Whipple remembers, "and he felt that I had betrayed his friendship. It was not that at all; I don't think Bart ever asked me about our behavior." Although Whipple never intended to get involved politically, he sympathized with Bok and Shapley: "They were both expressing their repugnance at the McCarthy operation, which was a despicable blot on the whole U.S. government attitude toward liberal thinkers. I was generally sympathetic but never wanted to be involved." Wright agreed with this view: "I think Bok made it seem more personal than it really was."

Radio Astronomy and the Discovery of Spiral Structure

Bok did not neglect his science during this difficult time. Although his career opportunities seemed to be slipping away in succession, scientific opportunities were not. With the Harvard Observatory directorship, and then Boyden station, out of his reach, Bok passionately thrust himself into the science of the Milky Way. On the horizon was a new 21-centimeter radio telescope whose penetrating ear would soon hear into the galaxy's heart. Perhaps this project would keep Harvard attractive to Bok. Almost as if it were a lifeline, Bok grabbed onto it. At first Bok was confident of success, since radio astronomy was now evolving rapidly into an important line of research.

But this completely new approach was only part of the story of how the Milky Way's spiral structure was actually found. The discovery was a long process involving both optical and radio telescopes. Although Bok was not the one to make the discovery, his approach to the problem certainly helped point the way.

Since the 1930s Bok was the acknowledged master of statistical studies of the structure of the galaxy and its interstellar material. His work on galactic structure had concentrated on the analysis of counts of stars; however, his results did not go far enough to indicate the concentrations of matter necessary to establish the existence of spiral arms.[29]

Walter Baade, a German astronomer at Mt. Wilson, followed a different strategy. In the mid-1930s he had lost his application papers for U.S. citizenship and consequently in 1941 was classified as an enemy alien virtually under house arrest at Mt. Wilson Observatory. With a monopoly of observing time on the 100-inch telescope there, and able to take advantage of the dark sky resulting from the Los Angeles wartime blackout, Baade studied the spiral patterns of nearby galaxies, defined two "populations" of stars, and identified regions of hydrogen gas that characterize the spiral arms.[30] He suggested that an examination of the so-called O- and B-type stars, with their associated hydrogen nebulosity, might reveal, or trace, a spiral shape to our own galaxy. For a while Baade and Bok corresponded on how Bok's Milky Way observations might be correlated with Baade's studies of M31 to indicate spiral structure in our galaxy. "From my studies of the Andromeda nebula," Baade wrote in 1949, "I would bet that the absorption for the 4 Cygnus Cepheids is due to the fact the line of sight (from them to us) runs in the absorption free— or at least absorption-poor—space between two neighboring spiral arms."[31]

In 1951 William W. Morgan, Stewart Sharpless, and Donald Osterbrock, all of Yerkes Observatory, followed up Baade's idea. By studying the distribution of stars of different populations in the solar neighborhood, they detected evidence of two spiral arms, which they called the Orion and Perseus arms, plus part of a third called the Sagittarius arm.[32]

The American Astronomical Society's 1951 meeting took place in Cleveland just a few months after Bok's return from Africa. Bok badly wanted to have discovered the galaxy's long suspected spiral structure. However, he knew that "Morgan had done the sensible thing in spectral classification and deserves all the credit for it. I just came too late."

The night before he read his seminal paper announcing the discovery, Morgan was kind enough to share his findings with Bart and Priscilla by asking them to meet with him in his dormitory room. Sitting on the bed, the stunned Boks first saw the data that showed evidence for the three arms. The following day, session chairman Otto Struve asked Bok to lead the commentary on Morgan's work. "Both Morgan and Struve were very kind to get me involved," said Bok, adding that they could have just as easily ignored the man who had clearly missed the boat.

Interestingly and incorrectly, Shapley did give Bok credit for completing similar work at the same time with the southern Milky Way.[33] Bok denied this; while in South Africa he concentrated on Eta Carinae and he did not complete the star counts that might have painted a picture of the spiral galaxy.

The advent of radio astronomy offered a totally new way to confirm and expand the discovery of spiral structure. While optical telescopes use mirrors or lenses to see deeply into the sky, radio telescopes employ large dish-shaped antennae to hear it. Barely eleven years had passed since Grote Reber's *Astrophysical Journal* paper about his backyard radio antenna (see chapter 5), but Bok fervently wanted a big radio telescope to work the problem from that direction. At first he was alone; even Baade held out little hope for this line of research and encouraged Bok to drop the idea.

In 1951, using a small pyramid-shaped horn antenna mounted on a roof of Harvard's Civics Building,[34] Harvard physicists Harold I. Ewen and Edward M. Purcell detected radiation from neutral hydrogen atoms at the 21-centimeter wavelength, as a radio signal from the Milky Way.[35] Before the advent of radio telescopes, the galaxy's shape lay hidden behind a dark veil of interstellar dust that optical telescopes cannot penetrate. But radio telescopes "see" a different wavelength of sky, and through them, the Milky Way's spiral shape could be mapped. The spiral arms are traceable by observing where hydrogen is especially concentrated. Not only could the Orion and Perseus arms be confirmed, but the arms could also be extended much further out, beyond the dark matter that blocks the view of the optical telescopes. Bok's old mentor Jan Oort, and also his colleague van de Hulst, then went on to publish a 21-centimeter map of the galaxy.

Bok was now trying to get a large radio telescope for Harvard. Meanwhile Menzel and Whipple, never believing he would succeed, were trying a very different route: getting the Army signal corps to pay for the telescope, but with a very different research goal—the observation of meteors. Bok hated the idea of the military funding science, and he even called it "blood money."

In an Observatory council meeting, Bok claimed, Menzel and Whipple argued that his Milky Way research would be very difficult to fund in the future. "Bart," Whipple said, "it is clear that we cannot now look forward to support Milky Way research at Harvard." Would it not be better, Whipple proposed, that the Signal Corps fund the radio telescope, and that it be used to study the deceleration of meteors at various heights in the upper atmosphere?

"Things were not very cheerful on the docks," Bok thought. Under the guise of financial constraints, he felt that the others were snatching his beloved Milky Way research from him. Behind his back, Menzel and Whipple also had lunch with some of Bok's students, asked them questions, and then debated amongst themselves how to make the proposal look good to the military.

If Bok was unnerved over the threat to his telescope, he tried his best not to show it in front of his students. "Bart had told us that he was turning the project over to Menzel and Whipple," Campbell Wade, then an undergraduate, emphasizes, "but at no point did he give any inkling of any hostility. He just said, 'They have access to certain sources of funds that I do not; so they are going to take it over.' He put it in a gentlemanly way."

Bok's judicious and quiet manner during this entire period was atypical, considering his usual energy level. Wade suspects that Priscilla might have suggested that he be "extremely circumspect; otherwise he could very easily turn a bad and discouraging situation into a totally hopeless one." Frances Wright recalled also that Bok was uncharacteristically distant and reserved during this period. However, Bok's caution extended even to his children. John comments that there was almost no discussion of these politics at home, but that he was aware of what was going on: "I think there was a strong feeling on the part of Whipple and Menzel and others that once the government, whatever that means, viewed you with suspicion and distaste, your ability to get funds for the kind of research they wanted to carry out were impeded. I think Whipple and Menzel saw that Shapley's involvement in these un-American activities committees, and to a lesser extent Dad's involvement, imperiled their own ability to carry out their research."[36]

Bok's self-control eventually paid off. When the military route proved unfruitful, Bok got another chance. In 1953 he arranged a $32,000 grant from the National Science Foundation for a small 25-meter radio telescope.[37] But that was not enough. Together with Shapley, now Professor Emeritus, he met with Mabel Agassiz, a member of one of Boston's most famous families, in an effort to persuade her to supply the remainder of the needed funds for the instrument. Agassiz had given money before, always in the name of her late husband, George Russell Agassiz. All the income from the endowment was intended to go toward Harvard's Agassiz Museum of Zoology. But over the years she developed a personal respect for Shapley and also became close enough to Bart and Priscilla that they often referred to her as "Aunt Mabel."

Their annual meetings were very friendly. Bart and Priscilla would arrived precisely at, say, four o'clock, driving around the block once or twice to pinpoint their arrival time. The butler would usher them in, and Agassiz would then offer sherry to Bart. Even though Priscilla enjoyed sherry as well, she did not get any during these visits; instead Agassiz poured orange juice for Priscilla and herself. Then Agassiz would inquire how the previous year had gone at the observatory. This was Bart's cue; he was expected to come up with a proposal for some item, like a spectrograph, that would cost in the neighborhood of five thousand dollars. Agassiz would write the check on the spot. Then, precisely at two minutes before five o'clock, Bart would thank Agassiz for the visit and the gift, and two minutes later the Boks were ushered out the door.

Their annual meeting near the end of 1952 was different. When Mabel Agassiz asked about the observatory, Bok decided to ask for $25,000 toward a twenty-five foot antenna intended as a precursor for a much larger sixty-foot radio telescope. Uncertain about a sum five times larger than usual, Mabel Agassiz told Bart and Priscilla she would need to think about it. A short time later she requested that Bart Bok and Harlow Shapley "make a little trip" with her. They were picked up in an opera Cadillac, in which the chauffeur sits in an open roofless area in front and the passengers sit in the back. They drove to the gate of the Mt. Auburn Avenue Cemetery. Having no idea what was about to happen, Shapley and Bok said little during their ride, occasionally looking toward each other like expectant children.

The Cadillac stopped at the cemetery. The three got out of the car and stood by the gate. "Harlow and Bart," Mabel Agassiz said, "I am going to give you the $25,000. But it is such a large amount; I just want to be near George when I do it." She then wrote out a check—not to Harvard but to Shapley personally—for the sum of $25,000. Combined with additional funds from the National Science Foundation, the gift finally put the telescope on its way to completion.

Divided into two twelve-foot sections, the antenna was finally moved to the Agassiz station on a frigid January morning in 1953 "with state police blocking the roads," Bok remembered; "it was lots of fun." Harvard was now poised to study radio sources in Cassiopeia and Cygnus as well as the diffuse nebulae, and to learn about hydrogen gas in the Milky Way. Soon after the telescope was finished, Bart, Priscilla, and graduate student David Heeschen sat quietly as they watched the pen of the telescope's data recorder rise and fall as it recorded the telescope's first data coming in from the Milky Way. Finally Priscilla broke the silence with a soft quote from Omar Khayyám: "The Moving Finger writes; and, having writ, / Moves on."

Encouraged by the early success from the small telescope, Bok was able to get Roger Revelle of the Office of Naval Research to start the process of funding a telescope three times larger. Apparently Bok didn't see this as military "blood money." After a lot of discussion, skeptical at first, he understood that the Office of Naval Research might be a precursor to a civilian National Science Foundation, and thus he was willing to work with Revelle. Bok eventually raised some two hundred thousand dollars from the fledgling National Science Foundation, partly through the graces of his friendship with Allan Waterman, its first director. Apparently unknown to Bok, his supposed nemesis Fred Whipple was asked to adjudicate the proposal to NSF for the telescope, and he recommended that it be built. "A negative vote from me," he added, "might well have killed the project."[38]

As the telescope was built, it became a marvelous sight. "At its topmost point," wrote David Heeschen, "the reflector rises as high as a seven-story building, affording a fine view of the countryside to anyone with the energy and boldness to climb it."[39]

The telescope was finally dedicated on April 28, 1956, on Bart Bok's fiftieth birthday. In a few short years Bok had so honed his skills with radio telescopes that he had become one of the country's top radio astronomers. He later helped select the site for the National Radio Astronomy Observatory in a valley near Greenbank, West Virginia, and remembered how his work with radio telescope design led to his meeting the architect Buckminster Fuller high in New York's tallest building: "Fuller came in with great zeal and gave us all sorts of tetrahedral designs," Bok noted. "He put his legs and his arms on the floor to demonstrate the stability. On the fortieth floor of the Empire State Building. It was out of this world."

Dr. Bok and the Subcommittee

By 1954 the McCarthy purge was nearing its zenith. In addition to HUAC, several states, not wanting to be left out, formed their own committees to ensure that the 1950s version of "politically correct" thinking was followed. The Massachusetts variant was the "Educational Sub-Committee of the Commonwealth Commission to Study Communism, Subversive and Related Activities." One frosty 1954 evening Bart and Priscilla were leaving their home to hear a Boston Symphony concert. Just as they were driving off a car pulled up. The Boks returned and asked if the driver was looking for someone. "Yes," he replied, "I'm looking for Bart J. Bok."

"Well, that's me."

"Fine. I have a subpoena for you."

A startled Bok was to appear before the educational subcommittee. In getting pre-hearing legal advice, he learned that the committee was essentially fishing for the names of people who had Communist leanings. The idea was that they would ask about the activities of people in an effort to get a witness to admit that a colleague might be a present or former Communist, "fellow traveler," or Communist sympathizer. Apparently the phrases "might be a Communist" or even "might have been one" were good enough to prompt the committee to look further. Bok did know people—a top physicist among others—who had admitted to him that they had belonged to the party at one time.

On Friday afternoon, February 19, 1954, Bok answered the subcommittee's summons in a forty-minute interview. Bok was administered the oath and then asked "Are you now, or have you ever been, a Communist?"[40] Although the committee counsel told Bok that he was not even suspected of being a Communist, the committee, in its intimidating fashion, demanded to know his position anyway. Bok challenged the subcommittee to "bring in a whole stack of Bibles: I will put my left hand on the Bibles, raise my right hand, and swear that I had never been a Communist; nor was I invited to become a communist." Bok's forceful manner worked. Some members found that "very refreshing; instead of simply pleading the fifth amendment, which was what many witnesses do." Bok claims their reaction set "a very nice tone" for the rest of the hearing.[41]

With some strange logic, the subcommittee next asked why he would not have joined the party had he been approached. Bok replied that one important reason was that he had been repelled by the 1937 purge of Boris Gerasimovicz. Stalin had the Soviet astronomer killed and then had his name removed from all Soviet references. Next came a key question: Bok had supported the formation of the new national Progressive Party a few years earlier; one commission member wanted to know why he had done this. He answered that he had been unhappy with some of President Truman's policies and was looking in new directions. The counsel wanted to know why he had left that party. Bok explained that the new party also did not meet his expectations.

The discussion then turned to the central issue, Bok's membership in the American Association of Scientific Workers. Here the questions were very specific. Did Bok recollect any times when any of his friends, notably Isadore Amdur, the co-writer of his letter on UNESCO to the *New York Times* (see chapter 6), had attempted to "throttle" free debate? After Bok answered no, they spent some time discussing the AAScW's program, specifically why Bok felt attracted to it. Lastly, Bok summarized his campaign against astrology and his efforts with Amdur to bring science into UNESCO.

One final question: How could Communist infiltration of voluntary organizations be avoided in the future? While answering this, Bok, as he put it later, "let the committee know what he thought of them." Bok suggested that they distinguish between Communist Party members of the late 1930s, who genuinely might have been working to stop the spread of Fascism, and those who were presently joining the Party: "To join the Communist Party at this time, one would have to be either a fool, a real revolutionary dissatisfied with all of our Democratic system, or a psychopathic pervert. I said I knew of no one, faculty or student, at Harvard whom I suspected of being an active Communist Party member at this time."[42]

Bok then leveled his sights on the subcommittee's central agenda and methods. First he said that there was little risk of Communist infiltration of voluntary liberal organizations. However, he added this caveat: "A far greater risk seems to me that excessive protective legislation will tend to discourage the best younger scientists in the country from participation in any 'extra-curricular' activities like those in which I and many of my colleagues engaged during the late 1930s and early and middle 1940s. Already there is a premium on the wearing of blinders by anyone of the younger generation of scientists. It is notable that the physicists under 35 or 40 years of age watch the old-timers perform without daring to participate themselves any longer in public affairs where, because of their special training, their competent advice is needed. I said that I fear that we are encouraging the training of narrow science-specialists, who know that it is dangerous to participate freely in public discussion relating to the social and political implication of their work."[43]

Enter the Smithsonian

By Menzel's third year of directorship, Harvard College Observatory had changed direction completely by inviting, through the efforts of Fred Whipple, the Smithsonian Astrophysical Observatory (SAO) to move to campus. Fred Whipple had wanted to set up an optical satellite tracking system, a project he estimated would cost several million dollars but would be invaluable for the artificial satellites that were soon to come. Whipple was almost rhapsodic about the potential of artificial earth satellites. In November 1955 he told the American Astronomical Society that "first matter and energy, and now space will have become the slaves of man."[44] At the same time the SAO was looking for someone to head its solar operations. Whipple saw the opportunity to join the SAO with Harvard, with a resulting growth in strength for both institutions.

So in 1955, the Smithsonian became heavily involved in meteor and satellite tracking, and Harvard College Observatory suddenly became a much larger place. By now Bok was so unhappy with Harvard that he would not go along with what the others proposed. Feeling that the Smithsonian was a big organization that would devour the observatory, he also said later that neither he nor his colleague Cecilia Payne-Gaposchkin had been properly consulted about the merger.

According to Bok, Menzel called an "emergency meeting" of the Observatory Council, consisting of himself, Whipple, Cecilia Payne-Gaposchkin, and Bok. He announced, Bok recalled, that "Cecilia and Bart should be informed that we have decided to ask Smithsonian Astrophysical Observatory to come to Harvard. Fred will be director." Then Menzel said that Harvard dean McGeorge Bundy had insisted that Bok and Payne-Gaposchkin sign a document relating to the issue, and that since he had an appointment with Bundy he would like the signatures immediately. Menzel then explained that the joint venture would result in a huge influx of funds, allowing the combined observatory, as Bok interpreted the insult, "to deal with expensive people like Bart Bok." Bok insisted that this meeting was the first he had heard about this proposed new arrangement.

Around the same time Bart and Priscilla asked their old friend Otto Struve (the former *Astronomical Journal* editor, see chapter 5) to visit one evening. Before dinner they were standing on the front porch, enjoying the Boston twilight, when Struve nervously said that he had brought a message.

"From whom?"

Struve answered that it was "from your colleagues, Bart."

For a minute they said nothing. Then Bart asked, "What is it?"

"The message is that life will be so much easier at Harvard if you would stop your support of Harlow Shapley."

For some minutes there was silence while everyone was deep in thought and review. First had come the loss of the directorship. Second had come the loss of Boyden. Third, Bok felt his colleagues were trying to make him feel that the Milky Way was not a worthwhile field. Fourth, he didn't like the Smithsonian moving in. And now they were trying to make him stop supporting the man he admired more than anyone else.

"Life would have been very simple," Bok remembered years later, "if Priscilla and I had turned against Shapley. Shapley was accused of having been a 'dangerous Communist.' Actually, he was an independent thinker, a man who had the nerve to go after the globular clusters (see chapter 3) and straighten them up. He went after political things in exactly the same way and he believed in world peace and in world friendship and in the idea that astronomers had to do something about it."

With some alarm Struve looked at his friends. "Have I said something awful?"

"No, Otto, you haven't," Priscilla answered sadly. "But Bart, I think it is time we left Harvard."

Departure

By 1955 Bok was exploring a tentative offer, at about half his Harvard salary, to become director of Australia's Mount Stromlo Observatory and Professor of Astronomy at the Australian National University. McGeorge Bundy, then the dean at Harvard in charge of the Observatory, at the same time offered Bok a solution to his increasingly difficult problems. He would double Bok's salary, but in return, Bok would leave the observatory. His new position would be as professor in Harvard's School of Education with responsibility for development of high school science curricula.

It was a difficult choice. Bok was being offered four times the salary he could get in Australia, but he turned Bundy down. "I won't do it, Mac. I don't want it. I am an old Milky Way boy and an old Milky Way boy I want to stay."

Bundy looked back at his colleague. "What are you going to do then, Bart?" And he confirmed what Bok thought was obvious: "You can't stay in your department. There are too many fights going on." Interestingly enough, in only seven years the same Bundy who worried about Bok would be sitting on the executive committee of President Kennedy's National Security Council, faced with advising the President whether to invade Cuba to destroy Soviet ICBMs and possibly start a nuclear war.

By the end of 1955, the offer from Australia, as well as a "firm inquiry" about the directorship of the new National Radio Astronomy Observatory in West Virginia, were still several months away. But as Christmas approached, Bok met with Harvard's new President Nathan Pusey and presented him with his departure notice. Looking directly at the president, Bok made his opinion plain: "I came to say, Sir, that I will be off your reservation a year from now."

"Have you informed your colleagues and Dean Bundy?"

"No, Sir," Bok replied sadly. "That's what you get paid for."

The discussion went on informally a while longer. "Since I don't like Harvard," Bok explained, "there are two things I can do. One is to jump out of a window, but I don't love Harvard enough to do that. The other is to resign without a firm job offer. That's my way of saying I want to get the hell out."

On his final day at Harvard Bok did not even enter his office "to avoid sad goodbyes." The observatory he was leaving really did consist of excellent people, as careful in their science as they were active in other high-minded pursuits. Solar astronomer Donald Menzel was a weekend painter who also wrote science fiction. Years later he said: "I did everything in my power as acting director and director to make you feel at home. I failed completely." Bok noted sarcastically: "Well, he didn't do very well obviously, did he? He failed completely. Paragraph."

For Fred Whipple, Bok's departure marked the end of a long and fruitful friendship. Whipple later remembered happier days, for example when a group of Harvard professors crossed the border to Canada to attend a scientific meeting. In a previous crossing Bok had spent some time showing his identification papers to the border guards, so this time he decided to say he was a native-born American. When they reached the border, the other professors all claimed they were American-born. Finally the official reached the last person. "Where were you born, sir?" he asked. Bok sat up stiffly and, in his fullest Dutch accent, said loudly "Born in Cambridge, Massachusetts." That delayed the group for almost an hour.[45]

Bok waited to announce his departure publicly until May 10, 1956,[46] although much of the community knew about it at the opening of the Agassiz telescope two weeks earlier. For his students, with whom he was popular, it was a shock. Arthur Hoag, later director of Lowell Observatory, looks back on Bok's special lecturing method, whereby he expected his students to arrive fifteen minutes early to copy a set of extensive notes written on the blackboard and then to pay their full attention to the lecture, not notetaking. "Bok was severe but in a kindly way," Hoag recalled. "He insisted on making his students work, and he always levelled with us."[47] Astronomer Constance Sawyer, who graduated Harvard in 1953, agrees: "We felt we were headed toward solving universal mysteries, and some of us were. All of us took a lot of criticism and ribbing, and none of us doubted our ability to shape up and become the astronomers we were destined to be."[48]

Mabel Agassiz received the Boks one last time to say farewell. The Boks discussed their future plans and philosophy, about which they felt very deeply: "What are we?" asked Priscilla. "Are we for sale, or are we people in love with the Milky Way?" Priscilla felt that the new life could be taken two ways: "You could say the Boks are going into exile, or perhaps you could say it is the greatest opportunity in the world." Suddenly the Lady Bountiful of Harvard astronomy looked at them intently. "Unless I do something, Harvard will forget about you in two weeks." She thought further, then said that she would arrange with McGeorge Bundy to start a "Bok Prize"—to be given to a Harvard graduate student. Stunned, they graciously thanked Agassiz for her kindness, and Priscilla asked that the prize qualifications be extended to include women students at Radcliffe, Harvard's sister college.

They ended the meeting with drinks. Bart sipped sherry while Aunt Mabel and Priscilla shared orange juice.

10

The Australian Years

In the ten years following the end of World War II, the expansion of facilities for astronomy was as dramatic as it had been after 1609 when Galileo first turned his tiny spyglass toward Jupiter. In 1948 the 200-inch-diameter optical telescope opened on Palomar, and in 1957, half a world away in England, a 250-foot-diameter radio telescope was set to eavesdrop on galactic goings-on. These were exciting times to be an astronomer.

Despite his troubled years at Harvard, Bart Bok remained in the center of all this explosive growth in astronomy. New ideas about the structure of the Milky Way were appearing regularly, and although Bok did not develop any of these, he was a superb teacher who integrated each new find into the whole picture. Through regular reports in *Sky and Telescope, Scientific American*, and *Science Monthly,* Bok educated an international classroom on the shape of our galaxy and took them through the early development of radio telescopes, which made it possible to sift through the obscuring dust in our galaxy to determine how it is put together.

Bok was so well known by now that readers of the June 1956 *Sky and Telescope* were stunned to learn of his departure from Harvard. "An outstanding American astronomer," the lead article announced, "has been named director of the Commonwealth Observatory in Australia." Bart Bok was to leave for Mount Stromlo, near the Australian capital of Canberra. "There the new director will have excellent facilities for continuing and expanding the studies of the Milky Way on which he has been engaged for many years at Harvard."[1]

The Boks were leaving Harvard? Nobody *leaves* that eminent institution; once a Harvard professor, always one. But by moving to Australia he was positioning himself to be a much more central part of the surge of new astronomy than he could in Cambridge. The front page announcement seemed intended as a *bon voyage* for the Boks as they headed south. Bart and Priscilla arrived in Australia in March 1957.

But how did he get the Australian position? During Bok's last years at Harvard, a series of events completely unknown to him was taking place at Australia's Mount Stromlo Observatory, whose director, Richard Wooley, was departing for England to accept the position of Astronomer Royal. It was up to Joseph Pawsey of the radiophysics laboratory at Australia's Commonwealth Scientific and Industrial Research Organization (CSIRO) and Mark Oliphant, director of the Australian National University's Research School of Physical Sciences, to propose a successor. Because of Bok's strong support for the development of radio astronomy at Harvard, Pawsey supported Bok. Oliphant agreed, and Bok was offered the position. Oliphant considered Bok to be one of his most successful appointments.[2]

Astronomy has quite a tradition in Australia. In 1788 Admiral William Bligh (Captain of the *Bounty*) wrote of an observatory being constructed supposedly to observe a comet.[3] John Tebbutt, Australia's nineteenth-century comet hunter par excellence, discovered the great comets of 1861 and 1881, both of which became brilliant. By 1925 a national observatory was well under way at Mount Stromlo, and a 74-inch reflector was completed there in 1955. It was accompanied by a forest of telescopes, including a 26-inch refractor and 50-, 30-, and 20-inch reflectors. At the same time, Sweden's Uppsala Observatory had located their new 20-inch Schmidt telescope there.[4]

Bok was hired to expand on this tradition. Mount Stromlo, until then independent, was to become part of the Australian National University. As ANU's first full professor of astronomy, Bok's goal was to establish a graduate school as good as the one he had left at Harvard. ANU's vice chancellor then tried lamely to deflate Bok's interest in radio astronomy by saying that "I want to make it very clear, that we are basically an optical observatory." That might have been true, but Australian astronomy was already heading toward radio in a big way. In 1959 the Radiophysics Laboratory in Sydney, led by E. Bowen, issued the first of several contracts for a gigantic 210-foot steerable radio telescope.[5] Although Bok did not lead this project, he fostered a close relationship with the Radiophysics

Laboratory, including arranging for some students to complete joint Stromlo-Radiophysics graduate theses.[6]

Although the 210-foot would not be the world's largest radio telescope, it would be close. By the time Bok moved to Australia the mighty 250-foot dish was starting work at the University of Manchester's Jodrell Bank in England. For many years this fully steerable English dish would *be* radio astronomy in the eyes of the world. Through the medium of radio, astronomers in countries as cloud-covered as England could now be at the forefront of astronomical research. Now Australia would have a large radio telescope too. After seeing Harvard's radio telescope take shape amidst so much controversy, Bok was delighted to witness the construction of these mighty telescopes.

Of all his achievements in Australia, Bok considered his establishment of the graduate school at the Australian National University his most significant. His predecessor, Wooley, had started a few regular courses but nothing on the scale Bok foresaw. The top caliber students Bok attracted strengthened the work on Mount Stromlo,[7] and the Boks' supportive and outgoing personalities fed this constructive loop. "Bart and Priscilla devoted themselves to the school wholeheartedly," Stromlo senior staff scientist Ben Gascoigne recalled. "Their hospitality, especially to students, was legendary, and Bart himself was tireless in his travels up and down the country, lecturing to student groups everywhere."[8] Of the twenty-eight students accepted into the school, all but five were still active in the field at the time of Bok's death.[9]

Bok loved to recollect that on the day he officially took over as director of Stromlo (March 7, 1957), he found five telescopes, of which only one worked. That was an overstatement. Although the 74-inch had a problem with its mirror, it was an excellent telescope completed only two years earlier by the Grubb-Parsons firm. As its original mirror had been found to be slightly astigmatic, the telescope had a temporary replacement while Grubb-Parsons refigured it. The Schmidt camera from Sweden's Uppsala Astronomical Observatory was not working because it had just arrived and was still in boxes. In far more serious trouble was the 50-inch telescope, which Bok appraised to be utterly useless. That left the 30-inch Reynolds reflector as the only functioning instrument on Bok's opening night. The legend that Bok "always left his observatories in better shape than he found them" was about to get started as Bok set to work at Stromlo.[10]

Installing a large Coudé spectrograph on the 74-inch telescope was one of the first tasks he set himself. He asked Theodore Dunham, well re-spected for the spectrographs he built at Mount Wilson Observatory, to build it. The Coudé is so large that it cannot be attached to the end of a telescope. Instead, star light picked up by the telescope has to be diverted by small mirrors to travel through the telescope's mounting into an ad-jacent room where the Coudé spectrograph is housed. To create a path for light to reach the Coudé room, the telescope's massive concrete pier would have to be bored into, a challenging prospect that would require weeks of precision drilling. Dunham offered a highly innovative alter-native: to speed up the process, he would place tiny sticks of dynamite at precise locations in the pier and *explode* his way through it.

Bok was unnerved by this dangerous proposal. If it failed the entire telescope could shift away from its meticulous alignment on the southern celestial pole. Worse yet, the blast might reveal unknown stress points in the main mirror, causing it to crack.

After some study Dunham and Bok convinced themselves that the risk was acceptable, and the explosion took place on a Sunday morning in 1960: "I prayed first and Priscilla prayed too. Then Dunham and I and half a dozen of our workshop people went in there, set the dynamite and left." The charge did exactly what was intended, and by the end of 1960 the 74-inch had its Coudé spectrograph, becoming a far more versatile instrument.[11]

"Ambassador Bok"

In Australia Bok's exceptional qualities as a salesman for astronomy would reach their peak. Within a few years of his arrival there he had become so well known and liked that, by one account, he was the best known figure in the country after Prime Minister Robert Menzies. Bok received his first major taste of fame and adulation on October 4, 1957, when the Soviet Union launched Sputnik into orbit.

The news was exciting and shocking at the same time. Who would dominate this new age of space? At Stromlo Bok fully expected to hear from his former colleagues at the Smithsonian Astrophysical Observa-tory, who undoubtedly had observed the satellite and would provide an exact ephemeris for it that would allow observatories around the world to follow its path around the sky. When nothing arrived, Bok was angry, suspecting that the Smithsonian was deliberately not informing him. It

BELMONT UNIVERSITY LIBRARY

later turned out that they had not been able to observe Sputnik yet and that they were as much in the dark as he was.

By the end of Sputnik's first day in space Bok was approached by one of the local newspaper reporters who asked if the observatory was going to attempt to photograph the remarkable new object. "Of course not!" Bok bellowed with his usual effervescence. After all, he explained, the narrow fields of view of the Stromlo telescopes were not designed to find or track an object that hurtles across the sky in fifteen minutes. The only telescope he thought might work was Uppsala University's wide-field Schmidt.

But Tony Brzybylski, Stromlo's expert in positional astronomy and orbit calculation, had other ideas. With engineer Kurt Gottleib, Brzybylski stealthily opened the Uppsala Schmidt telescope without the knowledge of either Bok or the Uppsala officials. Having a vague idea where and when Sputnik would appear, the two observers loaded a large piece of film into the telescope, pointed the instrument in approximately the right direction, and waited for Sputnik to rise out of the western sky.

"There it is!" they yelled as the new artificial moon suddenly rose in the northwest. They could see the satellite's upper stage rocket, which was as bright as first magnitude, and, much fainter, the satellite, which was nearby and appeared clearly on the photograph. Gottlieb briskly centered the telescope's finder on it. He opened the shutter so swiftly and forcefully that the telescope shook. But the deviously acquired telescope time was worth it: a telescope at Mount Stromlo got the world's first picture of the moving trail of Sputnik I and its much brighter rocket upper-stage as they sped across the sky, and Brzybylski was able to use the exact positions of the beginning and end of the satellite's trail on the film to calculate a rough orbit for the satellite. Now totally converted by the surprising success at the Schmidt telescope, Bok was delighted to parade about with the picture it had taken and claim it as Stromlo's own.

So exciting was Sputnik that Bok was invited to give an extemporaneous address to both houses of the Australian parliament about it. Concerned about this evidence of Soviet military strength, the senators and representatives listened closely as Bok explained the consequences of the new technology. Although satellites were not Bok's specialty, he did expound on the possibilities of communications satellites. After Bok finished his talk, Sir Alister McMullin, the House Speaker, inquired if it would be possible for some of the audience to go out and see the satellite.

The speaker appointed a "committee" of six to go outdoors and watch for it at the time Brzybylski had calculated for the satellite's next appearance. Bok was a bit uneasy about the prediction, but he needn't have worried, for the satellite and its rocket appeared right on schedule.

By the end of that evening Bok had befriended at least half the audience of parliamentarians, and his reputation as a salesman for astronomy in Australia was made. And it was that evening that led to the start of a friendship with Australia's Prime Minister Robert Menzies.[12] It was a natural friendship between two men of strong will. Just before 1950 Menzies had become prime minister as head of a coalition government composed of the Liberal and Country parties, and he quickly developed a reputation as an orator as fine as Churchill's. He fully supported the Australian National University and had gained the respect of most of Australia's intellectual community. He was also a first-class politician. Bok's friend Oliphant would say, "I learned that Menzies could speak beautifully for half an hour, keeping me hanging on his every phrase, admiring his erudition and polish, and only when he had finished did I realise that he had really said nothing."[13]

Menzies occasionally took advantage of this friendship, and Bok allowed it. In 1961, as Bok was about to leave to attend the dedication of India's new Tata Institute Observatory, Menzies invited him to dinner and asked him to sound out the possibilities that Jawaharlal Nehru, India's legendary first prime minister, might wish to visit Australia. Bok was not a stranger to "Pandit Nehru" (as he and others referred to the well-educated leader).[14] Menzies and Nehru had known each other since their student days at Cambridge University, but they had been at utterly opposite political poles; Menzies was a "dyed in the wool royalist," while Nehru was a revolutionary who had devoted his life to the freeing of India from British yoke. "He and I really disliked each other for many, many years," Menzies told Bok. "But now I am the boss in Australia and he is the boss in India. Could you please tell Nehru that I am interested to know if he would like to visit Australia?"

When Bok arrived in India it was arranged that he would meet Nehru for tea. With Nehru preoccupied with a national election campaign, Bok was not sure what kind of reception he would get. Bok was ushered into Nehru's room and introduced. "Oh yes," Nehru smiled, "I remember Bart Bok from Harvard."

"Well, Mr. Prime Minister," Bok struggled to open the Menzies connection, "I am now in Australia, where I am director of Mount Stromlo Observatory." Bok paused briefly, then went on: "Sir Robert Menzies, our prime minister . . ."

"Yes, I know," Nehru interrupted, "I meet him at the Commonwealth prime ministers meetings."

"Well," Bok continued tentatively, "Sir Robert has asked me to tell you that he hopes that soon you will come and visit Australia. And," Bok added hopefully, "as it was my pleasure to show you around Harvard Observatory a few years ago, so I would like to have the pleasure of showing you my observatory in Australia."

Nehru gazed kindly at Bok. "Professor Bok," Bok emphasized his reply, "I always look back with pleasure on the day you showed me the observatory at Harvard. Please tell your Prime Minister that after I have visited South America and perhaps Africa, Australia shall be *near* the top of my list."

After Bok returned to his Australian home he dined again with Menzies. "Sir Robert," he said, "I didn't get a nice response." After hearing Bok's report, Menzies sighed. "Huh! The upstart hasn't changed a bit. He is still full of the same sort of stuff he always was. He is still a revolutionary and I am still the Queen's man." The two leaders eventually did meet, but in Nehru's own land.

Bok was able to put his friendship with Menzies to good use. While sitting next to him at dinner one evening, Bok proposed that a wide belt of land around Mount Stromlo be set aside to protect the observatory from the expanding suburbs of Canberra. Menzies declared thousands of acres of land to be state forest.[15]

A Decade for the Milky Way

During Bok's first year at Stromlo he published no major papers, a fact which is not surprising since he was busy settling in. However, *The Milky Way* soon came out in its third edition, which incorporated a major rewriting of the text. Completed in his last year at Harvard, the new text reflected a better understanding of the Milky Way than did the editions of 1941 and 1945. Its leading changes reflected the new work on spiral structure and the role played by radio astronomy.

When William Morgan and his colleagues from Yerkes announced their discovery of the Milky Way's spiral structure in 1952 (see chapter 9), astonishment was quickly allayed by caution. Unless astronomers could come up with a better way to "see" through the galaxy's dust lanes, it would be possible to see spiral structure no farther than about 15,000 light years away. To verify the spiral arms, astronomers needed to probe at least five times farther. During the early 1940s, Walter Baade had discovered that regions of hydrogen were the best way to trace the extent of spiral structure in the nearby galaxies. Now the new radio telescopes allowed the detection of hydrogen's distinctive 21-cm emission band to far greater distances. By 1955 radio telescopes were peering into the center of the galaxy and finding deuterium, or heavy hydrogen, at the 91.6 cm wavelength.[16] In the same year Americans R. X. McGee and J. G. Bolton found a bright radio source known as Sagittarius A and proposed, somewhat prematurely, that it could be the actual center of the galaxy.[17]

Bok saw that radio telescopes were less useful than optical telescopes for determining distances of objects. Partly because of this weakness, he felt strongly that a healthy approach to galactic studies needed to coordinate both optical and radio astronomy. He strongly urged his students not to consider themselves as either radio astronomers or optical astronomers, but just *astronomers*. Bok encouraged this approach throughout his career. As John Glaspey, one of his graduate students at Steward Observatory, wrote, "We should consider ourselves as being responsible for everything in astronomy, regardless of our personal field of specialization."[18]

From his graduate student days until his death, Bok searched to figure out just how our galaxy is put together. By 1958 radio studies had painted a complex picture of a galaxy with a nucleus that seemed to be relatively smaller than those in some other spiral galaxies. However, the Milky Way appeared to be surrounded by a huge swath of at least three spiral arms, one in the direction of Orion, another toward Perseus, and a third toward Sagittarius. (Arms are given names based on the constellations in which they are detected.)

Bok was troubled by a discrepancy between the spiral structure as revealed by the radio observations and the optical data. Morgan's canonical map showed the spiral arms as elliptical, but radio studies at the 21-cm wavelength revealed them to be more circular, like those in other galaxies.

Because of obscuring matter between the stars, it was still hard to tell whether a feature was a major arm or simply a small spur of a larger and hidden arm. The problem is similar to trying to map the shape of a forest from a thicket of trees near the edge; the cartographer knows the nearby trees but has only a vague view of the rest of the woods. With radio telescopes, astronomers can search the Milky Way for the dark clouds of hydrogen that, on the basis of their observations of other galaxies, they know are associated with a galaxy's spiral arms. With optical telescopes, they can locate certain types of stars that populate the spiral arms and can thus trace the extent of those arms. But the arms are so large and extensive that it is difficult to determine what constitutes a complete arm and what is just a spur off another arm.

Bok suspected that the arms were tightly wound up "like the spring of a watch." And in one of these arms, about 27,000 light years from the galaxy's center, is our Sun.[19]

A possible reconciliation of the apparent contradiction between radio and optical data came to Bok as he remembered a picture he had imagined while cruising through the Panama Canal with his family in 1933 (see chapter 8). It was a fanciful "Carina-Cygnus" spiral arm that Bok at one time had thought began in the southern sky constellation of Carina, crossed through the solar system, and continued on in the direction of the constellation of Cygnus in the northern sky. Could this be the tracing of a real spiral arm? Still pushing his Panama Canal notion, in a 1959 letter to *The Observatory* Bok proposed a revised model of the galaxy's spiral arms based on his Carina-Cygnus arm instead of Morgan's proposed Orion arm.

The way he saw the galaxy, the Orion feature is not a complete arm at all but a spur that is connected to a Carina-Cygnus arm. In this way, Bok's model allowed the arms to be circular, agreeing with the picture suggested from radio telescopes.[20]

Bok outlined his new theory in a popular article published that same year in *Scientific American*.[21] Summarizing the spectacular progress made during the 1950s in understanding spiral structure, Bok pointed out the new ways that spiral arms could be traced in our galaxy, using Cepheid variable stars with periods longer than fifteen days,[22] open or galactic clusters, and supergiant stars that shine ten to one hundred thousand times brighter than the Sun.[23]

In March 1963 fifty scientists came to Australia to discuss the implications of these pivotal discoveries at an IAU Symposium that Bok put together, using some funds he had garnered from UNESCO. The question of where the arms actually were was still largely unanswered; optical data showed them as elongated, while the radio telescopes painted them as more circular around the galaxy's center. Bok held to his belief that the Carina-Cygnus arm solved the discrepancy as "the major local spiral feature, from which protrudes a spur in Puppis and Vela."[24] But others, led by W. Becker, foresaw correctly that the Carina-Cygnus arm did not exist, and that the Carina concentration was simply a part of the Sagittarius arm.

How to correlate the optical data with the new information from the radio telescopes was the central question addressed at this IAU symposium. Using open star clusters as a tracer of spiral arms, Becker reported that the distances of over 150 galactic star clusters he studied showed a pattern of spiral structure, but not the same structure that the earlier 21-cm radio maps displayed. At this same 1963 meeting, McDonald Observatory astronomer Gerard de Vaucouleurs first suggested that our galaxy might have many arms, and that instead of having an oval center surrounded by arms, like a pinwheel, it might be a barred spiral, with a central bar of material surrounded by spiral arms. It was not until late 1990 that a slight barred feature was finally confirmed.[25]

With its good discussion and national publicity, the conference brought worldwide attention to Australian astronomy and accolades for Bok. In its wake, less than two weeks later, the Australian House of Representatives discussed the future of astronomy in that country (see chapter 11).

Bok's concept of a Carina-Cygnus arm remained popular for many years, finding its way into general astronomy books and other popular literature.[26] But with improving data, the idea did not survive, except to be divided into parts of two distinct arms moving off in different directions, as Becker had proposed. The last edition of *The Milky Way* was a "state of the galaxy" address for 1981. The book described the latest spiral arm structure—an arm in the directions of Orion and Cygnus, an arm in the outer Perseus region, and part of an arm in Sagittarius. In a sense the Carina-Cygnus arm lives, but only the southern half as a Sagittarius-Carina arm.

The ability of radio telescopes to "see" hydrogen enabled discoveries about the dark clouds in the galaxy to come thick and fast, answering old questions and raising new ones. The Bok globules yielded some important secrets to the radio telescope's ear. Bok now thought that most of these small clouds were short-lived objects that would become unstable as cosmic winds (the rush of energy blowing out from every star) blew them apart. But in an exquisite cosmic play, some globules would begin to contract under the influence of gravity leading to the formation of new stars.[27]

Radio studies also gave astronomers a clearer picture of how the galaxy rotates around its center; the clues were embedded in the radio emission spectra observed from the hydrogen clouds of what is known as the interstellar medium. The spectra contained a complex Doppler shift pattern, and for astronomers this was the telltale signature of the motion of the clouds. Originally detected by the 82-foot radio telescope in Holland in 1955, the hydrogen clouds led to the discovery three years later of a gargantuan outer halo surrounding the main disk of the galaxy.

Bok saw in radio astronomy the solution to many of the problems of star birth and growth, and he urged his fellow astronomers to obtain "as complete information as possible about the distribution, state of motion, and physical conditions in the interstellar medium."[28] His own research time would henceforth be divided between star formation and galactic structure.

Except for the three editions of the Boks' now classic work *The Milky Way*, Priscilla had yet to collaborate with her husband in any formal published research. This changed in the summer of 1960, when the Boks produced their first paper together. It was a report of some basic research that reported a series of magnitude measurements for fields of Southern Hemisphere stars. Using a photoelectric photometer, the Boks secured magnitudes of stars from as bright as magnitude 8 (bright enough for binoculars) to as faint as 15 (requiring a sizeable telescope).[29]

The Boks had started this project at Boyden, Africa, in 1950 and completed it at Stromlo nine years later.[30] This first paper was intended simply to establish a magnitude reference for what the Boks really wanted to do: a study of the magnitude vs. color of stars in the Large Magellanic Cloud, our galaxy's nearest neighbor. A few months after this first paper appeared, the Boks published a study of two small fields of blue supergiant stars surrounded by nebulosity in the Large Magellanic Cloud.[31] Their conclusion was surprising: these big stars are infants—less than ten million years old (our Sun, by comparison, is five billion years old). The Boks wanted to concentrate on these very young stars because they could reveal so much about the processes by which new stars are formed. By 1962, using the 26-inch reflector on Mount Bingar, Australia, the Boks had expanded their study to fourteen associations of similarly young stars. Now they were producing a steady stream of joint papers, some on their own, others jointly with students, that were probing the secrets of star formation.[32]

Hosted by Bok

With increasing interest in astronomy in Australia and an increase in the personal regard for Bok, the Australian Broadcasting Corporation proposed that he do a series of ten half-hour lectures on national television. Beginning with the Sun and solar system, the program traveled through the Milky Way and paraded out into the distant galaxies. "For each lecture I could have ten slides *maximum* of the old-fashioned large variety, which could be projected. That was the rule."

These broadcasts were so popular that people who had seen them would recognize the host, sometimes years afterwards. On one occasion Bok visited a gem and mineral show in Tucson. Among the jumble of local displays were international booths, including one from Australia. As Bok approached the stall, the man sitting there opened his eyes in wide surprise: "You were on my telly last week at home in Brisbane!" Apparently the series was still being rebroadcast on Australian TV.

Bok was also a hit on the down under lecture circuit, his series of four lectures at Canberra being especially popular. "It is reported," his friend Gascoigne noted later, "to have been the only such course in which more people attended the last lecture than the first." Bok's style was inimitable. His attempt at explaining parallax, commonly illustrated by parallel railway tracks appearing to converge, was particularly memorable. When he sensed that the slides being used to illustrate his lecture were a bit dry, Bok abruptly stopped talking. He moved to one side of the lecture stage, raised the blackboard pointer to shoulder height as if it were a bow and arrow, and then pretended to shoot out the slide projector in the back row. Then, stiffening up, he faced the other side of the stage, marched across, ordered himself to stop, swung around and shot again.[33]

Four lectures given at Canberra University College in 1957 resulted in one of Bok's most pleasurable books. However, *The Astronomer's Universe* was not a book of which Bart was especially proud. He had felt it had been "published in a great hurry," and lacked the scholarly depth of his more typical works. For *The Astronomer's Universe* Bok adopted an easy style, presenting his material at a less involved level than he had in *The*

Milky Way. It was written for high school students, beginning and enthusiastic amateurs, and for bright children at summer camps. "It never got very far, but at least there were copies of it in odd places. And the publisher especially tried to send it to high school groups in the United States." The author, while teaching astronomy at Camp Minnowbrook on Lake Placid, found a copy of this book in the camp's library.

The four lectures that comprised this book were the foundation on which Bok built a frenetic agenda of continent-wide appearances on many topics. While his topics stressed astronomy, Bok occasionally lectured on other important subjects as well. A January 13, 1964, address in Hobart, for example, called for a "real crusade" in support of better education of women. Calling attention to the one-in-four ratio of women to men doctoral candidates whom he had directed, Bok claimed that it seemed "natural that women should press for equal job opportunities and equal pay for men and women of all ages."[34]

"I had a rule that I would talk to any organization countrywide that would listen to me," Bok stressed. "But I had a price. That same afternoon, or the following day, I must be permitted to address the children at the local high school."

Bart J. Bok, associate professor at Harvard. Harvard College Observatory photograph, circa 1934.

Priscilla Fairfield in 1928, the year she met Bok.

*Bok is about to demonstrate something exciting to the audience.
Shapley is on the left. Circa 1948.*

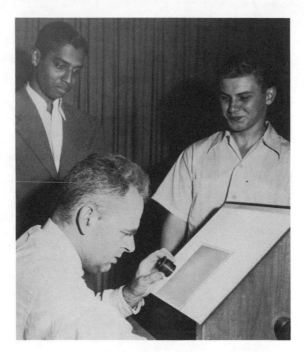

*Vainu Bappu and Gordon Newkirk look on as Bok
examines the discovery photograph of Comet Bappu-
Bok-Newkirk, 1949. Harvard College Observatory
photograph.*

The 12-foot radio dish in transit, 1953.

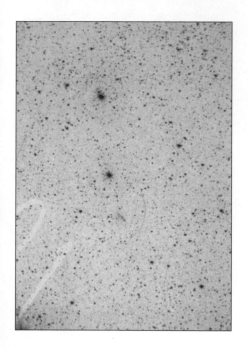

Discovery plate of Comet Bappu-Bok-Newkirk.
Photograph by Vainu Bappu, 1949.
Reproduced courtesy of Harvard College
Observatory.

Bart Bok next to the Agassiz telescope. Circa 1956.

Mealtime at Stromlo. Priscilla is about to feed a group of magpies.

Mount Stromlo. (Observatory)

Bart Bok and his detailed blackboard notes. Circa 1975.

Bart Bok in his last year, 1983. Photograph by the author.

Bart and Priscilla at Stromlo. Circa 1960.

Barnard 335, a classic Bok globule. The globule is about four arcminutes in diameter, about a seventh of the diameter of the full moon. Bok discovered that globules represent an early stage in the formation of stars. Photograph by Bart J. Bok, using the 90-inch reflector at Steward Observatory. Courtesy of University of Arizona Library, Special Collections.

A Bok photograph of the Keyhole Nebula, the center of the Eta Carinae complex.
Courtesy of University of Arizona Library, Special Collections.

The Milky Way, centered in Scutum. Photograph by the author, March 19, 1993.

11

The Anglo-Australian Observatory

"Siding Spring Observatory owes its existence to Bart Bok."
—S. C. B. Gascoigne, 1990[1]

While he was Mount Stromlo's director, Richard Wooley proposed a large new optical telescope for Australia, by some reports as large as Mount Palomar's 200-inch reflector. When Bart Bok took over, he first suggested, according to Sir Mark Oliphant, a collaborative effort between Australia and the United States. "The whole [Anglo-Australian Telescope] project arose from Bart Bok's advocacy of an U.S.-Australian telescope, which failed, for largely Australian reasons, to get off the ground."[2]

Bok gave Prime Minister Menzies an earful on how valuable a remote field station under the darkest Australian sky would be. Bok's first proposal was an immediate start on a site-testing survey over the entire southern half of the continent. When and if the big telescope should start, a site already would have been selected with care and not with haste. Menzies went along with this farsighted idea and agreed to provide about twenty thousand pounds per year for a site search.

"Within a short time," Gascoigne wrote, "and with characteristic energy, Bok set about finding a site where a field station for future Mount Stromlo Observatory telescopes could be established without too much delay, and which might also serve as a site for a possible large telescope; he had this in mind from the beginning."[3] Bok appointed A. R. Hogg of the Stromlo staff to coordinate the survey.

It was a prudent course of action. Because of increasing light pollution, within a decade the sky at Stromlo would be too bright for most observing.[4] By April 1960 the level of interest was more for a new site than for a big new telescope.[5] The astronomers wanted a site that would have as many clear nights as possible, especially, Bok was sure to emphasize, from September to March when the Magellanic Clouds are most favorably placed.[6] A final interesting priority was that the site be free from Australia's frequent smoke from brushfires.[7] Bok was quite favorably impressed with Mount Bingar, near a small town named Yenda north of Adelaide and north of the large Murray irrigation area. The site had been home to a successful 26-inch telescope since 1959.[8] Nineteen other sites, including Coonabarabran's Siding Spring, some 300 miles north of Canberra, were also included in a survey that included sky cloudiness levels, the quality of seeing, and tests of how badly the atmosphere dims objects just rising or setting. For the promising sites, a record of night cloudiness over two years was carried out, and over one year for the less hopeful sites.

Interestingly, after Siding Spring was suggested by Harley Wood, from New South Wales, it was rejected the first time around since the search committee mistakenly thought that the mountain was not high enough. As Gascoigne relates, the committee of four was treated in Coonabarabran "to a memorable dinner which included such delicacies as Roast Turkey Virginis, Sirloin Tauri and Coffee Milky Way, then pushed on south and east."[9]

By 1961 Siding Spring and Mount Bingar were the finalists. Bok wanted Bingar; survey coordinator Hogg fought for Siding Spring. Finally Sir Leonard Huxley, Australian National University's vice chancellor, met with both men to resolve the issue,[10] and Siding Spring was selected. Although at 3800 feet it is not a very high site, it still offered a dark and steady sky, promising a fine field station for Mount Stromlo Observatory.[11]

Although Bok lost on his choice for the field station, he passionately led the effort to turn the remote mountaintop into an observatory.

If acquiring a site was relatively straightforward, building a large international telescope on it was definitely not. It was expensive enough to require a collaborative effort between at least two countries, the two most promising partners being either Britain or the United States. But other ideas for international telescope projects were on the horizon as well, especially one for the new European Southern Observatory, and there was a prospect of Australia's joining that one. In the wake of this uncertainty, the whole idea cooled off early in the 1960s.[12]

At first Menzies struck Bok as overly cautious: "We have to take this a little slow," he remembered the prime minister's words. "Before I make such a major scientific decision, I am asked about having food on the table." Agreement over a joint Anglo-Australian telescope was hardly unanimous in the astronomical community; some astronomers preferred a collaboration with the United States instead.[13] And still others, fearing that the project would bleed funds from already existing programs, did not want a large telescope at all. "So what I'll do," Menzies told Bok, "is submit this proposal to the Australian Academy of Sciences as I must do about all matters of scientific inquiry." Thus, a formal proposal requested the Academy to approve the idea of the country joining Britain in a project to build a large telescope.

The request seemed a mere formality, until Menzies received the Academy's response. It suggested a delay of two to three *years* while proposals for other kinds of scientific collaborations were examined. The reply suggested almost a dozen possibilities, including, Bok mused with dismay, an international flower garden.[14]

Bok responded quickly and vehemently to the Academy. On August 21, 1962, he addressed the Australia-New Zealand Association for the Advancement of Science (ANZAAS) at its congress in Sydney.[15] "I wanted to make this address a firm one," he said, "telling the Academy to get off their high horse and help things along; not erect obstacles." Rumors had already spread that Bok planned a controversial address, and his friends at the Australian Broadcasting Corporation heard about it. "Bart," they said, "if you have something you want to tell the Australian people, it is up to us to provide you with a soapbox."

Bok's address was broadcast throughout the country. The auditorium filled quickly the day of his speech, with Thomas Cherry, president of the Academy, sitting in the third row. Bok began with some traditional director-type comments, and then he struck.

"Since I am remaining an American citizen," Bok warmed up to his topic, "I have thus far refrained from commenting on the general policies, but I feel that now the time has come for me to speak frankly, for I am deeply concerned about the future of Australian science.

"To begin with, I should hand out some bouquets. The Australian people and their political leaders deserve one for the sympathetic understanding that they have shown towards proposals for pure scientific research. . . ."[16]

Bok then tendered three areas in which he thought the Academy had failed. "My first objection arises from the fact that the Council of the Academy did not consult its own National Committee on Astronomy [which] has a good representation of the younger astronomers of the country and the council thus ignored an obvious channel of communication with the younger generation."[17]

Then Bok attacked what he thought was the Academy's highhandedness. "Second, to the best of my knowledge, no Australian optical astronomer was consulted by the Council of the Academy at the time of the preparation of the Academy report and, since optical astronomy was not represented on the council, no Australian optical astronomer has been permitted to see the report. I was asked to appear before the Council once, in March 1960; this was only for a brief and informal testimony— long before the Report was apparently prepared."[18]

Bok's final complaint considered other nations, as the question of international collaboration in science had become a national issue. "Thirdly, to my mind the Academy did not show a sufficient awareness of the urgency for a friendly and positive response at the time when the first inquiries came from overseas."[19]

Academy president Cherry turned so pale that Bok thought he might have given him a heart attack, but Cherry left the meeting in good enough shape to draft a seething letter. A few days later the message arrived accusing Bok of having "offended the Establishment. . . . Bok understood the Establishment to mean the prime minister."[20] As Bok remembered the letter's end: "You have outlived your usefulness to this country and should now return to the United States."

Bok was in trouble again. Wondering what to do, he thought that "I couldn't just call the prime minister and say, 'May I have an appointment please, sir? Have I offended you? I'm so sorry. What can I do to make it up?'"

Bok had his chance less than a week later. King Bhumibhol Adulyadej of Thailand, with his wife Sirikit, was visiting Australia. There was an official tour of the observatory,[21] and finally a state reception at University House. This was quite a party. With a small orchestra playing Handel, the university faculty in full academic dress lined up along the path where the dignitaries would pass.[22]

Until the procession began the prime minister did not say a word to Bok. As Menzies paraded slowly by, he looked straight ahead, avoiding the astronomer's anxious glance. Hoping to get at least a friendly look, Bok tried hard to catch his eye, but Menzies stared straight ahead as if to ignore Bok purposefully. "I stood there," Bok recalled, "and thought, 'Oh my God, he doesn't even want to look at me!'"

As the procession moved along, Menzies stiffly approached Bok's position in line. He never faced Bok. But at the instant he passed by, he poked him hard in the belly and whispered: "You are a bad, bad boy!"

Bok's fears vanished with the prime ministerial ribbing. He knew he was going to stay in Australia and he was confident that sooner or later, he would get his telescope. "Only Bob Menzies could have delivered his message so nicely, briefly, and eloquently," Bok later confided.[23]

By early 1963, Menzies was showing new interest in the original proposal between Australia and Britain.[24] He saw only one technical problem. When the Australian National University was founded, it was not permitted to own land outside of the area around the Canberra region. This was remedied on March 28, 1963, when Menzies introduced a bill declaring that the "powers of the University extend to the making of astronomical and meteorological observations in any part of the Commonwealth."[25] The bill was designed to allow the Australian National University to own land near Coonabarabran in order to construct an observatory. Menzies stressed that "since the present functions of the university are defined in the act with reference to the Australian Capital Territory, it seemed wise to vest the university with a specific power, not confined to the Australian Capital Territory, to undertake astronomical observations."[26]

However, partly because this was a big-ticket international project, Menzies's real hope was that the bill would stir a sophisticated discussion on the future of astronomy in Australia. In an undertone of tribute to Bok, he went on: "I believe that we will all be happy to see the university pressing on so energetically in this field of inquiry and, therefore, I am pleased to be able to commend this bill to the House and to move that it be read a second time."[27]

Menzies got his wish in a long session on April 10, 1963. With the opposition parties supporting the measure at the start, it appeared that a friendly discussion about astronomy was under way, one in which Bok was quoted liberally as stating that "Australian and British astronomers appear to be agreed on the desirability of a 150-inch Reflector. . . ."[28]

When the subject then turned to the status of astronomical research in Australia, it was clear that Bok and other astronomers had coached the debate leaders well, especially Representative William Charles Wentworth. A member of the House of Representatives since 1949 from Mackellar, New South Wales, Wentworth was well known for having developed a defense plan against Japan in 1939. He became Social Services Minister in 1968.[29] "Perhaps the House does not realize," Wentworth claimed, "the world importance of the work done by Australian pioneers in the field of radio astronomy . . . a new science that has developed in the postwar period." He then described how differently the sky appeared when studied through a radio telescope: "The surprise finding was that the intense waves were coming not necessarily from the brightest objects in the sky. In other words, we were able to open a new window in the universe through which we could locate objects, the existence of which had not been suspected."[30]

The discussion shifted to how Australia's Parkes radio telescope would actually do better than its larger rival at England's Jodrell Bank, a revelation intended to stir the patriotic juices on both sides of the aisle.

"Yes, it will do a much better job," insisted Wentworth. "Although it is not quite as big as the Jodrell Bank instrument, it has been built to much finer tolerances. . . . This is particularly important because it allows focussing of the 21 centimeter hydrogen line. . . . From having conversations with Professor Bok and other people I know that at Parkes we have an instrument that is way ahead of anything available in this field anywhere else in the world."[31]

Wentworth then continued with an informed discussion of the advantages that a 150-inch optical telescope at Siding Spring would have over the originally proposed 120-inch instrument. "It is more convenient," he said, "to have the observer placed at the prime focus than to reflect the light from a mirror. Because of the physical size of the human body, and the space it occupies at the prime focus, it is desirable to have the bigger instrument."[32]

Bok was thrilled with the results of this part of the discussion. As he somewhat whimsically put it later, the sense in the House was akin to: "Now, look. The astronomer has to sit at the telescope's focus. If we have a 120-inch, the astronomer's elbows have to be too close together. Aren't we proud of our astronomers? Let's give them elbow space! A 150-inch it is."

The debate was a resounding success for Bok. The bill passed handily, and it was obvious that the crisis of the previous August had passed. The only reference to his controversial address criticizing the Academy had come from Laurence J. Failes of Coonabarabran, who quoted from it only to emphasize that Bok was urging that work begin on the new site. He also referred to the "magnificent" response to Bok's lectures across the country.[33]

In late 1963, a 40-inch Boller and Chivens telescope arrived, and on February 12, 1964, Gascoigne took Siding Springs' first photographic plate.[34] A 16-inch and a 24-inch reflector soon followed.

Although the smaller telescopes were operating, Siding Spring was not opened officially until April 5, 1965, less than a year before Bok returned to the United States.[35] The big telescopes would come even later than that. "The advent of the AAT," Gascoigne wrote, "then of the UK Schmidt, and the ANU 2.3 meter in its rectangular building, led to sweeping changes. Not even Bart Bok, most sanguine of directors, could have imagined such a transformation in so short a space of time."[36]

Late in 1963, Bok visited England for two weeks to help move along the complex negotiations for the bi-national venture in the 150-inch telescope.[37] The telescope was not built before Bok left Australia; that was one of his few disappointments about his sojourn there. In his final visit to Menzies before leaving for the United States, the prime minister acknowledged his disappointment but told him, "You mustn't worry over your big telescope, Bart; these things take time."[38]

Despite all the good words, the 150-inch telescope did not actually get the final go-ahead until 1967, eight years after the earliest British attempts in 1959 to begin the joint project. Bernard Lovell of England's Jodrell Bank Radio Telescope wrote that the delay was political even on the British side: "The problems and difficulties that beset the concept until 1967 and almost led to its abandonment were not primarily financial. The issues were political ones coupled with protracted indecision amongst the astronomers and scientists both in the United Kingdom and Australia."[39]

The situation between Bok and President Cherry of the Australian Academy of Sciences remained tense. In April 1965 Bok showed fellow observatory staff members copies of some notes relating to a report of the Academy's Telescope Committee. As he did three years earlier, Cherry wrote a furious letter to Bok, demanding, in so many words, that he mind his own business. Criticizing Bok's "assumption of other people's responsibilities for the Telescope Project," Cherry pointed out that the material he circulated so freely was part of a confidential report between the Academy and the Royal Society. "Will you never realize (1) that by the Academy (Australian Academy of Sciences) and (British) Royal Society taking over the sponsorship of the Telescope Project the chances of its success have been vastly increased, and (2) that through your back seat driving you are in the opinion of your academy friends biting the hand that feeds you."[40] Cherry pettily demanded that Bok submit to the Royal Society a copy of the list of those who received this letter, and to assure him that spare copies, as well as the stencil, had been destroyed. Bok was quite upset by this letter. "I am quite worried about the whole business of the 150-inch Reflector," he wrote to Mark Oliphant. "Tom Cherry let off a nasty blast at me before he quit as President of the Academy . . . not very pleasant . . . all around a very sad situation."[41]

Despite such stabs at Bok, there was no question of his pivotal role in the project. Both the Australians and the British lauded him at the telescope's dedication in 1974: "Your telegram," Sir Mark Oliphant wrote to Bok, "was read out by Fred Hoyle, who gave you full credit for having been the initiator of the whole enterprise."[42] And the Australian people generally admired Bok, in no small measure because of his frequent appearances on radio and television. During a particularly moving television interview held on the "Bok Walk," a catwalk that stretched just below the dome of the new 40-inch reflector at Siding Spring, Bok talked about the telescopes that would grow there in the coming years. He pointed to where the Anglo-Australian telescope would go, indicated the future location for the U. K. Schmidt telescope, and, as the camera followed, recited the names of the surrounding mountaintops as they passed across the screens of televisions across the country. "I knew them all. Oh, we had a lovely half-hour session from that Bok Walk."

12

Of Birds and Presidents

Not all the Boks' Australian friends were human, as they quickly learned after they moved into their large, 15-room director's residence near the 74-inch dome on top of Mount Stromlo. "They built the director's residence first and the observatory next; that's the way it was done. It was a really nice house, and Priscilla and I decided to live in it and really use it." Built of yellow brick and stucco, the two-storey house overlooked the Molonglo River to the west. Bok always loved the view of the river and the mountains beyond it.[1]

About six months after they moved in, early in September and at the beginning of Australian spring, they found a young magpie lying with a broken leg. Bart wanted to pick it up and try to save it, but Priscilla had qualms: "No, it is a young bird and its mother will abandon it if it has been touched by a human hand. Besides," she added sadly, "we can't do much. It looks as if that bird is going to die."

"Then we must touch him," Bart insisted, "for that is the only way he can stay alive!"

They placed a small dish of bread crumbs for the little bird, and then set the sprinkler going, "very softly," over where he lay. The magpie did pull through, albeit on one leg. The Boks named him Eibeen. And when he one day found a mate, the Boks christened the other Tweebeen. Nesting near the house, the two birds adopted the Boks. "They used to wake us up in the morning and they would come out and sit in the tree and try to look in the bedroom and say, 'Time for our breakfast; come down.'"

The two magpies preferred cheese for their meals, especially, Bart noted with a wink, imported Dutch cheese. The birds even shared their family problems with their caretakers. When one of their young was run over by a car, Bart remembered, they "came to mourn on our lawn right near the house, and we noticed how sad they were."

When the Boks dined outdoors, the birds loved to strip the meat scraps off the T-bone steaks after the Boks were through with them. "I would walk home," Bart remarked, "around 5:30 in the evening. When I came out of the building, Eibeen and Tweebeen would fly to the kitchen window squawking 'aak! aak! aak!'—an indication for Priscilla that Bart was on his way home. We often had our dinner outside on a little glassed-in porch. The two of them sat outside, and when they felt we had had enough they would say, 'Aii, aii, aii,' and that was the signal to throw the rest to them."

The Boks were convinced that Eibeen and Tweebeen kept the common—but poisonous—brown and yellow snakes away. "We had lived all this time at Stromlo and never saw a snake, and we lived right where there were lots around. The birds followed Priscilla around when she went digging in the garden to get the worms and other things that she dug up. They talked to her; they loved her; they were very sociable birds who acted as though they had permitted us to live there."

The birds' "permission" was stretched after the Boks returned from a four-month vacation planned around the IAU meeting in August 1958 in the Soviet Union. This was the latest of the triennial congresses the Boks had attended since they met at the one in Leiden in 1928. The Moscow meeting was far larger, providing portable radios and headphones for simultaneous translation for a thousand English, French, and Russian-speaking astronomers. In Bok's own scientific area, the IAU decided in keeping with current radio research to adopt a new position for the pole of the Milky Way Galaxy, shifting it about a degree and a half from the value in use for the previous quarter-century.[2]

The Boks had a delightful return trip that included an excursion on the ship *Pobeda* across the Black Sea from Odessa to Istanbul.[3] But when they finally arrived home, Bok took out some cheese—"We had taken the precaution of bringing some cheese home with us"—only to find Eibeen and Tweebeen gone. Bok called loudly, even yodelled, but his magpie friends did not answer. But then Priscilla looked down. "Well wait a minute!" she said. "Look who's here!" And there, at Bart's foot, was lonely Tweebeen.

"Aak! aak!" (Bart's translation: "For crying out loud, you've been away a long time. Don't stand on ceremony, just drop your cheese! I'm hungry!")

The 'beens never liked the Boks to "upset the apple cart," and they definitely disapproved of the garden parties the Boks put on from time to time. Both birds would hang over by a nearby tree and complain as the Boks cleaned up from such parties. A typical exchange:

"Aak! aak!"

"You shut up, Tweebeen and Eibeen!"

"Aak! aak!"

"If I feel like having friends over for a party, I'm not going to ask your permission first!"

"Aak! aak!"

"Forget it! I'm damn well going to have a party! Shut up!"

Meantime, a gardener helping with the cleanup came by and stood at the end of the garden path. "The old boy," Bart thought he heard him mutter, "has finally gone bonkers."

Neither storm nor drought kept Bart and Priscilla from taking care of their beloved magpies. "During a drought we could not use water on our lawns. Well, I cheated! I thought that our magpies had to have water or else they would die. I used a soaker hose turned on very slightly so that just a little water would come out. So what happened as a result of that? Magpies came out from all over the place to our yard, for that was the only place where there was water. Not only magpies, but crows and other birds too. So my soaker hose became a segregated bar, fifty feet long. At the end were the crows, other birds would be in the middle, and the magpies would be in the front—always our magpies right at the front. They had a pecking system and if one bird would get in the way, then the pecking system would work. And if a bird went to the wrong place, then he would be sent to the bottom of the hose."

A man of order, Bart did not tolerate fighting for the scraps of cheese he would bring for his growing flock. Somehow he managed to train the magpies to stand in a semicircle with him at the center. Whenever they would fight, Bart would simply leave them, and go indoors.

This worked for all the magpies but one who had a predilection for calling "Aak! aak!" from the roof. That was Bart's clue to throw up a piece for him too. At its height, the whole circus included some sixty magpies.

One day Bart returned home to some upsetting news. "There is a very serious situation in our family," Priscilla said.

"What do you mean?"

"Eibeen and Tweebeen got into a big fight this morning. There was another bird. They were battling high up in the sky, squawking and diving; and then this afternoon Tweebeen came back with a new mate." She and the new mate had murdered poor, one-legged Eibeen.

Priscilla had even lectured Tweebeen. "I don't like this at all," she said. "We don't believe in this sort of thing in our family." But Tweebeen was resolute. "Aak! aak!" she said defiantly. (Translation: "Forget it! Meet my new mate.") Granddaughter Sara later named the new bird Greyback.

As the Boks had discovered, magpies can be vicious, even to themselves. In fact, most Canberrans were not as fond of these birds as the Boks were, for at times these very aggressive birds could attack any creature, including a human, whom they saw as an invader. The birds were especially active at the observatory. The magpies somehow had an intense dislike for one graduate student, and they took to dive-bombing him at every opportunity. But this unpleasant fellow's colleagues seemed to agree with the birds. Often inappropriately vocal, the young astronomer would regale the other students with his opinions about all subjects, and seemed to take delight in harassing others over perceived inadequacies. Naturally, he quickly became one of the least popular students at Stromlo. He even relished the thought of challenging Bok at every opportunity—not a good basis for a relationship between graduate student and supervisor—and the director had to control his abrupt temper to be evenhanded in his treatment of this student.

The Boks gave lots of garden parties. Like Shapley at Harvard, they kept a high level of morale among the observatory family. But at one of these gatherings the obnoxious student started criticizing Priscilla over her feeding the magpies. This student apparently hated the birds with a passion. Surprised, Priscilla stared at him without responding. Warming to his subject, he then accused Priscilla of "criminal activity in the feeding of these horrible animals."

As he got louder, other students came by to pull him away. That didn't work; instead he became even more insolent. Puzzled by the commotion, Bok came out of the house to find the student yelling at Priscilla. Bok was enraged. In a brief and intense confrontation Bok reproached the student from top to bottom, ordered him to stay away from Priscilla, and finally told him to leave the party.

Another graduate student at that party, Richard Price, witnessed the

consequences of Bok's anger. He recalled that Bok "had endured personally many insults and jibes, but he could not forgive the attack on Priscilla. In fact, this was one of only two students I ever heard Bok speak
unflatteringly of. The other tried to fake his way through oral exams with
bluster, lighting and relighting his pipe, and showing general unwilling-
ness to admit areas of ignorance."[4]

The other parties were conspicuously successful, whether they were
just for the students, for political figures, or for family members. One
event occurred during a visit of daughter Joyce and her family. This party
was formal, with government officials in attendance. Bok's granddaughter
Jeanne, about three years old, was exploring the ground near the formally
dressed adult guests. She discovered a knob and decided to experiment
with it to see what happened. As water sprinklers turned on all over the
observatory grounds, the startled guests rushed for cover. Grandfather was
thrilled, and Jeanne never forgot his delight.

The appearance of a very bright comet marked Bok's closing months
in Australia. Even though it was well announced in the weeks preceding
its rounding of the Sun, Comet Ikeya-Seki's magnificent ghostly presence
attracted little public attention until the morning of October 31, when
Bok awoke to go to the bathroom. His attention was kindled by what he
thought was a bright searchlight beam dominating the eastern sky, but he
quickly grasped the opportunity for public education in the face of this
majestic apparition. Within the next few hours the media all over Australia had published Bok's effervescent account of the comet, and on the
morning of November 1 thousands of Australians arose to see it.[5]

The Boks lived happily at their Mount Stromlo residence for nine
years. But on March 31, 1966, it was time to return to the United States
to take up a new directorship, this time at the University of Arizona's
Steward Observatory in Tucson. Bart rose at 5:00 that morning "to say
goodbye to my magpies." Stealing a half pound of cheese from the
kitchen, he and his birds had their final breakfast together.

Australian Legacy

Bok left Australia a much better place, astronomically speaking, than he
had found it. He had provided the country with top facilities, a good graduate school, and perhaps most important of all, through his public appearances he left the people with a good understanding of what the sky

was all about. Bok was on a first-name basis with almost every public official in Australia, and shortly before he left he even explained the operation of the 74-inch to Australia's new Governor-General, Lord Casey.[6]

By May 1968 the Boks were well settled in their new lives in Tucson. Menzies had retired as Australia's prime minister, replaced by John Gorton. Meanwhile, Lyndon Johnson had announced that he would not seek reelection as President of the United States. On May 17, Bok received an invitation from the Johnson White House to attend a dinner for the Australian prime minister.[7] A telefax arrived almost at the same time, clarifying that the invitation was for both "Professor and Mrs. Bok."[8] The delighted Boks were given an impromptu sendoff by their Steward Observatory colleagues and students, including a banner which said "Goodbye Steward, Hello Lyndon—Bon voyage."

The full state dinner began with a formal reception line that included the President and Mrs. Johnson, as well as Prime Minister and Mrs. Gorton. Each guest was introduced formally: "Professor and Mrs. Bok, the University of Arizona, Tucson, Arizona."

But as soon as the Boks shook hands with the President, Gorton could wait no longer. "Bart, Priscilla, it is so good to see you. Are you doing as well as you were in Australia?" The two men then had a warm conversation about the progress of the Siding Spring Observatory. Johnson looked on for a moment and then smiled. "It is obvious," the Chief Executive observed, "that you two know each other very well."

It was a spectacular dinner, with Chesapeake Crabmeat for appetizer, an entree of Roast Duckling Bigarade, and Paul Masson Emerald Dry for the dinner wine.[9] Among the guests were actor Charlton Heston and broadcaster Art Linkletter. The event ended with a formal address from the president which, Bok wrote, "would help set the stage for continued good relations between Australia and the United States."[10]

Ten years later, in 1978, Bart Bok returned to Australia for a two-month lecture tour sponsored by the Australian Academy of Science. His reputation in Australia hadn't diminished. Upon hearing of Bok's return, a local newspaper hailed him as the "grandfather of Siding Spring."[11]

Near the end of his visit, Bok lunched with then-director Donald Mathewson before flying to Perth. Bok was having too good a time, recalled Mathewson, to keep his mind on the clock, even though Mathewson repeatedly looked at his watch and reminded Bok that he had a plane to catch. When Bok was finally ready to leave, the two of them rushed to the airport in time to see the plane's door being slammed shut. Mathewson pleaded frantically with the airport staff, but they wouldn't let Bok board.

Desperate but confident, Bok took the predicament into his own hands. After some discussion—Mathewson couldn't hear what was being said—Bok was ushered away from the gate area only to return a minute later riding on one arm of a forklift. When it reached the plane the forklift rose majestically and deposited Bok and his suitcase at the reopened aircraft door.

As he disappeared into the aircraft, the former Mount Stromlo director turned toward his colleague, smiled broadly, and waved.[12]

13

Arizona
The Last Directorship

"Your long-range need is for a good crop of graduate students who, if you have treated them well, can establish your good name around the world." —Bok's advice to UA's Astronomy Department, 1964[1]

The Move from Australia

When the *Arizona Daily Star* trumpeted early in 1966 that "one of the world's leading astronomers, Dr. Bart J. Bok, will join the growing astronomy department of the University of Arizona," few people on the Steward Observatory staff were really surprised. Unlike the tempestuous move from Harvard to Australia a decade earlier, Bok's ascendancy to the directorship at the University of Arizona's Steward Observatory was a career move in the works since the Boks left for Australia.

Tucson was a city the Boks had known and loved since their first visit in 1941 to speak before a group of Harvard alumni. By the mid-1950s Tucson was beginning to lose its identity as a frontier town. In astronomy, the setting up of the national observatory at Kitt Peak meant that the University of Arizona would want to develop its astronomy program just as Harvard had done many years earlier. Early in 1957 the Boks stopped there again on their journey to Australia. Like other journeys across the United States, this once included stops to visit other prominent astronomers, including the famous comet finder, Leslie Peltier, in Ohio.[2] They also called on Aden Meinel, founding director of the National Astronomical Observatory, in the observatory's temporary headquarters in Phoenix. Meinel remembers that the Boks, who drove up in a "flashy new yellow and black Ford convertible," were already considering a return to Tucson after their stay in Australia.[3]

The Boks arrived in Tucson ostensibly to consult with University of Arizona officials on the question of whether Steward Observatory should be involved with radio astronomy; with giant radio telescopes sprouting in England and Australia, some faculty members thought this was a direction to which the Arizona astronomers should turn as well. Bok did not agree. With the embryonic national optical observatory well along, Bok thought that Steward would be much better off building a large optical telescope that would establish the university as a international leader in observational astronomy. At a dinner party with Steward Observatory director Edwin Carpenter, Priscilla talked excitedly about how much they loved Tucson and said that they would likely retire there after their return from Australia. Dinner guest David Patrick, the university's vice president for research, overheard Priscilla's comment and saw an opportunity. "Why just come here to retire?" he asked. "Why not just come back a few years early and earn an honest living with us?"

"Is that an offer?" the Boks wanted to know. Although that friendly dinner conversation did not immediately result in a formal contract, the Boks assumed that the offer was open. The university really did want the Boks to return. Its officials kept up a low-key courtship by mail throughout his time in Australia, during which they consulted him on key policy decisions.

About five years after the Boks moved to Australia, Gerard Peter Kuiper, Bok's old friend from Leiden days, unexpectedly decided to retire from McDonald Observatory in Texas and move to Arizona. So confident was Kuiper that he would have a job waiting for him there that he allegedly bought a house in Tucson before the university even hired him.[4] The arrival of Kuiper signaled a whole new direction in the university's astronomy program. Within a few years Kuiper formed an institute for lunar and planetary studies, and had a new 61-inch planetary telescope built in the Santa Catalina mountains northeast of the city.

Kuiper was a genius with a photographic memory and an ability to accomplish large amounts of work; he was also arrogant, and insisted on going in his own direction. When Kuiper arrived at the university he almost immediately clashed with Carpenter, who had developed a plan to move the observatory's 36-inch reflector away from its campus home to a dark sky site. Arrangements were almost complete to set aside some land at the new national facility, whose site had by now been selected at Kitt Peak, southwest of Tucson. Carpenter looked forward to Steward's first major telescope expansion in almost thirty years. His heart was set on moving the grand old telescope up to the mountaintop.

But Kuiper objected to this idea. Going over Carpenter's head, he told University of Arizona President Richard Harvill that "moving that old telescope is a totally foolish idea," suggesting as an alternative that a completely new 61-inch reflector be built and installed there. Upset by this interference, Carpenter persuaded Harvill to keep to the plan already agreed upon. Harvill did suggest one important compromise. Why not build the Kitt Peak dome larger than needed so that a bigger telescope could eventually replace the smaller one? (In 1993 the 36-inch telescope was still actively in use searching for asteroids approaching the Earth.)[5]

When Carpenter died in 1963, the university needed Bok earlier than they expected to take over Steward Observatory. Dean Herbert Rhodes asked Bok if he would like to come immediately. But Bok was not ready. Because he needed more time to finish doing what he had set out to do in Australia, including helping with the development of Siding Spring's 150-inch telescope, he asked for a delay until 1966. But the University of Arizona's astronomy-related programs were expanding rapidly. Steward Observatory and the astronomy department were getting new office and laboratory space, Kuiper's dream of a Space Sciences Center was also close to reality, and Aden Meinel had come to the university from Kitt Peak in hopes of launching an Optical Sciences Center. President Harvill asked Meinel to become director of both the observatory and the astronomy department; he accepted on the condition that he would resign as soon as Bok arrived from Australia.[6]

On June 10, 1964, the Boks arrived in Tucson for a month-long stay.[7] In a pre-visit letter to Meinel, Bok expressed an important hope that "we shall have a chance to talk at some length about the whole philosophy of astronomical education, for it is in this area, along with research and writing on the Milky Way, that I feel that I have my biggest contribution to make."[8] Away from director's obligations at Mount Stromlo, Bok planned an intensive period of research and writing; and he even declined Meinel's request to give a series of lectures. "I am really looking forward," Bok confided to his friend, "to the time in Tucson as providing a fine opportunity for getting some work done without interruption."[9] However, Bok did use that June visit to finalize the arrangements for him to assume the directorship two years later.

During this visit the *Tucson Daily Citizen's* June 18th issue published an interview with Bok, who praised the city's growing astronomical importance: "Developments at the university and at Kitt Peak," he said, "will mean that this is a place no astronomer can afford to miss."

Bok's correspondence with Aden Meinel and the university administration shows that he influenced both departmental policies and its staffing for at least two years before he took over as director.[10] At the end of 1964 Dean Rhodes wrote to Bok about when the appointment, still eighteen months away, would be announced, and noted that the Australian National University had already started a search for Bok's successor there.[11]

Early Days

In July 1966 Bok became director of Steward Observatory and head of the University of Arizona's Department of Astronomy, and Aden Meinel went on to direct the Optical Sciences Center. Bok quickly persuaded the university to double the department's size from six faculty members to twelve.

At the start of his first semester that fall, Bok delivered the first of the department's Monday evening public lectures, naturally on his favorite topic, the Milky Way. Although this was not a course lecture, Art Hoag, a Kitt Peak astronomer who had completed his Ph.D. under Bok at Harvard, remembered how Bok always expected his students to arrive early and copy down his blackboard notes (see chapter 9). As if by habit, Hoag arrived some time before the lecture was to begin. There was only one other person in the room that early—Dr. John Graham—who, Hoag knew, had studied under Bok in Australia and had also been trained to arrive early at a Bok lecture.

To get acquainted with his new students, Bok organized a series of seminars for the staff astronomers to describe their research. "This was a great way for Bart to find out what other people were doing," writes John Glaspey, then a new graduate student. It also provided the incoming students a chance to assess which professors would be the most interesting to work with.[12]

The new director began a policy that all graduate students would participate in three observatory functions: for example, taking turns showing slides at colloquia, participating in an informal "Journal club" where students present short papers on astronomy topics not related to their research, and helping with public tours at the telescope at Kitt Peak. Bok quickly became active in student-faculty relations at the university and was even appointed to the its prestigious "Committee of Eleven." This group of senior faculty members advised the administration on sensitive university matters, including how to react to student protests against the Vietnam War. So popular did Bok become that the night before his sixty-fourth birthday in 1970 he was named "outstanding UA faculty member of the year" by the senior men's class on its traditional UA Men's Night.[13]

Bok was a busy and concerned director, but he did have a tendency to micromanage his department. His intense style had not changed from his Australian days, when a bright light going on in the 74-inch telescope dome, meaning that observing had stopped for some reason, would prompt an immediate call from the director's nearby house. Although the Bok house in Tucson was seventy miles from Kitt Peak, observers at the 36-inch telescope would often expect a call from the director at four or five in the morning just to ask how the night of observing went.[14] While most of the observers expected, and even appreciated, this early morning call, a few resented what they saw as interference. But that was Bok's way. He once berated Professor Ray White at the telescope for using finder charts that he thought were too small, never mind that they worked efficiently for the younger professor. Bok did have a nasty streak that affected even those who were close to him. When one student did poorly on her Graduate Record Exams, a national standardized test used for admission to graduate school, Bok stung her by insisting she apologize to the professor in charge of admissions. Even though she admired Bok, the incident still upset her when she recalled it twenty-five years later.

Bok also did not mind dressing down a student or employee in full view of everyone else. One day, as astronomer John Glaspey remembers, Bok learned that an error had crept into the position of a telescope field in a published paper. "Bart found us all at the coffee hour (always held prior to departmental seminars) and in front of several of us gathered there, confronted my wife, who had been responsible for doing the calculation, with the bad news. Nonplussed, she told him to write back to the fellow and tell him to wait a couple of thousand years [when, supposedly, the Earth's motion of precession might make the position closer to being correct]. Bart was speechless (which didn't happen often) and left the room mumbling under his breath without a come-back, much to the amusement of Priscilla, among others."[15] Not long after Bok wrote a letter of recommendation for another student, the student was involved in some minor college prank. In a fit of rage after finding out about the incident, Bok threatened to retract his letter of reference, and it was only after soothing words from Priscilla that Bok calmed down. When he learned that yet another student had allegedly cheated on his wife, Bok became so upset that he threatened to expel the young man.

The Bok temper was so unnerving because it seemed so out of character and was just as likely to flash on people he liked as those he did not. The author was the recipient of one such outburst. In most cases Bok would calm down after a short while, but he was not a man known to apologize.

To build morale and to honor those who had achieved well, Bok arranged frequent pizza lunches for the department. At social events Bok was a real performer. He rarely looked another person in the eye or had the patience to listen to a stranger's sorrows. Although he was rarely belligerent, Bok always dominated conversations, often following up a story told by another with a story of his own that he thought was better.

Bok was friendly to everyone at Steward, calling employees by name, including the custodians. The people he worked with generally found him very considerate to them: he would never demand, always ask. By the start of his Tucson years, Bart's parties had become legendary and sophisticated, serving both to boost student morale and entertain visitors. Glaspey writes: "I remember the first time Bart had convinced, as he put it, Jan Oort (the famous astronomer and Bok's mentor, see chapters 2 and 9) to visit him in Tucson. Bart had his usual sherry party; at one point he grabbed me literally by the arm, plus Myron Smith and one other student, led us over to Prof. Oort, shooed away whoever was already talking to him, introduced us to Prof. Oort, then walked away, forcing us to make conversation with the great man on our own! That sort of trick was always something of a shock, but it worked, since we soon learned that the great men of science were usually very friendly and understanding, and we quickly got over our sense of awe."[16]

At each of the Boks' student parties, it was traditional for his own students and "grandstudents"—students of his former students—to come early and help out. At one of the Christmas parties his "gofers" were his

Harvard Ph.D. student Art Hoag and Ray White of Steward Observatory. White had received his Ph.D. from Ivan King, one of Bok's students, and hence was considered Bok's "grandstudent." Hoag and White arrived early for the Christmas party. White went to set up the sherry, always a staple at these events, and promptly found that the Bok household was fresh out.

Giving White ten dollars, Bok asked his grandstudent to buy two gallons of cheap Gallo sherry. As soon as White returned, Bok took one of the bottles and started pouring it into an empty bottle of the far more expensive Louis Martini. White was astounded. With a broad grin, Bok shrugged his shoulders. "These bottles are too inconvenient," he said, trying vainly to hide his deceit. "It'll be much easier to pour from this smaller bottle!"[17]

Notwithstanding such little tricks, the Boks' many colleagues, students, and friends cherish their memories of those parties. "Bart was a marvelous host," recalled David Crawford of Kitt Peak. "He created a beautiful, ambient environment, and his guests went away feeling really good."[18]

The 90-inch Telescope

In the years before Bok arrived at Steward Observatory, he assisted Aden Meinel, who was writing a proposal for the National Science Foundation's Centers of Excellence program to improve the quality of Steward Observatory through the construction of one of two telescopes, a 60-inch or a 100-inch reflector, that would be built on Kitt Peak.

Bok's recollection of the response of Director Lee Hayworth is probably apocryphal: "Bart, you know how to build observatories. You know how to run observatories. Let's turn the '6' upside down to a '9' and give Steward a 90-inch." Steward Observatory was given a single two-million-dollar grant for a "Science Development Program." After Hayworth's decision there was some question for a time as to the exact size, depending on the availability of the glass, of the new telescope. A year before he arrived in Tucson Bok speculated that the telescope might be as large as 84 or even 100 inches.[19] By March 1966, when construction began, the size had been finalized at 90 inches.

Looking a bit like a huge can of spray paint, the 90-inch observatory building's design was an interesting departure from the conventional hemisphere used in observatory domes. This Aden Meinel design saved money by avoiding the need for the expensive curved steel structure of traditional domes.[20] Moreover, the building was unusually tall for its time, bringing its telescope far above the eddying air currents close to the ground which result in poor seeing and inferior images of celestial objects. For the telescope itself, the designers saved money by virtually copying the mechanical and optical design of Kitt Peak's 84-inch Ritchey-Chrétien reflector, an optical system offering wider fields of view than those of classical Cassegrain telescopes.

But glass and steel are only part of a telescope. The detector—the instrument that records the light—is just as important. Just before the Boks left for America they received a telegram from Merle Tuve of the Carnegie Institution that announced the arrival in Australia of a new kind of electronic technology: "Your many friends in U.S. astronomy and physics will be delighted that one of the Carnegie NSF Image tube sets is prepared and being sent for Mount Stromlo staff use before you leave Australia as symbol of universal affectionate regard for you both and as another continuing reminder to them of your dedication to the southern sky."[21] (Within fifteen years the image tube technology would be abandoned in favor of the much more efficient light-gathering computer chip called a charge-coupled device, or CCD.)

As early as 1964, image orthicons (the TV cameras then in use) were becoming popular as a convenience in observing, allowing astronomers to guide their exposures from the comfort of heated control rooms.[22] By the end of the 1960s the technology had rapidly improved, in part spurred by the U.S. military for use in night operations in Vietnam. Thus, observers waiting for the new telescope were counting on the use of an image-tube with ten times the sensitivity of the most common photographic film then in use, hypersensitized Kodak IIa-O.[23]

For all this to work, many systems, parts, and technologies must come together, and no matter how many tests a telescope's optical and mechanical parts undergo, there is a moment when, on a clear night, the entire instrument must face the sky as a complete unit. Any number of things can go wrong, from minor errors in the telescope's motors to an astigmatic mirror which would give flawed star images, as astronomers painfully learned years later, after the launch of the Hubble Space Telescope. On the evening of May 28, 1969, Bart Bok, Ray White, and several other observers drove up to the 90-inch to celebrate the ritual of "first light" for what they hoped would be a fine new telescope.

The telescope was hardly fine-tuned for observing. The mirror did not even have its coat of reflective aluminum. There were no motors to move the huge structure rapidly from one object to another. There was, however, a motor drive to follow a star in right ascension (a celestial equivalent of longitude), but no similar motor to make adjustments in declination (latitude).

When the group arrived they threw a switch that started to open the dome's two huge shutters. It was a thrilling moment. As the space between the opening door grew larger the group watched the darkening sky and gibbous moon whose light, they hoped, would soon grace their telescope.

To move the telescope Bok and his team attached ropes, and as some people pulled on the ropes others pushed the telescope along. The instrument inched closer to their first target, the Moon. Suddenly they had it, and someone called out "There it is! Stop!" But by now the telescope's momentum allowed it to travel a little farther before stopping, and they had to repeat the push-pull routine. Finally they centered the telescope on the Moon, and with some difficulty focused it. Once they had calibrated the telescope's setting circles on the Moon's position, they had less difficulty finding the next target, Jupiter.

"OK, gentlemen," Bok then announced, "let us see if we have a telescope." By now they had locked onto a new target, Messier 13, the globular cluster in the constellation Hercules. "Raywhite!" Bok yelled, slurring the two names into one, his usual reference to White. "Are the plateholders ready?" With the plateholder mounted in the telescope, Bok opened the shutter. He steadied the huge steel structure by keeping one of the cluster's stars in the center of the eyepiece as the film recorded the light of M13 for ten minutes. It was White's turn next. He guided a similar exposure of the Ring Nebula, Messier 57. Finally he took both plates to the darkroom.

Within a few minutes Bok grew impatient and started pacing around. He pounded on the darkroom door. "Still in the fixer!" White answered. "Well, be quick, Raywhite!" White had just enough time to splash water to remove the fixer chemical when Bok rushed in to examine the M13 plate. The stars were round and beautiful across the glass. Relaxing in triumph, Bok stood up, put the plate back in the wash, and proclaimed: "Well, gentlemen, we have a telescope!"[24]

Bok's Early Retirement

One of the more surprising aspects of Bok's directorship was that about a year and a half after he arrived in Tucson, he asked to be relieved of it. "I am now almost 62 years old," he wrote Dean Bowen Dees in February 1968, "and I find I get terribly tired from the day to day pressures. Also, I would like more time for research and writing than I seem to have now."[25] Although Bart and Priscilla had moved to Tucson with the intention of retiring there, it seems strange that he would start the process so shortly after his arrival, particularly in view of the strides his career was taking forward: two months after his letter he was elected to the prestigious National Academy of Sciences.[26]

Bok added that he did not want to give up the directorship until the 90-inch was operating smoothly, an event he knew was still a year away.[27] But less than two weeks before their happy 90-inch first light episode, Bok wrote Dees reminding him to "do everything possible to have my successor appointed to take over by September 1, 1970."[28]

Bok never indicated that there was any problem with other people in the department that was influencing his decision to step down. However, other faculty members suggest that there was a conflict on the horizon, this time with Ray Weymann, a young and forceful professor who was already beginning to influence the direction that research at the 90-inch was going to take. Although Bok suggested Weymann as a possible director as early as his February 1968 letter, some observatory staff felt that the Weymann choice was a mistake. The good feeling and family atmosphere that Bok was trying to germinate, one professor claimed, was threatened by Weymann, who had turned the observatory into "an armed camp." More than one other Steward Observatory faculty member remembered that Bok appeared to be subjugated by Weymann and consulted him before he made almost any decision. Articulating the feeling of some of his colleagues, one professor felt that Weymann was taking over the telescope from the other staff who had been involved in its construction. A theoretical astrophysicist, Weymann was emphasizing research more into galaxies and less into the stars of Bok's beloved Milky Way.

Apparently it was Weymann's idea that observing time on the telescope be allotted not by one person but by a telescope allocation committee. Groups of astronomers were already forming such committees to review proposals for use of the telescopes at the national observatories at Kitt Peak and at Cerro Tololo Interamerican Observatory in Chile, and this communal peer-review approach certainly seemed to be gaining favor.

However, if there was a conflict between Weymann and some of the staff, Bok did not appear to let it bother him, and Weymann denies that there was any controversy. Bok felt friendship and respect towards Weymann, and he encouraged Weymann in his desire to be director and even nominated him for the honor of membership in the National Academy of Sciences. "When I was offered the job as Director of Steward Observatory I had serious reservations about accepting the position," Weymann writes. "Bart and Priscilla invited my wife and me over for dinner one night, and he turned on his usual charm and plied me with wine and did, in fact, make a major impact on my decision to accept the position. Priscilla told me later that she thought he had come on too strong and twisted my arm too hard!"[29]

By the late 1960s Bart and Priscilla were thinking about how to enjoy many years of retirement in Tucson, and a comfortable relationship with Steward Observatory was to be a big part of that happiness. Ten years Bart's senior, in 1968 Priscilla was 72 years old, and Bart looked forward to spending more time with her rather than with administrative duties.

In any event, Bok would leave a very healthy department. By June 1969 it had twenty graduate students, of whom seven were leaving temporarily because of the military draft. The 90-inch began scheduled operation that fall.[30] More exciting news came in January 1971, when *U.S. News and World Report* published a rating of graduate programs across the United States. In its previous report in 1966, Arizona's astronomy program was not listed at all, but now it placed fifth in the nation. The good news had a particularly satisfying corollary: Harvard placed sixth. Bok was thrilled, and he admits that he and Priscilla "had a strong martini that night: four to one."

As it turned out, Bok retired in 1970, only a year before his sixty-fifth birthday. That year was filled with professional achievement. At its general assembly in Brighton, England, Bok was elected vice-president of the International Astronomical Union, representing the more than one quarter of the IAU's individual members coming from the United States. The same year he was elected president of the American Astronomical Society.

Star Birth in the Milky Way

In Tucson, a group led by astronomer Beverly Lynds organized a conference on "Dark Nebulae, Globules, and Protostars" with the intention of honoring Bok. The two-day meeting that began on March 26, 1970, attracted sixty scientists from all over the country. Ray White handled most of the day-to-day operation of the conference, and in addition to her other duties, Lynds edited the book that contained the meeting papers. White always thought that Bok was a little suspicious that there was an underlying purpose of the conference, and that it was to oust him a bit early. Considering the great honor this meeting produced for Bok, that is unlikely. "At the age of 64 years," Jesse Greenstein wrote in the dedication to the conference book, "he has decided to retire early from the directorship of Steward Observatory, presumably to channel his energy more efficiently into work on his loved Milky Way."[31]

In an important way, this conference represented a subtle turn for Bok's scientific interests, which had concentrated on the Milky Way's spiral structure. Bok now wanted to focus once more on the galaxy's dark matter—the globules and the other dark clouds of the interstellar medium—which had dominated his work in the late 1940s, when he and Edith Reilly discovered the importance of the small dark nebulae in the Lagoon Nebula, Messier 8, that are now known as Bok globules. By 1970 there were already some 200 known globules, of which half were very small ones detectable only through their location in front of a bright nebula like the Lagoon.[32] Because the smallest are no larger than ten thousand astronomical units in diameter (ten thousand times the distance between the Sun and Earth), Bok suspected that the globules were in a state of slow collapse toward the birth of new stars. "I don't think," Bok said at that meeting, "that these small units have a choice other than to collapse." The globules are also very cold; astronomers had known that since Carl Heiles discovered the presence of the hydroxyl, or OH, radical in the nebula south of Rho Ophiuchi. Since the free hydroxyl radical is highly reactive and exists only at temperatures very close to absolute zero, the globule environment must have a temperature close to that. What would it be like inside a globule? A large amount of unlit gas—perhaps the equivalent of nine times the mass of the Sun—would pass through the globule over a period of one hundred million years. Some of this gas would be captured by the globule's own frigid particles. Over this period of time the whole globule would shrink. The small globules would collapse to form single stars, and the large ones would form clusters of stars.[33]

Of all the other circumstances that could trigger the birth of new stars, the best known is the outburst of a supernova. As the shock waves from the outburst push outward, they pass through thick concentrations of interstellar gas, creating an environment where star formation can occur.

Using the new image-tube on the telescopes at Steward and at Cerro Tololo, Bok and his colleagues Carolyn Cordwell and Richard Cromwell discovered a series of globules which were much larger than the globules in which he was originally interested. These new clouds had diameters almost double the distance between the Sun and Proxima Centauri, the nearest star. Through his own observations as well as the research by his team into others, Bok's team prepared a listing of 16 representative globules that would be useful to optical and radio astronomers. These globules were selected by Bok and Cordwell by going through the original Barnard catalogs as well as more recent studies. One of the aims of their research was to calculate masses of these globules. The large globules, Bok found, ranged in mass from 2 to 50 times that of the Sun, the largest mass belonging to Barnard 361, a round globule in the constellation Cygnus.[34]

Although Bok was clearly steering away from spiral structure, he did not ignore this other research love during his Steward period. The most visible change in Bok's view of the galaxy was the demise of his idea of a Carina-Cygnus arm (see chapters 8 and 10). He was, however, even more convinced that there was a major spiral feature in Carina. To prepare for a thorough exploration of this feature, Bart and Priscilla continued their work on Southern Hemisphere photometric standard stars.[35] With these standards as a base, they explored stars from a section of the feature at a distance of 6,500 light years. Finally, they observed stars at double that distance, or 13,000 light years.

Whether the Carina arm was actually one of the spiral arms of the galaxy or simply a part of a larger structure depended partly on semantics. Bok defined spiral arms as "long-connected streamers of hydrogen gas, many of which resemble logarithmic spirals."

In 1972 Piddington published a paper criticizing this definition.[36] In an unpublished rebuttal, Bok explained that he had always referred to the Carina arm as a "spiral feature," not an arm, but that he had now traced its extent to eight kiloparsecs, or almost 25,000 light years, from the Sun. Bok admitted that one could not tell for certain whether the Carina feature was a complete spiral arm by itself or merely a part of an even larger spiral arm.[37]

Another big change in thought about galactic structure was the demise of the idea that magnetic effects could affect the development of spiral arms, an idea quite readily accepted only ten years earlier (see chapter 10). In the intervening time, the discovery by Jocelyn Bell and Anthony Hewish of pulsating neutron stars (or pulsars) allowed astronomers to refine downward their estimates of the strength of magnetic fields in the galaxy. By 1970 the strength of a galactic magnetic field was thought to be much too low to have an effect in creating a spiral arm.[38] Since the pulsars tended to be found in known spiral structures, they were being hailed as a new way of tracing the extent of spiral arms.[39]

Of all their work during the Steward Observatory period, the Boks enjoyed the time spent at Chile's Cerro Tololo Interamerican Observatory more than anything else. Away from director's duties at Steward Observatory, Cerro Tololo meant studying the structure of the Carina feature or photographing the Eta Carinae and Gum nebulae in search of answers to their questions about the birth of stars. "Probably our most useful work," Bart remembered, "was done under very favorable conditions at Cerro Tololo. Our visits to Cerro Tololo marked about the best days in the lives of Priscilla and Bart Bok."[40]

Although Bart loved to observe, he sometimes was careless. During one Cerro Tololo observing run he arbitrarily substituted his own guesses for exposure times that had been carefully worked out by Ellis Miller and Alice Hine, two of his students, resulting in a series of pretty but scientifically useless photographic plates.[41]

When the staff of Kitt Peak National Observatory decided to prepare a film on Cerro Tololo, its sister facility in Chile, the producers wanted to show Bok working at one of the Cerro Tololo telescopes. However, as a fund-saving maneuver they suggested that Bok perform the scene using the 36-inch reflector at nearby Kitt Peak, since it was rather similar in appearance and operation to the Chilean telescope. "To hell with you!" Bok shot back. "I won't do this fake thing under any circumstances. Everyone, especially my graduate students, will know it is not the 36-inch at Cerro Tololo; it's the one at Kitt Peak. They will say the damn fool doesn't even know where the controls are!" Bok had had an unfortunate experience at Harvard, where he had agreed to such a picture. "First thing I did," he said, "I closed one eye, which I never do, to look through the telescope. Got photographed, got printed in the newspaper, and one of the Harvard graduate students put it on the bulletin board with a sign under it: "Peeping Tom Finally Caught."

Bok got his way this time. The scene was produced at Tololo and was shown for many years to thousands of visitors at both observatories.

On November 3, 1970, Salvador Allende was elected as Chile's Marxist president, inciting a widespread movement in the United States to reduce ties with that country, even to cutting off relations altogether. The political change alarmed Bok, who had always fought the intrusion of international politics into science, and who once again let his feelings be known: "I wish to protest as vigorously as I know how against this approach," Bok announced at the Chicago meeting of the American Association for the Advancement of Science. Fearing that these developments would block international scientific exchanges and the resulting benefits between countries, Bok insisted: "Astronomers have traditionally had the habit of continuing foreign correspondence and associations during times of war and of political stress between nations." This was the same attitude that led to his AAScW activities (chapter 7), and his pro–South Africa article (chapter 9). International cooperation in science was one of the canons of Bok's life, and his commitment to it led to such efforts as the building of the Anglo-Australian telescope. "International collaboration between our scientists and scientists from nations which hold political beliefs different from ours can form bridges of understanding. . . . I hope that as a nation we may have enough sense to strengthen our political relations with Chile by increasing rather than decreasing our scientific involvement with that nation."[42]

Prison: Public Service with a Twist

Arriving in Tucson with a legacy of bringing astronomy to the people, Bok expected so many invitations to give public lectures that he would have to turn them away. But his extracurricular teaching life in Arizona turned out to be serene, with few demands on his time. This apparent lack of public interest bothered him.

One notable exception to this disappointing response came in the form of an unsolicited letter he received from inmates at the state prison in

Florence, Arizona, some sixty miles north of Tucson. Inmates there had asked that Professor Bok assign one of his staff to come to the prison and give them a lecture. Bok saw a wonderful opportunity in this letter, and always remembered fondly the thoughts he had while answering it: "No. I won't assign anybody. I am not in the habit as a director to assign people to give lectures. That is not the way we run this university. But I will be delighted to come myself and lecture to your group, and tell you some of the latest things about astronomy."

Not long after came an unusual reply, considering the lack of interest Bok perceived in other Arizonans. The prisoners wished to prepare themselves for the lectures, and they requested some information so that they could read up on Bok's subject. In their letter acknowledging the material he had sent them, the inmates had a final request: "We notice, Professor Bok, that your wife is an astronomer of distinction too. Would you bring her along with you? And would you like to come to dinner with us?"

The Boks arrived at the prison early one evening, identified themselves, and walked in as the huge gates opened and then slammed shut behind them. It was a highly successful evening, and even the chocolate cake was good. Showing them slides from his massive collection on the Milky Way, Bart took the inmates on a tour beyond their prison walls, to the planets, the nearby stars, and the distant suns of the Milky Way. The Boks left happy but undoubtedly relieved when the event was over.

A few weeks later the Boks received another letter, this time from the Women's Self Improvement Society at the state women's prison, also in Florence. Again they had a very successful evening, but this time the women followed up, asking the Boks to return. After that the lecture became an annual event: "A year wouldn't be right without a lecture by Professor Bok," Bart recalled one of the women saying.

The evening's program was highly structured. A chairperson would handle the discussion, and questions would be asked only in a specific order. If a prisoner wished to ask a question out of turn, she would be turned down quickly with a sharp "You're out of order." They did this, the Boks were told, to prepare themselves for reentry into society. So relaxed did these evenings become that one prisoner, helping the Boks return their slides and materials to their car, said, "Gee, Dr. Bok, you know—I could escape tonight." Looking round at the quiet street, the Boks realized that two prisoners were indeed outside the front gate. But the women went back inside uneventfully. "There was a very warm-hearted feeling," Bart said, "that we wouldn't have missed for anything." The feeling was obviously shared by the prisoners who wrote Dr. Bok from time to time asking for more information about articles they had read or new discoveries about which they had heard.

A tasty Mexican dinner at a U-shaped table preceded the 1970 lecture. The Boks sat among different groups of prisoners, talking and joking about prison life and to a lesser extent about astronomy. Priscilla sat next to a woman around sixty, and the two women struck up a conversation.

After the dinner Bok stood up and was about to begin his lecture when one of the prisoners caught his attention. "Professor Bok," she whispered. "Did you know that the woman sitting next to your wife is none other than Winnie Judd?" Startled, Bart looked and saw Priscilla engaged in an animated conversation with Judd.

On the way home Priscilla was positively glowing. The Boks had never made a point of asking any prisoner why she was there. "Boy, Bart, I've had a good time tonight sitting with this bright woman. Her father was a minister like my father was. She has been to Mexico. She has worked in California. We had so much to talk about. I had a wonderful time. I hope we can keep in touch with that woman, even see her next year."

"But Priscilla," Bart answered, "do you know who that very nice, bright, woman is?"

"No."

"That's Winnie Judd!"

"Oh. Really? *The* Winnie Judd?" For a second Priscilla was stunned, but only for a second. "Well! You know what? I don't care. So what if it was Winnie Judd! I like her. I think she is a wonderful woman. She has traveled, and she talks nicely. She knows what she is talking about. She listened carefully to your lecture. She is a great woman and don't you start tearing her down!"

Priscilla was being uncommonly forgiving. Her partner in conversation was the "trunk slayer," one of the most notorious murderers in Arizona's history. On October 16, 1931, Judd fatally shot two women who were allegedly her two best friends, Agnes Anne LeRoi, a Phoenix X-ray technician, and Helvig "Sammy" Samuelson, an Alaskan school teacher with tuberculosis who had just moved to Phoenix on funds provided by her friends. After dismembering Samuelson, Judd put both bodies in trunks, took the trunks to the railway depot and shipped them off to California. A baggage handler discovered the crime when he saw blood dripping from one of the trunks. She was noticeably uncooperative and hot-tempered during her 1932 trial, pleading that the murder was self-defense.[43]

Judd was sentenced to death by hanging on April 28, 1933 (coincidentally Bart's birthday). But three days before the execution was to occur, Judd was found insane and her sentence was commuted to life imprisonment. After she had escaped seven times from the Arizona State Hospital in Phoenix, she was transferred to the women's prison.[44]

At the Boks' 1971 lecture to the Women's Self Improvement Society, Priscilla sat down with Winnie Judd again, and they had another conversation. After that, a series of escapes (not by Judd) put an end to all outside lectures in the prisons. But so strongly was Priscilla attracted to this woman that when the time came for Judd's parole hearing she thought that she and Bart should intervene on her behalf. "If we ever need a housekeeper," Priscilla said trustingly, "I would rather have Winnie Judd than anybody else."

Hoping that he could win her release, Bart wrote a letter to Governor Jack Williams of Arizona: "We are well aware of the circumstances under which she came to the State Penitentiary, but we are equally impressed with the fact that by now she is fully ready to return to society and that she has, moreover, been in prison long enough to have served her time for the crime committed about 40 years ago. She is clearly a reformed person, and one who is ready to take her place again in Society."[45]

Governor Williams was not impressed with Bok's plea. "You must understand," he wrote Bok in June 1970, "that those who knew and loved Helvig Samuelson, when she lived in Alaska, and took up a collection because she contracted tuberculosis and sent her to Phoenix to get well, are equally concerned that Mrs. Judd not be released!

"I want you to realize that when the decision is finally made, it will be my decision, not yours, and I will have to live with it."[46] Four months later, Williams did commute Winnie Judd's sentence. Judd moved to California to become a housekeeper, and she changed her name to Marian Lane.[47]

14

*

A Far and Radiant Resting Place

"We have been married for 46 years and you should not worry. From now on, I am your memory. I'll stick with you."
—Bart Bok, around 1974, talking with Priscilla, now suffering from progressive memory loss[1]

A tire blew out on takeoff as a plane carrying Bart and Priscilla took off for Chicago. As the plane began its descent, the crew was not sure if the landing gear would hold on touchdown. The captain announced that as far as they could tell the gear was in place and the landing, though rough, would be a safe one. However, he warned his passengers, there was a chance the plane would crash. The flight crew taught the passengers how to brace for this emergency landing, and then there was nothing to do but wait.

Sitting there helpless, Bart held Priscilla's hand. "Oh, this is terrible, Priscilla, frightful." At first his wife said nothing. Then she looked up and said, "Bart, look around you." As Bart looked at the other passengers, Priscilla said, "Look at all the young people on this plane. People who have their whole lives ahead of them! Haven't we had a beautiful life together?"

The couple sat quietly as Priscilla made her point. "If we crash, and everybody rushes out—we are going to sit right here and let the young people out first."[2]

The plane landed safely. When they returned home, Bok acrimoniously demanded that the airline explain the near disaster and justify the state of their tires; and he was angrier still when he discovered that the airlines commonly retread them.

In that time of their lives, the activities they shared meant the most to them, including their trips to Chile's Cerro Tololo observatory, where

Bart took long exposures of the southern Milky Way, especially the region of Eta Carinae. After placing a photographic glass plate into its holder on a typical night, Bok loaded it into the telescope and checked his large finder charts one more time. He then swung the gigantic metal sail of a telescope across the sky, expertly stopping it near Eta Carinae. For the umpteenth time he prepared to photograph the seemingly tranquil nebulosity that surrounds that mysterious star. Then he opened the shutter. For an hour Bart carefully guided the telescope, moving it ever so slightly slower, then faster with the touch of a button, always keeping Eta Carinae in the center of the telescope's field of view. Every now and then he lifted his eyes from the eyepiece and looked out through the dome to glance at the sky, which remained black as ink, completely free of clouds.

The hour was up. Bart closed the shutter, gently removed the plateholder from the telescope, and took it to the darkroom. Only when all the lights were off could the next operation begin. The plate, taken from its protective holder, was bathed in a developer. Bart grasped the edges of the plate as the chemical did its work, coaxing the latent star images to appear on the emulsioned surface. Then a buzzer went off. Bart lifted the plate clear of the developer and briefly soaked it in an acid bath. Finally he immersed the plate in a third chemical designed to neutralize the developer and harden the emulsion. Having done this procedure often over many years, Bart was used to the pitch darkness.

With a snap of a switch the light was on. Putting the plate under a magnifier, he looked at the result. From one side to the other, the star images were true, sharp points of light surrounded by the dramatic haze of the surrounding nebula. "Priscilla," he would call, "come look at this. It's beautiful."

To describe the intricacies of the Eta Carinae region, including the nearby Keyhole nebula, as "beautiful" is an understatement. The complex, delicate combination of star and nebula make the Eta Carinae region one of the most breathtaking in the entire sky (see chapter 4). Looking like a fuzzy star to the unaided eye, the region becomes a group of bright stars surrounded by wisps of cloudiness when magnified. The larger the telescope, the more there is to see.

Both the Eta Carinae region itself and what we understand about it have changed during the Boks' half-century delight in this corner of space 6,800 light years away.[3] Near the star system of Eta Carinae itself is a pattern of gaseous knots, first observed in 1944, that looks a bit like a manikin or homunculus, complete with "head pointing northwest, legs opposite and arms folded over a fat body" around the central stars.[4] By 1972 these knots had rushed outward a quarter of their 1949 distance from the star, indicating that the material might have been thrust from the star around 1860,[5] some twenty years after it underwent an explosion that briefly made it one of the brightest stars in the sky.[6]

The nebula is a highly concentrated region of brightly lit hydrogen gas that glows very much like a fluorescent light. Hydrogen is very common throughout the galaxy's spiral arms and is the main ingredient in the formation of new stars. Most of the hot, blue stars in the region may be only a few million years old—almost newborns by celestial standards.[7] As Bok loved to repeat in his public lectures, "the good Lord is cooking up there at a much faster rate than he does near us, so you can see much more clearly what the hell is going on when stars are formed."[8]

Only on the first night of an observing run would Priscilla join Bart at the telescope to help ensure that everything was working well. Otherwise the two Boks seldom worked as a team at the telescope. Bart explained that it never worked out well "with one person in charge of the night, and the other taking orders. Priscilla wasn't made for that, and neither was I." As the collaboration matured over the years, Bart became the observer, and Priscilla would prepare the observing data for later analysis. After a night of observing at Mt. Stromlo, for example, Bart would lay out the long paper record of the night's data on the carpet in the hallway of their director's residence, and the following morning Priscilla would try to make sense of the data as Bart slept. By early afternoon Priscilla would have the last night's observations ready for analysis.

Eta Carinae was just one course on the Boks' busy observing menu. Whether they were observing the Milky Way's neighbor the Large Magellanic Cloud or obtaining photometric data on standard stars, the Boks worked in their separate ways to produce solid results. During one of their Australian Christmas holidays, the Boks traveled to Stromlo's remote observing station at Mount Bingar for two weeks of photoelectric photometry, obtaining brightness data on stars. Upon arrival Bart told the "screwdriver boys" (as he humorously—not disdainfully—called observatory technical staff) to go home and have a merry Christmas, and he then proceeded to set up the telescope for photometric observing of several stars.

The purpose of these photometric observations was to obtain a series of accurate measurements of each star's brightness to establish a roster of standard stars from which further research could be accomplished. Once the telescope had been pointed directly at a chosen star, the photometer would begin the first of a series of measurements needed to get a good average brightness value. Afterwards the telescope would be moved slightly away from the star so that the photometer could measure the sky background, a value to be subtracted so that the brightness of the sky would not influence the perceived brightness of the star. The same procedure was repeated using standard stars whose brightnesses were already known.

The Boks were on their own that Christmas. Had anything gone seriously wrong with the telescope, they would have packed up and gone home. "Priscilla and I had a hell of a good time working together," Bart stressed, "and out of that collaboration came one of the most important papers on integrated magnitudes for the brightest nebulae regions in the Large Magellanic Cloud."[9]

From the earliest days of their marriage, Priscilla insisted that their professional collaboration always be a fifty-fifty bargain. "I'll never *assist* you," Priscilla insisted, "but we can do things together. We'll sit at different desks, not across from each other; I don't want you looking on." This approach worked well for the Boks. In fact, from the earliest days, when Priscilla completed her paper on the proper motions of the RR Lyrae variable stars, this way of working did much to increase the respect each had for the other.[10]

Over the decades Bok loved to reminisce how he loved those happy times. Usually, Bart would observe all night, taking detailed notes in the observing logs, so that Priscilla could reduce the data the next day and be ready for the following night's work. Frequently, brief notes of love and affection appeared in the margins of these observing logs.[11]

One night, just before dawn, while Bart was working alone at the 74-inch telescope not far from his home, Priscilla was awakened by a long wail coming from the darkened dome. Startled, she thought that Bart had possibly fallen off the observing platform. As she got up to investigate, she heard another booming sound, this one unmistakable:

"Day-o."

And then she heard the rest of Bart's melody: "Come with the tally, man, tally me bananas. Daylight come and me want to go home. Day-o. Day-o. Daylight come and me want to go home."

Relieved that her husband was unhurt, just busy loading a Jamaican banana boat, Priscilla laughed to herself and went back to sleep.

By 1970 Priscilla's letters were showing a greater-than-ever pride in her husband's accomplishments. The teasing and "I'm better than you" attitude that Bart had ascribed to her in jest certainly was not apparent in letters like this 1971 epistle:

> Dearest Bart,
>   Did you see the beautiful certificate that came for you from KTUC?
> You have been selected as our
> Star of the Day
> in recognition of
> your continued
> distinguished contributions
> to astronomical science
> and your receiving the
> International Astronomy
> Medal for 1971
> Radio KTUC will salute you throughout the day Sunday, August 22, 1971.[12]

By 1971, Priscilla's letters began noting the little things in their marriage that had now become very important: "This morning was cooler than it has been," she wrote to her husband in 1971, "so I spent a couple of hours out in the garden cleaning up the rose bushes, so they'll look nice when you come back."[13]

The International Astronomical Union

The spring of 1970 was a good time to relinquish the administrative chores of Steward Observatory and the graduate school: the 90-inch was operating, and the school was doing very well indeed (see chapter 12). However, Bok was hardly slowing down. During this time he became increasingly more involved in the American Astronomical Society and the International Astronomical Union. He also kept up his teaching duties until he retired from the university in 1974. University of Arizona President John Schaefer made him professor emeritus one month later.

The IAU had always had personal meaning to both Boks. The most important IAU meeting they attended was their first, in 1928. That was where, of course, Bart met and fell in love with Priscilla. "Our marriage," he bragged, "was IAU sponsored." It was easy to attend the next IAU congress three years later in 1931, for it met at Harvard. "It was just before a total eclipse of the Sun in nearby Maine," Bart quipped, "during which I earned fifty bucks and bought a chair for our house." With rare exceptions he attended every subsequent IAU meeting, making new friends like Viktor Ambartsumian (Stockholm 1937, see chapter 5). Bart was elected to several IAU commissions over the years, including president of Commission 33 on Galactic Structure, as well as membership in Stellar Photometry (Commission 25), Radio Astronomy (Commission 40), and the Magellanic Clouds Subcommission of Galaxies (Commission 28).

In 1970 IAU president Otto Ackmund formally invited Bok to be nominated for a vice-presidency, a position which would give him a seat on the IAU's prestigious Executive Committee. For Bok, the nomination was a great honor, and he was subsequently elected during the 1970 assembly in Brighton, England. Bart saw the Executive Committee as a "steering committee for astronomy on a worldwide basis." It provided a chance to influence the directions in which astronomy was headed, a task he always relished. According to Bok, the Executive Committee suggested which kinds of symposia, for example, would be emphasized and which discouraged. Consisting of about a dozen members, the Executive Committee met once each year. With this position came the possibility that someday Bok would become president of the IAU. But that was not to be.

Priscilla's Illness

In late May 1972, while Bart was in Albany at IAU symposium 52 on Interstellar Dust,[14] Priscilla had what he called a very mild stroke. She appeared to recover quickly and there seemed to be no discernible effect; she continued working on final revisions to *The Milky Way*'s fourth edition and at age 77 single-handedly completed its index.[15]

But within a few months she began to exhibit a slight loss of memory. At first it was barely noticeable; she might wake up and briefly not recognize her husband. But it became much more serious. "I know that you are kind to me and that I love you," she said one morning, "but what is your name again?"

Priscilla's illness was some form of senile dementia, a term encompassing a number of severe and irreversible illnesses that all have similar symptoms of memory loss and dramatic changes in behavior. Although it was never diagnosed as such, Priscilla's symptoms resembled those of Alzheimer's disease.

Whatever its name, the course of the disease that Priscilla was now starting would consume her life, and because Bart would have to care for her, he would put his life on hold for a long time. This disease was as hard for the family as it was for the patient. There was absolutely nothing Bart could do as he watched the mind of his strong, intellectual, passionate wife wither away to a shadow.

The illness is so devastating, so tragic, that some husbands and wives actually pull away from their sick spouses, mourning them while they are still alive. However, despite the lack of social services and counseling that are now available, Bart's handling of the tragedy was astute and effective. He brought to bear his phenomenal will and intelligence, and for a man known to be blunt and impatient at times, Bart treated his fading wife with extraordinary patience, compassion, and good humor. First, he mounted a portrait of the family in their bedroom, and he kept a small blackboard handy. Each morning he would patiently introduce his wife to each of her children and grandchildren, and he would do it again whenever needed or asked for. Granddaughter Jeanne Sherry noted that this was an example of how Bart turned a potential calamity into something "positive and fun: Bart liked to repeat things anyway, he was a great one for that, and he repeated them joyfully for Priscilla."[16]

As Priscilla's memory declined ominously, her personality changed with it. When Bart discovered one afternoon that all the oven burners had been left on, he knew that Priscilla could no longer be left alone, not even for a few minutes. "Now it's clear, Bart," Priscilla said softly. "I'm a nitwit, and I can't cook anymore." In her lucid moments, however, Priscilla was able to teach her husband how to cook, an activity at which he became quite proficient and enjoyed to the end of his life.

As Priscilla's memory grew worse, she had difficulty concentrating. Fighting her illness with all her remaining resources, she continued going over the proofs of the fourth edition of their classic *The Milky Way*, struggling endlessly over individual sentences. She marked material she did not like, but was not able to explain why. Eventually Bart quietly took away the proofs she had been examining. He did not fight the disease, as Priscilla did; as her condition became worse he patiently tried to work with her step by step.

The next watershed event occurred in 1973 when Gerard Kuiper, Bart's friend from Leiden and head of the university's Lunar and Planetary Lab, died suddenly while on a visit to Mexico. The funeral took place at Tucson's Unitarian Church, and as prominent astronomers and friends of Kuiper, the Boks sat in the front row. As they took their seats, Priscilla looked around and became instantly uncomfortable. "Why are we here?" she whispered to her husband. The service consisted of a series of eulogies given by friends. When Bart sat down after his eulogy, Priscilla stated that she wanted to leave. "But we can't, Priscilla. We're sitting in the front row!"

"But this is all so false! Everybody is saying all these nice things about Gerard. Don't you remember how he put me in the wrong taxi at Leiden?"

"Yes, the taxi drove you all across town. But we have to stay here anyway."

After a few more minutes Priscilla again demanded that they leave, but Bart still resisted. Knowing that if he argued too vehemently, she would only become more adamant, he smiled and tried his best to keep her calm. Finally, as the service ended and someone brought out refreshments, Priscilla reached her limit. "Bart," she said, "I know Unitarian churches. My father was a good Unitarian minister, and every church has a fire escape someplace." Bart looked around, and sure enough, there was a fire escape nearby that they could use without being too obvious. Stealthily they moved toward the exit, opened the door, and left.

This could have been a calamity, but it turned into a beautiful moment as they stood in the warm sunlight on the balcony of the fire escape, relieved that they had exited unseen. As they were about to start down, Priscilla motioned for Bart to wait. There at the top of the fire escape, Priscilla insisted that Bart make her a promise. "If I should die before you, I want you to promise me that you will have no service, no memorial event of any sort."

As her husband listened, Priscilla went on: "You like a good show, Bart. But I want absolutely no show when I die." She paused a moment, and then smiled. "You know, I'm from New England, just like the witches were. If you have a memorial service, I will come down in the middle of it, on a broomstick, and I'll remind you of what I said on this fire escape!"

Bart laughed and agreed. "No service, Priscilla." Arm in arm, they descended the stairs. But somehow Bart was so impressed with his wife's thought that a year later he wrote that the same instruction should hold for himself: "If the time should come to pass that I die, then I do *not* wish to have a Memorial Service. My body is to go to the U of A School of Medicine, Department of Anatomy."[17]

In 1974 Bart resigned his vice-presidency of the IAU. "The IAU was a large family," Bok felt, "and the executive would have been furious if I had not resigned. My IAU assignment was precise: take good care of Priscilla." His resignation served to alert the community of the urgency of Priscilla's illness: "As always," Steward Observatory director Ray Weymann wrote, "Barbara and I stand ready at a moment's notice to help out at any time if needed."[18]

Almost to the end Priscilla was quite capable of putting on a good show for visitors. When newspaper reporter David Dietz visited from Cleveland to write a series of astronomy articles, Bart cooked dinner while his wife took the reporter on a tour of the garden of which she was so proud.[19] The reporter came back enthralled. "She was the perfect hostess," he told a relieved Bart. "The only evidence of her memory loss was that she would repeat things often." But other events did not go so well. Not recognizing members of her own family, she would sometimes demand to know who was intruding in her house.

"Priscilla knew precisely what was going on with her illness," Bart felt, "for she was a well-informed, intellectual woman." One day she insisted, "Bart, you'd better drop me because I'm becoming a dope. I'm no use, and you must have a life to live."

"No, Priscilla," Bart answered her. "We have been married for 46 years and you should not worry. From now on, I am your memory. I'll stick with you." In another conversation he told his wife, "I have this past year been happier with you than I have ever been before. We have become very close to each other."

With a slight wave of her hand, Priscilla said, "Same here."

That he could discuss Priscilla's fragile memory and behavior change with her was a source of hope for Bart. But it was a tense time. She had, as much of her family recollected, a strong independent Yankee streak in her, and she did not wish to be babied. As her personality changed further, there would be moments when she would return instantly into exactly the person she once was, as if a machine shorting out would suddenly, but so briefly, function as it had in years past. Such times lasted only a minute or two, but when they occurred Bart had to transform himself instantly from caregiver into loving husband and not act as though she were a child.

For example, once as they were both sitting in their living room, Priscilla suddenly started reflecting on the state of their Milky Way research. "Bart," she said, "get out of spiral structure. The future is in star formation." In this cogent piece of advice, Priscilla was urging her husband to continue the work she knew was closest to his heart—the globules, Eta Carinae, and all the other aspects of how stars are formed. Her amazed husband said that he would, and he did.

The Boks continued to enjoy doing simple things together, like their daily late afternoon drives north of Tucson. Driving north on Campbell Avenue one day, they felt their car being virtually lifted up by a giant explosion. Later they learned that three careless riflemen had been shooting at a dynamite cache when the dynamite blew up, killing them all. Priscilla boasted that her husband was an expert driver who kept both hands on the wheel and was prepared for contingencies.

Visiting the Arizona-Sonora Desert Museum west of Tucson became a favorite activity. Their favorite part of this combination botanical garden and zoo was the large enclosure for birds, a place that reminded them of their days in Australia. Priscilla had grown especially fond of a roadrunner who seemed to dominate the entire enclosure. Bart considered it "a really firm boss who told all the other birds where to get off"—a quality with which he would have had some empathy. In any case, this roadrunner had apparently taken a liking to Priscilla, staying near her and sometimes sitting on her shoulder.

The aviary had one small problem, however, in that once people reached it there was no comfortable place to rest. "We've walked all the way from the main building to here," Priscilla said wearily, "and you'd think there would be a place to sit down. Like the old New England saying, 'What the Lord has forgotten, be padded with cotton.'"

Most of all, the Boks loved spending time outside in their garden. Priscilla planted flowers, and occasionally Bart worked outside as well. But on one such afternoon Bart noticed a strange quiet. Priscilla could not be found anywhere. With an uneasy feeling he rushed to his car and drove up and down their sleepy street, Sierra Vista Drive. When he still could not find her on the neighboring streets he drove toward Campbell Avenue, one of Tucson's busiest thoroughfares. Now thoroughly frightened, Bart decided that if he didn't find her in a very few minutes he would call the police.

What a sense of relief he felt to see Priscilla walking safely, if not prudently, past the church a few blocks from their home. He stopped the car and asked her where she thought she was going.

"I am on my way to the university to speak with [President] John Schaefer," she replied. "I want to tell him that you are basically a very hard worker but that you are lazy. He's got to find you a teaching job, for it is clear that you are out of work."

On another morning, colleague Ray White found Bart sitting morosely in the office the university still provided him beneath the campus telescope dome. Despondently Bart told his astonished friend that during the night Priscilla had left the house and wandered about the neighborhood dressed only in her nightgown, but that an alert neighbor brought her back. Priscilla hadn't recalled a thing about her nocturnal walk.[20]

As his wife fell deeper into her disease, Bart noticed that she assumed a more carefree attitude. In the late summer of 1975 they sat in the middle of the front row for a performance of Mozart's *The Marriage of Figaro*. As the orchestra struck up the overture, Priscilla started to hum along. As the music grew to a crescendo so did Priscilla's voice, and Bart gently but frantically tried to induce her to stop. His doctor had warned him not to interfere, for patients can get rebellious when asked to stop such behavior. Bart need not have worried. The conductor knew the Boks and solved the quandary himself. With a flourish he thrust the baton toward the strings, then the winds, and then turned around and with a smile and a bow, directly toward Priscilla.

On October 16, 1975, the Boks attended a concert put on by the Arizona Chamber Orchestra.[21] Conducted by Dean Robert Hull, the program opened with a performance of Handel's *Water Music* that was so enrapturing that again, Priscilla hummed along to it. Before the *Water Music* ended Priscilla turned to her husband. "Bart, I now want to go home. I have heard the most beautiful music I can imagine." So entranced was Priscilla that Bart later wrote Hull to congratulate him on what he considered to be a triumph: "The Chamber Orchestra's performance on October 16," he concluded, "was the last time she attended a concert. She reached for my hand during the playing of the *Water Music* and the memory of that occasion is one of the richest ones I have. Thank you from the bottom of my heart.

"Not knowing about the October 16 concert, our daughter, Joyce, who lives in England, sent us for Christmas a beautiful recording of the *Water Music*. . . . I am listening to the record several times each week."[22]

Hull was deeply affected by Priscilla's reaction. "Seldom have I received such a moving comment," he replied; "indeed, it is difficult for me to find adequate means for response. . . . It is good to know sometimes that what one does touches people in unusual ways and to a greater degree than could have been imagined."[23]

The week around November 15, 1975, promised to be a busy one. The Boks were invited to three events, a dinner with Senator Barry Goldwater (which was subsequently canceled), the dedication of the Dartmouth-MIT reflector on the west slope of Kitt Peak, and a symposium to celebrate the opening of the university's Flandrau Planetarium. Priscilla was strong enough to attend only one, and of the three the symposium at the Planetarium was obviously the simplest. It was just a few minutes drive from their home, and they could enter and leave the planetarium comfortably whenever they pleased.

The Boks arrived as soon as the planetarium doors opened, and Bart excitedly took his wife to the exhibits in the large "Galaxy Room" on the east side of the building. They were so early that Bart had to ask one of the guides to turn on the exhibit lights. As the exhibit surged to life, it revealed a beautiful multi-picture panorama of the entire Milky Way. It even had tiny red lights that could be turned on and off to point out specific Milky Way features.

Priscilla pressed one of the buttons, and a faint red light turned on to identify the Eta Carinae nebula far away in the Milky Way of the southern sky. They stood there quietly for a moment, remembering the stunning photographs they had taken of it during years of observing. Finally Priscilla spoke. "You know, Bart," Priscilla said, "when I am gone, that is where I am going. I will ask St. Peter to give me a front row seat right at the center of the nebula. I'll see stars forming right before my eyes!"

Overwhelmed by this profound merging of his two greatest loves, Bart tried to hold back tears as he hugged Priscilla. "Eta Carinae," Priscilla repeated as they walked into the planetarium theater, "that is where I want to be."

The Boks sat near the front, but by the end of the first lecture Priscilla had grown tired and they went home. Four days later, on the bright morning of November 19, Priscilla swam in the pool at their home. As she climbed out she walked by a flower bed and stopped to admire the pansies. Standing near them, enjoying their fragrance, she chatted with her husband. "These pansies are doing very well indeed. I planted these pansies, not you, so let's keep that in mind. They should survive the winter and should look lovely next spring. But never forget that they are *my* pansies!"

She paused again, then tensed and looked quizzically at her husband. "I feel funny," she whispered. "I have a pain in my chest." Bart looked toward her, then noted that she had been hanging clothes earlier that morning as well as swimming. "Maybe you did a little much; maybe you stretched a muscle."

"I don't know," she said, now more sharply, "it feels very funny." Bart then led his wife toward the bedroom to lie down.

Suddenly Priscilla turned white. "Oh God, it's worse!" She clutched at her chest, shut her eyes in agony for a few seconds, then fell unconscious as Bart rushed for the phone. In a moment an ambulance arrived to carry the Boks the few blocks to University Medical Center where a cardiac resuscitation team was ready. "They worked so fast," Bart remembered. But in half an hour it was over.

Bart stood there stunned as the doctor told him that Priscilla was gone. He walked into the trauma room to see her one last time. Almost without thinking, he cut off a lock of her hair. Too quickly, the hospital staff asked what arrangements should be made. He mumbled that some time earlier both he and Priscilla had signed forms authorizing that their bodies were to be donated to the University Medical Center for teaching and research.[24]

Less than an hour earlier Bart and Priscilla had been talking about a flower bed. Now Bart left the Medical Center and walked slowly back to his house alone. He paced the rooms for a short while, then sat down in his study to call his children. Ray and Barbara Weymann and Bart's secretary Maxine Howlett came over. "It was the only time I had ever seen him tearful," Weymann writes, "and I vividly remember him saying how he had been able to save a lock of Priscilla's hair and this meant a great deal to him."[25]

By the following morning Bart started to think that Priscilla's attack might have been a blessing, sparing her even more misery as her mind continued to fail. A few days after Priscilla's death, Bart returned to the planetarium to look again at Eta Carinae's position in the Milky Way montage. Then the staff asked him to enter the theater. On the seat Priscilla had used four days before she died, second row from the front, second seat on the left, a small plaque read simply:

Priscilla F. Bok
November 15, 1975

Of Birds, Act II

Priscilla's death was the start of a long and lonely period in Bart's life, a period of withdrawal from his usual ebullience. His change in mood was so marked that almost everyone I interviewed noted it. However, he was not idle. Keeping in mind their fire escape discussion from two years before, he also thought of the many pleasant hours they had spent at the aviary at the Desert Museum. He decided to create a fund to maintain the enclosure and to provide a concrete bench in his wife's memory.

Because they could see the possibility of many memorials turning the place into a cemetery, at first the museum staff disliked the plan. But as Bart persisted, saying that he did not even want her name on it, they eventually caught on to the idea. Inscribed into the concrete were a series of intaglios, symbols of "the edge-on appearance and spiral structure of our Milky Way system. . . . Actually," Bart added, "her name is on the bench, but it is hidden underneath where nobody can see it." It is a handsome and fitting seat.

On a dismal morning around Christmas 1975, Bart remembered the birds. Priscilla was gone, as Bart said, "somewhere in the Eta Carinae nebula; I felt very lonesome and sorry for myself. I had opened all my presents; there was enough liquor to turn me into a permanent drunkard and enough candy to make me weigh 225 pounds. I sat here and felt terrible." But then he decided to visit the aviary. As he walked into the enclosure, the roadrunner that Priscilla had enjoyed so much walked out and then hopped on his shoulder: "It then jumped off my shoulder, and I thought that would be the end of it. But then the bird came back with a twig. We had a lovely time playing with the twig. She would give me the twig: 'thank you, that's a beautiful twig; may I hold it for a moment? Now I give it back to you.' We had a lovely time playing fiddlesticks with the twig. I said to the roadrunner, 'Did Priscilla send you?'"

But much as the roadrunner wanted to monopolize Bart's affection that day, there was soon competition. Two turkey buzzards came along.

"They came and looked at me and decided that my shoe strings were worms. So between the two of them they unlaced my shoestrings. I was being worked on by two turkey buzzards at the bottom, while at the top sat the roadrunner with the twig."

As Bart walked around the enclosure, the roadrunner remained comfortably on his shoulder. "When you deal with birds, you must always talk in a soft voice so that they know precisely where you are and what you are doing. If you stop talking, they get scared and fly off. And this roadrunner and I became very good friends."

Valley of Delight

Shortly after Priscilla's death Bok decided to get out of Tucson. As he described it, he planned to "go underground" in San Francisco. But no sooner had he registered in a hotel near Market Square than the phone rang. It was his former student Ivan King, now at the astronomy department at Berkeley, who had been alerted by Bok's secretary, Maxine Howlett. Identifying himself as a member of some secret organization whose task it was to know who moved where, King quipped, "It has been reported to me that you are about in San Francisco. We want you to join us for Thanksgiving dinner."

Just after Christmas Bart left for New York for a second try at "going underground," and also to consider his son John's urging that he move back to Boston. Walking along Broadway, he decided to see if he could get a ticket to a show, and quite by chance he found a performance of Aaron Copland's *Appalachian Spring*, a ballet suite first performed at the Library of Congress by Martha Graham in 1944. Bart recalled that when Priscilla was a young professor at Smith College, she had known Graham. The story of *Appalachian Spring* involves a young couple who decide to marry and build a home in the wooded mountains of Appalachia. Their wedding is presided over by an older lady, a mistress of ceremonies, and a revivalist minister surrounded by six small girl dancers. After a beautiful cotillion the dancers gradually vanish, leaving at the end the newlyweds amid the scaffolding of their home. Finally, in a quiet number that Priscilla had adored, they dance to an adaptation of an old Shaker hymn called *Simple Gifts*. As Bart watched the New York performance of this number he wept:

'Tis a gift to be simple
'Tis a gift to be free,
'Tis a gift to come down
Where we ought to be.
And when we find ourselves
In the place just right
It will be in the valley
Of love and delight.[26]

As Bart walked out of the theater into the darkening December afternoon, he felt reborn. In an instant he realized that he and Priscilla had been living in a valley of love and delight all along. His mind was made up; Tucson's valley of delight would remain his home.

On May 14, 1976, Bart formally dedicated Priscilla's aviary bench with a small ceremony at the Desert Museum: "Priscilla, here is your bench. It comes with my deepest love and affection and the love of your children and grandchildren. . . . May your soul rest in peace with the birds near you and with small figures symbolizing our beloved Milky Way on the back of your bench."[27]

The bench became a noble retreat for Bart. In the coming years he visited it frequently, sometimes alone, more often with friends. Another audience with the roadrunner soon took place: "Out from the bushes she came, scampering through, sitting on my shoulder." As he watched this roadrunner, Bart's thoughts wandered back to a far off place and time. A memory of Priscilla, happy and alert as she fed a group of magpies, filled his mind. Slowly the image faded, and he imagined once again the exquisite swirls of the nebula in Carina.

15

From Astrology to Valentine's Night

"The young have a right to look toward professional astronomers for guidance. It is high time that each of us does his or her best to make it clear that our futures lie in ourselves and not in our stars."
—Bart Bok on astrology, 1970

Had Bart Bok not been engrossed in a highly enjoyable battle against astrology at the time Priscilla died, his recovery from his loss would likely have taken much longer. This battle was the culmination of a lifelong campaign opposing astrology, a crusade which ironically brought him more publicity than he had ever received for a lifetime of scientific research and political activities.

"Every ten years or so it is time to have an anti-astrology campaign," Bok thought as he sat on his sofa during one summer day in 1975, gathering names to sign for a statement against the popular pseudoscience. "I took an old directory of the National Academy of Sciences," Bok noted, "an old directory of the American Astronomical Society, a couple of bottles of beer, and checked off who I thought were good people to send the request to."

Bok attacked astrology and astrologers with the same frenetic energy he always brought to the many areas of his life. His campaign's vigor and effectiveness rested in its two-pronged approach; he battled astrology at the same time as he championed a strong public educational program that emphasized the excitement of real astronomy over pseudoscience. He aimed his formidable rhetorical arsenal against the professional astrologers more than at the millions of people who believed in it. For those deluded souls Bok thought that there was nothing to do, despite the fact that, as he noted, "even the Catholic Church, thank God, has been very helpful," passing an edict against the practice of astrology several hundred years ago.

Bok's crusade against astrology was the result of a string of assaults that began in the late 1930s at Harvard College Observatory, where Harlow Shapley took the fight against pseudoscience seriously. He suggested that each professor become involved in disproving a single fringe belief. Donald Menzel's task was to debunk the UFO scare, which during the early 1950s had the planet being visited regularly by extraterrestrials in cigar- or saucer-shaped craft. Cecilia Payne-Gaposchkin concentrated on unmasking Immanuel Velikovsky, a psychiatrist whose 1950 book *Worlds in Collision* postulated that a huge comet had been ejected from Jupiter's region and repeatedly encountered the Earth, causing the Red Sea to part and the Earth to stop rotating during the Battle of Jericho before finally settling down and becoming the peaceful planet we now know as Venus. (Years later an astronomy student dubbed Velikovsky's notion "veli-unlikli.")[1]

By having each staff member concentrate on debunking a single pseudoscience, Shapley was able to conduct an important public education activity in a professional way without taking too much time from astronomy: "Otherwise," Bok argued, "you become a do-gooder and don't do any astronomy."

Bok was assigned astrology, and took it on as chairman of the American Association of Scientific Workers' committee investigating it. Published in 1941 in *The Scientific Monthly,* the committee's report sharply criticized the practices of astrologers. "What have scientists done," he demanded, "to correct such misconceptions? Individuals have occasionally voiced a protest, but active concern in the spreading of astrology has generally been considered below the dignity of scientists."[2]

If astrologers were to limit themselves to simply portraying the celestial sphere and not making predictions, Bok would call it harmless but "stupid astronomy." As Bok later wrote, "The abracadabra begins when the astrologer starts to interpret a person's horoscope."[3] This approach could be seen as an echo of Gerard Manley Hopkins, the famous Victorian-era poet and amateur astronomer who wrote that "astrology is astronomy, ordinary science, with an extraordinary science added,"[4] although most astronomers object to "astrology" and "science" being used in the same phrase. They find the idea of seeing the stars through horoscopes quite annoying, preferring to see some cosmic significance directly through the data collected by their telescopes. But astrology can become worse than annoying when people, especially political leaders, start to plan their basic lives by those charts. During the years of World War II it was commonly believed that Hitler used an astrologer, and there is evidence that Canada's wartime prime minister William Lyon Mackenzie King did so too. One would have hoped that by the 1980s politicians and their families had outgrown such behavior, so many people were distressed to learn that Nancy Reagan influenced the President's schedule according to the dictates of her astrologer.[5]

Seeking to know his enemy, Bok learned how to cast a horoscope, using the November 23, 1907, birthdate of his colleague Francis Wright. He presented the results in *Scientific Monthly*, showing how the horizon and celestial meridian divide the celestial sphere into four parts; and how each part was then divided into three equal sections by great circles passing through the north and south points on the horizon; and how this formed a total of twelve "houses" with the points of intersection of their boundaries called "cusps."[6]

"Scientists would feel justified in considering astrology as a legitimate field of scientific inquiry," the *Scientific Monthly* article said, "if astrologers could claim that its basic rules had been established through a rigorous study of correlations. But such a study has not been made. The rules by which astrologers interpret their horoscopes have not been derived from any known experiments or observations. Astrologers frequently claim an observational basis in the experience of forgotten generations far back in antiquity, but pure superstition can claim as sound a basis. In the cases of planets discovered in our times (Uranus, Neptune, Pluto) the evidence is conclusive that their influences on men were ascribed by the astrologers before preliminary observational tests of the influences could have been made, and even before accurate orbits could be assigned to the planets."[7]

The article in *Scientific Monthly* ended with a proclamation: "Astrologers have failed to suggest a workable mechanism by which the stars and planets can exert their influence on human destiny. The doctrine of astrology cannot claim that it is in any way supported by statistical evidence from observed correlations, and until such correlations are established scientists cannot accept the precepts of astrology."[8]

In the wake of that article, on November 22, 1941, Bok appeared before an association of amateur astronomers in New York City. Although he arrived with a prepared talk, he was shocked to discover that, incredibly, the society had also assembled a group of several New York astrologers, acting, Bok noted, as a "steering group" for the evening. The team included Ernest Grant of the oxymoronic American Federation of Scientific Astrologers, Edward Wagner, editor of *Horoscope* magazine, and well-known astrologer Carl Payne Tobey.

Startled that he would not have been consulted about such a plan, Bok canceled his prepared talk. He could take no other course. To refuse even to participate with a committee of "reasonable men" would give the impression that the representative of the astronomers was being just as hardheaded as the group he was poised to fight. He reluctantly participated in a debate with these people on the value of astrology. It didn't go well for Bok. Pitted against the astrologers, Bok tried to put his best face forward, describing his days in high school when he had an interest in the mechanisms of astrology.

In line with his *Scientific Monthly* criticisms, he even recommended that a committee of astronomers and astrologers be formed for the purpose of conducting scientific tests of astrological predictions. The astrologers agreed. But Bok quickly learned after the meeting, to no great surprise, that the "tests" that the astrologers were willing to participate in had nothing to do with the scientific method, with its requirements to adhere to strict controls and avoid preconceptions about results.

"Professor Bok," one of the astrologers challenged, "you say there are no professional astronomers who believe in astrology. How about Professor Kuno Foelsch in Florida?" Bok's reply—"I've never heard of the man"—prompted a taunt from the astrologer, who asked the audience, "How can I debate with this man Bok? He doesn't even know the people in his own field!"[9]

The evening ended with the two sides calling themselves "friendly enemies." Bok advised the amateur astronomers to take an *intelligent* interest in astrology. On the surface that seemed fair enough, but Bok was confident enough that any intelligent study of it would reveal its flaws.

After that experience Bok decided not to debate astrology again, but instead to fight it in print. "Oh, my God," Bok concluded, "astrology is *not* a thing to play with! There is too much money involved, and they don't want to undermine the interest of the believers." Because he subverted, as they claimed, the faith of the American people, some astrologers declared Bart one of the most dangerous characters in America.

Since Hitler supposedly followed astrology, these astrologers proposed that the army have an astrological division. They even suggested that the plan include some *astronomers*—"so long," Bart noted, "as that prejudiced guy Bok wasn't included."

After the *Scientific Monthly* attack against astrology in 1941, Bok continued his campaign but on a lower key. Then in 1970, alarmed by a resurgence of astrology, especially on college campuses, he felt compelled to lash out again. "We cannot give the soapbox to the goddamned astrologers to stand on," he said in making his case. "For when they get a soapbox, they take it. Brother, they can be tough because they're not tied down by the rules of physics, astronomy, or anything. They can say anything they wish."

Bok asked the American Astronomical Society, of which he was vice-president, to issue an official statement against the astrology cult during its annual meeting held in December 1970 in Tampa, Florida. Since it was enjoying a sudden resurgence in the late sixties, especially among young people, he was most concerned for college students who, he believed, "have scientific knowledge at their reach, but don't see through this pseudoscience." Bok told a reporter for the University of Arizona student newspaper that "astrology is okay as a diversion if it's not taken seriously, but I've found a lot of people at this University who follow it almost as a religion and half-seriously use it to direct their lives."[10] Bok clearly understood that the permissiveness that pervaded the nation's campuses at that time was a fertilizer for the growth of astrology.

Despite his efforts, the AAS council refused his request for its condemnation of astrology. Bok, who considered it a serious threat to a centuries-old tradition of rational thought, accused his more reticent colleagues of "behaving like ostriches." But according to colleague Beverly T. Lynds, Bok behaved like a "Don Quixote attacking the evil empire, and some of us in the society felt that it was a bit overdramatic. . . . The Man of La Mancha wanted us all to embark on a united extermination of it."[11]

These astronomers saw astrology as only one of many serious issues: "I felt," wrote Lynds, "that it was indeed a nearly impossible task in the first place and that the AAS had many more important windmills to confront. For example, the repression of scientific doctrines as found in certain religions—leading to things like the [Scopes] monkey trial—seem to me to be more unhealthy for astronomy than highly paid astrologers, who generally leave the science alone."[12]

Bok attacked astrology again in an address to the American Association for the Advancement of Science shortly after the AAS meeting. Blaming astronomers for failing to oppose astrology strongly through popular articles and lectures, he demanded that they not forsake the next generation of astronomers: "The young have a right to look toward professional astronomers for guidance. It is high time that each of us does his or her best to make it clear that our futures lie in ourselves and not in our stars."[13]

These two earlier major efforts against astrology were a prelude to the major assault that began in the summer of 1975. Instead of going back to the AAS Council Bok now approached the scientific community directly, member by member. With the help of Paul Kurtz, editor of *The Humanist*, Bok assembled a group of 192 well-known scientists, including 19 Nobel Prize winners, to sign a statement condemning the practice of astrology. Parenthetically, Bok later admitted that "I wasn't very conscious of who was a Nobel Prize winner and who wasn't. I just wrote to people I knew and respected."

To compile his list, Bok included names of those he thought would be reachable that summer. The list could have been longer still, by perhaps sixty names, had he waited for others to return from summer activities. But Bok was in a hurry. As it was, the manifesto against astrology was signed by such well-known scientists as Sir Francis Crick, Linus Pauling, Glenn Seaborg, George Wald, Frank Drake, Fred Hoyle, Jan Oort, and Fred Whipple.[14]

Amidst the flood of acceptances were a few negative comments. "I am very fond of Bart Bok and admire his courage, enthusiasm, and foresight, but I'm afraid I do not feel very strongly about astrology," wrote astronomer Roger Revelle. "If some people are comforted by a belief in astrology we should not try to take away their security blanket. . . . If I were to take a strong stand against astrology I would feel it necessary to be equally forceful about the Pope, Norman Vincent Peale and Billy Graham."[15]

Complaining about the arrogance of the campaign, one writer found Bok's statement "much too dogmatic, too much like: 'scientists say it is nonsense; so the public better believe it!'"[16]

The manifesto, accompanied by two articles by Bok and science writer Lawrence Jerome, appeared in the September/October 1975 issue of *The Humanist*, and it was reprinted in a book called *Objections to Astrology*. "One would imagine," it said, "in this day of widespread enlightenment and education, that it would be unnecessary to debunk beliefs based on magic and superstition. . . . We believe that the time has come to challenge directly and forcefully the pretentious claims of astrological charlatans."[17]

"No one can blame the Egyptians, the Greeks, the Arabs, or the people of India," Bok's article went on, "for having established systems of astrology at times when they were also laying the foundations of astronomy. . . . However, all this changed when the first measurements were made of the distances to the sun, planets, and stars and when the masses of these objects were determined."[18] Bok slammed the newspapers who "print this daily nonsense,"[19] and called yet again on his astronomical colleagues to join in the crusade.[20]

Bok got more public reaction to this than to all of his scientific efforts put together. "186 Scientists Call Astrologers Charlatans," the *Boston Globe* trumpeted in an article typical of stories around the country.[21] *The Humanist* had to run a follow-up in its November/December issue to publish some of the avalanche of letters it received.[22] Cartoonists had a field day too: the September 24, 1975 issue of the cartoon "Dunagin's People" said: "Your horoscope for today advises you to travel, make financial decisions, and forget what those scientists said about astrology."

People magazine ran an article, a picture, and, courtesy of astrologer Svetlana Godillo, a horoscope for Bok:

> This is a man who desires and needs to be prominent and to acquire fame and be recognized for his original and different thinking. His mind can be brilliant but his creativity and originality are very often put in the wrong direction. He has probably had a tendency throughout his life to find himself fighting losing battles. He very often leaps toward the things that are irrational. Really a nice person, and could have a sense of humor if he tried, but sometimes overcritical of himself and other people. I can only forewarn him that probably this Christmas and February of next year are very important to him and will probably alter his life, his career or maybe his standing in the community.[23]

Nothing out of the ordinary happened.

Of the flood of comments, one of the more thoughtful came from columnist George Will: "That astrology is preposterous is, of course, obvious to everyone except people with stupendous capacities for the willful suspension of disbelief." But he added a caveat: "Astrology bestows on its believers a sense of being not completely adrift on turbulent seas. . . . The distressed scientists insist, 'We must all face the world.' . . . But there is no 'must' about it."[24]

Bok's battle against astrology was also picked up by the February 1976 issue of *Psychology Today*, which ran his comment: "The gravitational forces at birth produced by the doctor and nurse and by the furniture in the delivery room far outweigh the celestial forces."[25]

That article also brought responses. "I would like to draw attention to the fact," one reader complained, "that the assertively suppressive attitude of Professor Bok and his colleagues in their criticism of astrology . . . is in marked contrast to the bland straightforwardness shown generally in *Psychology Today*."

In a private letter, another concerned reader wrote: "Doesn't this suppressive attitude seem to indicate a possible unscientific closed-mindedness on the part of these self-styled protectors of human mental health?"[26]

With an appeal in *Physics Today*, a publication for members of the physics and astronomy communities, Bok once again urged other scientists to join the "guerilla warfare" of the anti-astrology campaign.[27] He later stressed in an interview with the author that here was a useful role for nonprofessional astronomers. "The amateurs could spend time on an anti-astrology campaign: I think it's too bad that they have paid so little attention to it."

Thanks partly to Bok's efforts, many newspapers now publish disclaimers with their astrology columns: "Astrological forecasts should be read for their entertainment value only. They have no basis in fact." But perhaps the finest symbol of what Bok was up against was supplied by John Eddy, a Colorado solar astronomer who sent him a copy of a full-page advertisement for Inter-Continental Hotels in Bombay and Bangkok. The ad stated that "we have an astrologer-in-residence at the service of every guest, day or night." Eddy added a balloon showing the astrologer taunting, "Eat your heart out, Bart Bok!"[28]

Bok's Re-emergence

Despite the onslaught of publicity from the astrology campaign, Bok kept to himself for several months after Priscilla's death, frankly enjoying the fallout from his battles. By June 1976, he felt ready to return to the American Astronomical Society, at its meeting at Haverford, Pennsylvania. As he sat in the front row at the opening session, his colleague Beverly Lynds held his hand as Priscilla's name was called from the list of those members who had passed away.[29]

The recovery from the end of a marriage as intense and as close as the Boks' was very difficult. As he sat alone in his living room one evening, Bart suddenly thought of something Priscilla had told him: "When I get to Eta Carinae, I will ask St. Peter to assign me to watch over you. And as long as you are happy and busy, and especially as long as you have a girlfriend, that's fine. But if I see you moping, that's it! I'll tell St. Peter to forget about you, and give me a harp."

So Bart left his home and visited the Blue Note Café. Sitting alone in the cabaret, he ordered his drink and looked around him. The music was louder than he wanted. The crowd was noisy. What was he doing here? He watched the dancers pulsate gracefully to the music, and as the evening wore on, he became more relaxed.

"Well now, do you live in Tucson?"

"Hmmm?" Bart looked up at the gorgeous young dancer who had come by his table.

"Are you from out of town?"

"Oh, I'm sorry. Yes, yes. In fact," Bart went on, trying to hide his thick Dutch accent, "I am an executive from the Phillips company, and I travel all over the world." Bart's disguise was successful. The dancer, who gave only her stage name, said that she had just moved to Tucson and had no family in town. The discussion was friendly enough, and Bart left the Blue Note feeling that the evening had been a success. At least it had gotten him out of the house.

Soon afterwards, Bart picked up the morning paper and read of a murder. It was one of the dancers at the cabaret. As Bart read the ensuing paragraphs he learned to his relief that the victim's stage name was not the same as that of the dancer he had met. He thought how clever he had been to introduce himself as a business executive, for he surely would not want to be involved in any way with such a terrible event.

But as the day wore on Bart thought more about the lonely dancer at the Blue Note and what she must be going through. "B. J. Bok, you are a bad man," he concluded as he put pen to paper and wrote the young woman: "This is a note from the traveling executive," he recalled writing. "But I am not an executive, nor do I come from out of town. I am a recently widowed professor of astronomy at the University right here in Tucson. I can't begin to imagine what you must be going through right now."

He ended the note by providing his name, address, and phone number. Not long afterwards the dancer, whose real name was Judy, did call, and they quickly got to know each other. "Never any lovemaking," Bart recalled, "just happy company. But Judy came by frequently and we became very close friends. When she met the man who later became her husband she brought him to me, almost as if I were her father." Bart's friendship with Judy lasted until the end of his life.[30]

An increasingly hectic schedule of travel and lecturing helped return Bok to the astronomical fast track. At the IAU general assembly held in 1976, Bart introduced astro-celebrity Carl Sagan, who was to give a lecture about Mars. The auditorium was jammed. Giving the introduction in French, Bok explained the importance of Sagan's work on Mars. But as he spoke, he noticed Sagan looking thoughtfully heavenward—his later *Cosmos* look—as if collecting his thoughts for the talk to come. Pausing in his prepared text, Bok looked out at the audience and asked the women in perfect French, "*Avez-vous déja vu un profile comme ça?*" The audience roared with laughter.[31]

In early 1977 Bok spent two months in Chile, observing many nights from dusk to dawn despite the emergence of a mild heart condition. By the end of that year, Bok's slightly enlarged heart prompted his doctor, Gerald Giordano, to insist he slow down. Bok could travel, but he must rest each day after lunch and give only one colloquium or lecture each day.[32]

That same year promised an exciting trip to China for Bok as part of an American delegation. Ever since President Nixon had opened the door to closer relations between the two countries, Bok, as dedicated as always to good international relations among scientists, longed to be part of the first American astronomical deputation. The visitors would "survey the state of astronomy in China," wrote delegation chairman Leo Goldberg, "by visiting major centers of activity."[33]

Bok had known Goldberg since his Harvard days. He remembered how Goldberg had transferred into his undergraduate astronomy class there. Goldberg was unhappy in his mathematics class, but at the time Harvard imposed a fee of $5 for a transfer. "Leo Goldberg was the only one of my students," Bok contended, "who had to pay an admission fee!"

Although Bok had not had much contact in the interim with Goldberg, he fully expected to be one of the ten astronomers chosen for the China trip and he longed to become a part of it. Bok felt that he surely would be chosen. "I had been a very strong proponent of China getting into the IAU," Bok remembered. So certain was he of going to China that he turned down an invitation to join a cruise to see the October 12, 1977, total solar eclipse fifteen hundred miles west of Acapulco.

But time passed with no word. Finally a committee secretary telephoned. "Dr. Bok," she said, "I have a difficult assignment." As Bok listened in amazement, she went on: "Dr. Goldberg has asked me to inform you that you are number eleven on a list of ten chosen. Would you mind being available as a standby?"[34]

Bok was so upset he could hardly reply. Not being on the list upset him enough, but why could not Goldberg, who was in Tucson at the time, tell him the news himself? Bok breathed quickly a couple of times to collect his thoughts and then responded to the secretary. This is how he remembered the conversation:

"Sister, have you got a piece of paper?"

The secretary replied uneasily that she had.

"Have you got a pencil?"

"Yes, sir."

"Then would you convey my compliments to Leo Goldberg and all the members of his damn committee. And would you please tell them that they can go individually and collectively to hell. Finally, since you are such a nice person I will spell out that last word for you so you don't have to say it: h-e-double-l hell."

At the other end of the line the secretary was near tears. "I feel so sad that you are not one of the ten, and I especially admire you for what you did for Priscilla. But the committee felt that during the past five years you have been out of touch with astronomy and with Washington."

When asked later about this incident, Goldberg refused to discuss any aspect of his relationship with Bok, saying instead, "I'm like Bambi; if you can't say anything nice, don't say anything at all."

In the long run, Goldberg did his former associate a favor, for Bok was able to get reinstated on the eclipse trip to the Pacific Ocean. During the trip he met an amateur astronomer from California named Laura.[35] Unlike the friendship with Judy, this new relationship became intensely important to Bok, despite the fact that she lived hundreds of miles away and was already married. The couple would meet occasionally in Tucson, occasionally in California, and often traveled together. Whenever Bart would leave Tucson he would leave copies of his itinerary with several friends, all of whom clearly understood what a three-day visit to "the L. A. area" really meant.

By the end of 1977 Bart Bok was reborn. Proud of all his women friends, he even numbered them, publicly and to each other: Bart always referred to Laura as girlfriend number one, Judy as girlfriend number two, and Elizabeth Maggio as girlfriend number three. Only the first was a love affair. He loved to brag how Judy was his friend to go to the opera with and Elizabeth his friend for theater. Sometimes his friends would occasionally see him going to the theater or opera "with an attractive young woman on each arm."[36]

A science reporter for the *Arizona Daily Star*, Elizabeth Maggio had met the Boks during their Steward Observatory years. Recognizing her as one of the top science writers in the country, Bok frequently provided astronomical background for her stories, and continued to do so after she joined the university's information office. He would have been especially proud when, in 1989, Maggio became an assistant director at Steward Observatory.

Bok continued to increase his lecture schedule, including in many talks a colored slide of the Eta Carinae nebula and the story that Priscilla was there. "But when I pop off," he would add with a wink and a finger pointing downwards, "I'll probably be going in the other direction!" In September 1979 he visited Sonoma College in California, and had his entire audience sing happy birthday to granddaughter Jeanne, who was a student there.

A lecture trip to Australia in October 1978 culminated in his receiving the Selby Fellowship for 1978 of the Australian Academy of Sciences. Returning to the country of his happiest memories (see chapter 11), Bok had come full circle. From the unfriendly letters he had received from the President of the Australian Academy of Sciences fifteen years earlier, he was now an honorary member of the academy. His public lectures concentrated on "The Promise of the Space Shuttle and Space Telescope,"[37] "Globules and Star Formation," "The Big and Beautiful Milky Way," and "The Star Clouds of Magellan," clearly indicating that he had taken Priscilla's advice (chapter 14) to get out of spiral structure.[38]

His trip to Australia was a delight. The Australian Broadcasting Commission provided a camera crew that consisted largely of people he knew when he lived there, and they seemed to enjoy his return as much as he did. Before one of his lectures he was asked to stand in front of the camera and speak briefly for a microphone level test. With a big smile he stood up quickly and began, "Oh Laura, my Laura, I love you dearly. You are the most wonderful woman in the whole world!"

The evening kicked off with a long introduction that incorporated highlights of Bok's career in Australia, including the now-famous incident when Menzies poked him in the belly and said, "You are a bad, bad boy."[39] Then Bok approached the podium, thanked the speaker and the officials for inviting him, and then began his talk. When it was over and the crew told him that the tape record they had made was a success, he asked them if they could send a copy of the talk to Laura.

They did. The covertly edited tape began with Bart's thanking the speaker and the officials for inviting him, continued with "Oh Laura, my Laura, I love you dearly. You are the most wonderful woman in the whole world!"—and concluded with the talk.

Valentine's Night

With a paper in *Nature* and two others out elsewhere, all on the globules and the formation of stars, by 1977 Bok had also fully resumed his scientific activities, and in the direction Priscilla had prescribed.[40] The *Nature* paper built on the research done by Tapia (see chapter 12) on the extraordinarily large numbers of globules found in the dark nebulae known as the Southern Coalsack.[41]

These were busy and happy years. In 1977 Bok received the highly prestigious Catherine Wolfe-Bruce Gold Medal from the Astronomical Society of the Pacific;[42] in 1978 he received an honorary doctorate of science from Arizona State University; and in 1979 he received another honorary doctorate from the University of Nevada at Las Vegas. He was asked to contribute to three eminent publications, a University of Arizona book called *Man's Place in the Universe*,[43] and a popular-level article on the Magellanic Clouds for *Natural History*.[44] Finally, he had the chance to write a short biographical memoir about his late mentor and hero, Harlow Shapley, for the National Academy of Sciences (see end of chapter 4).[45]

In early 1978 Bok returned to Chile's Cerro Tololo Observatory with time granted on the largest telescope there, the four meter reflector, and a missive from Laura to take a special Valentine's Night photograph for her.

Experimenting with a new, infrared-sensitive emulsion known as IV-N (pron. 4-N), Bok photographed a Bok globule associated with the nebulous clouds that are the result of a supernova that blew up in the constellation of Vela over 20,000 years ago. After he processed the plate, he discovered, at the edge of the globule, two starlike bright nebulae that appeared to be connected by a thin thread of light. He recognized these at once as two stars literally being formed right out of the dark cosmic abyss of the globule.

First described in the 1950s by G. H. Herbig and Guillermo Haro, these objects consist of tiny bright nebulae that tend to appear near the edges of globules and that are thought to be either protostars or newly formed stars hidden by dust. They typically coexist with the winds of protons and electrons that stream from nearby stars. In an important sense, these so-called Herbig-Haro objects confirm Bok's 1940s suspicion that the globules he and Edith Reilly discovered at Harvard represented a step in the birth of stars.

Bok's photograph, which he took for Laura, is a magnificently painted celestial still-life showing the nebulosity left over from the ancient Vela supernova, the dark, almost absolute-zero-cold globules that have formed out of it, and the two Herbig-Haro stellar neonates.

The photo surfaced in several scientific papers, but what delighted Bok the most was its appearance in the *Sydney Morning Herald* under this headline: "'Darling, It's Twins,' Stargazer said on Valentine's Day."[46]

16

Last Years

"Brothers and sisters, you ain't seen nothing yet!"
—End of "The Promise of the Space Telescope," Bok's lecture
which was published in the *Congressional Record*

"I want to pee in all the great rivers of the world," declared Bok, who had his earthy as well as his stellar side. Fulfilling this ambition was a priority in his travels. When the Boks arrived at their hotel during their frequent jaunts and Priscilla wanted to take a nap, Bart would then leave to take a walk. "Whenever that happened Priscilla knew exactly where I was going," Bart reminisced. "She would think, 'Bart's gone off to pee in the river.'"

By the end of 1979, Bart Bok was working and playing at an energy level as high as he had at earlier stages in his life. Despite his slowly weakening heart, his life now was a series of travels and lectures all over the world.

Each of his public lectures stands out in a special way for the audiences that had heard him. One such presentation occurred at the Southeastern Planetarium Association in Memphis, Tennessee. Keith Johnson, who had worked with Bok during the early 1970s at Steward Observatory, decided to attend the lecture with his wife Mary. "We had some trouble finding the planetarium," Johnson writes, "and arrived midway through the talk. We slipped in through a side entrance as unobtrusively as possible. In spite of the fact that Dr. Bok did not know we were coming, and the auditorium was quite dim for his slide presentation, he glanced up at the two newcomers, and without a break exclaimed in his strong Dutch accent, 'Good morning, Keith! Good morning, Mary! I'll see you after we are done here!'"

"As it happened, the conference photograph was to be taken immediately after Dr. Bok's talk. We got outside; Dr. Bok insisted that Mary and I stand on either side of him for the photo. . . . Most of the group had no notion who we were. . . . I, of course, did nothing to clear up the situation, hoping that they would assume I was simply a world-famous astronomer dropping in to discuss theories of galactic structure with an old friend. This impression was strengthened when Dr. Bok insisted we sit with him at the banquet that evening. What we actually discussed was his Tucson fruit trees, his swimming pool, and the proper way to feed birds in Australia" (see soaker hose, chapter 12).[1]

In 1981 Bok addressed the Riverside Telescope Makers Conference at their mountaintop site near Big Bear Lake, California. He had just arrived from Los Angeles, where his beautiful slide collection had been stolen from his hotel room. Not about to be undone by this sad event, he began his lecture with the story of why he had no illustrations. "Never mind, though," he pronounced, stretching his arms forward, "I will give my talk with gestures."

The talk was a masterpiece. Forced to rely on his own abilities in public speaking, Bok captivated his audience. It was his small stories, usually left out of his slide presentations, that made this talk so special. For example, in one or two long breaths he told, in his strongest Dutch accent, how one time an astronomer asked a trivial question at a party with wine glasses clinking, and Bok nonchalantly said something that might or might not have made sense. But years later he found his statement quoted in a formal journal and footnoted "B. J. Bok, personal communication." The talk was repeatedly interrupted by applause, one person laughed so hard he pounded his fist on the floor, and when it was over the crowd gave him a long and loving standing ovation.

The Milky Way

During his time at home in Tucson he began his revisions on a new and expanded fifth edition of *The Milky Way*. He looked forward to many hours at this task and enjoyed telling people about a conversation he had had with Priscilla just three weeks before her death. In a moment of clarity, Priscilla had suddenly asked her husband to sit down and listen while she reminded him of the different audiences for which their opus was intended. Although high school students with some math and physics were the primary constituency (they had thought frequently of their high school-age grandchildren during the preparation of the fourth edition), the Boks were reaching out also to astronomy graduate students and scientists in other fields who needed an overview of the state of research into the Milky Way. They were writing also for informed amateur astronomers. Preparing a book to satisfy these diverse audiences was a challenge: "Don't increase the number of illustrations," she had warned. "Increase their quality. For every new one that goes in, throw an old one out." Bart took this somewhat arbitrary advice literally, and when *The Milky Way*'s fifth edition appeared on the eve of his seventy-fifth birthday, it was about as thick as the fourth.

During Bok's lifetime, the accepted picture of the Milky Way galaxy underwent several changes. What started out as a relatively tiny galactic system envisioned by Kapteyn, with the Sun in the center, was completely uprooted around 1920 by Shapley, whose studies of the globular clusters dotting the galaxy's outskirts proved that the galactic center was far from the Sun.[2] The five editions of *The Milky Way*, the Boks' greatest work, are a permanent record of the evolution of our understanding over half a century of what the galaxy in which we live is really like. For example, the book's first edition in 1941 didn't even have a chapter on spiral structure. Not until the 1956 third edition were Bart and Priscilla able to report William Morgan's discovery of the nature of the galaxy's spiral shape.[3]

The distance of the center of the galaxy provides another example. Even a question as simple as that yielded a slightly oscillating answer over the various editions, down from Shapley's original estimate of 50,000 light years to 30,000 light years in the first edition to 27,000 light years in the third, up to 33,000 light years (now expressed as 10,000 parsecs) in the fourth edition, and down again to 28,000 light years or 8,500 parsecs in the fifth.[4]

The third edition set an agenda for astronomers studying the Milky Way: "Our primary task for the next few years," he wrote, "is to build equipment—especially radio equipment—capable of tracing with precision the spiral structure of our galaxy. While there is always room for theorizing, the emphasis must first of all be on careful observation and unbiased analysis of the observations."[5] By the 1974 publication of the fourth edition, these radio telescopes had been built. "The happiest aspect of present-day studies of galactic spiral structure," the Boks now wrote, "is that the problems are being studied simultaneously from many angles. The theorists and users of large computers are hard at work on many aspects of the problem. Observing optical and radio astronomers consult and argue with one another uninterruptedly, and the astrophysicists are probing as best they can into the physical conditions of interstellar matter in spiral arms and in the regions between spiral arms. The full study of the spiral structure of the galaxy is providing a stimulus for astronomical research on many fronts."[6]

Although the existence of the galaxy's vast outer regions was suspected by the time the fourth edition appeared, it was not until the 1981 publication of the book's fifth edition that their importance and extent was understood. We now understand the galaxy to consist of at least three components—the disk, which includes the center and the spiral arms, the spheroidal component, which includes a bulge around the nucleus as well as a halo of thinly distributed stars around the disk, and a huge "corona" of material that is so vast that it couples the Milky Way with other large structures including some very distant globular clusters, the Magellanic Clouds, and seven dwarf galaxies.[7] In the late sixties, most scientists were comfortable theorizing that the Milky Way had a mass equivalent to 200 billion suns. But if the galaxy's corona extends as far as 300,000 parsecs, then the galaxy's mass would be ten times that.[8]

With the appearance of the fifth edition, Bok intensified his public speaking, accepting invitations from around the world. Of his several subjects, "The Big and Beautiful Milky Way" was by far Bok's favorite.[9] But with new research showing that the galaxy's outskirts extended farther than previously thought, he modified the title to "The Bigger and Better Milky Way." Bok loved to explain, in terms far more colloquial than he allowed himself in his book, how much larger and more complex our galaxy was than was previously thought. "We used to think that Andromeda Galaxy (the nearest major galaxy) was twice as large as the Milky Way," he would begin a lecture. "Now we think that Andromeda still is bigger," he emphasized with a wink, *"but not by as much."* He then added that the Milky Way seemed more complex as well. For example, it was previously thought that the galaxy rotated "nicely and politely" like the Earth does. But now, he would go on, astronomers recognize that different parts of the galaxy rotate at different rates, the inner section much more rapidly than the outer.

Although the fifth edition discussed the prospects that the Bok globules were a vital step in the early evolution of stars, Bok would never know for certain just how right he was about them. In 1991, eight years after his death, two astronomers found strong new evidence that Bok's suspicion was correct. Using observations obtained by the Infrared Astronomical Satellite, Joao Lin Yun and Dan P. Clemens of Boston University examined 248 Bok globules and found that 57 of them had hidden in them at least one young star with a mass of at least two-thirds of the Sun. Very likely the remaining globules harbor less massive suns.[10]

"The Promise of the Space Telescope" ran a close second as Bok's favorite popular lecture topic. He was utterly sold on the prospects of a 90-inch-diameter telescope in Earth orbit. Absolutely certain that it would instantly render its ground-based cousins obsolete, Bok seemed to think that scientific research should simply stop and wait for it. When someone asked him after the lecture what astronomers should do to prepare for the golden era of the space telescope, Bok replied (somewhat laconically): "Get yourself a good pencil sharpener and sharpen all your pencils, so that you'll be ready for the data the space telescope sends you." Arizona's Senator Barry Goldwater thought enough of Bok's arguments and enthusiasm that he even had the space telescope lecture reprinted in the *Congressional Record* (vol. 125, pt. 11 [1979], 13504–6).

The Milky Way was the coup de grace of an astronomer who felt religiously that teaching and public lecturing were every bit as important as research. "The scientist has the immediate day-to-day contact with the research and the advances. In Australia, if I hadn't made a big educational effort, I would have been criticized. I think it is the function of astronomers to be available for public lectures."

Bok felt that the study of the universe was a worthy public enterprise, but at the same time teaching was necessary to keep the profession healthy. "Astronomers have responsibilities to attract promising young students into the profession," he wrote in Australia, "and we should make special efforts to show them the fine opportunities that lie ahead."[11] He was in favor of a spectrum of initiatives, from producing pamphlets for the public to offering overseas research experiences for students. "At all stages in the teaching of astronomy," he went on, "we should keep the student aware of the beauty and grandeur of the universe that we are privileged to study. The teaching of astronomy at all levels should include regular observing periods. The beginning student should learn his constellations, know the planets and learn to follow their paths across the heavens and observe the Milky Way and its beautiful clusters and nebulae. At a more advanced stage, work at the telescope—optical or radio—should be a part of his training course."[12]

Wherever he lived, whenever he traveled, Bok sold the Milky Way, the sky, and the universe, both for fun and as a career opportunity. More than any other astronomer of his generation, he took as much pride in selling his profession as a jeweler would take in selling a diamond: "Astronomers should not hesitate to get out into the marketplace and recruit!"[13]

Ambassador Bok: Travels and Controversies

To the end of his life, Bok was as committed to the idea that the study of the universe should know no national boundaries as he was to astronomy itself. Between 1980 and 1983 Bok took a series of trips to India, the Soviet Union, China, and Indonesia. Bok's honest desire to lecture to public audiences about the Milky Way was coupled with an equal yearning to see how astronomers in other parts of the world were doing, learn what their observatory plans were, and make suggestions on their future growth.

Accompanied by his girlfriend Laura in early 1980, Bok visited India to lecture, visit observatories, and see a total eclipse of the Sun. He was always willing to give advice. During his visit to the University of Kumaon's observatory at Naini Tai, for instance, he learned of their plans for a large telescope, possibly with a mirror as big as four meters. Feeling that it was too ambitious a step for the small staff there, Bok strongly urged that the astronomers there not jump into the project too quickly, suggesting that they visit other large observatories to see how those astronomers had completed their buildings and solved their problems.[14]

What had started out as a pleasant retirement trip to India in the spring of 1980 got Bok into trouble when in Bombay he drafted a guest editorial for the *Bulletin of the Astronomical Society of India* regarding the observatory at Osmania University at Hyderabad. True to form, Bok did not mince words when he wrote that "all is not well with Indian Astronomy. The telescope equipment at Hyderabad's Observatory is not in good operational condition. . . . The theoretical work is at a high level, but they lack proper observational backing for their work. . . . To develop properly, the State Universities and Observatories must attract good young staff. This means that they must be prepared to pay good salaries, but that is their problem—not mine."[15]

The editorial created a storm of controversy in India before it was even printed. Bok's remarks became so controversial that one person wrote suggesting that they might lead to the demise of India's Astronomical Society. "I had hoped," Bok insisted, "that the paragraph in question would draw firm attention to the urgent need for better telescope equipment and higher salaries at Hyderabad and elsewhere."[16] He also admitted that his initial impressions of the Uttar Pradesh State Observatory at Naini Tal were "written in too much of a hurry during my last days at Bombay."[17] Through this little tempest, perhaps Bok hoped to use his prestige to nudge Indian astronomy into the modern age. However, his hastily prepared opinion piece backfired, embarrassing his friends for rather little gain.

Throughout the second half of his life, Bok followed the cyclical changes in relations between the United States and the Soviet Union. Through both frosty periods and detente, he had kept up his friendship with the Armenian astronomer Viktor Ambartsumian. In the summer of 1981, Bok joined a group of amateur astronomers traveling to Siberia to witness a total eclipse of the Sun. Since it had been some years since he had seen Ambartsumian, Bok anxiously looked forward to the trip to the Byurakan Observatory near Yerevan. As the group started walking down the observatory path, Ambartsumian appeared at the front door. As soon as he noticed Bok he broke into a run, arms wide open, and hugged his old friend. "My relationship with Ambartsumian was a very open one," Bok recollected, "in which either of us could tell the other precisely what he wanted."

Bok's visit to the Soviet Union took place at a nadir of American-Soviet relations. With President Reagan only a few months in office and Premier Brezhnev at the height of his adventure into Afghanistan, neither country was in a mood for compromise or trust. In the October 1981 issue of *Sky and Telescope* Bok wrote sympathetically about the state of astronomy in the Soviet Union, his friendship with Ambartsumian, and of his own continued efforts to discuss the plight of dissident scientists with Soviet astronomers he knew.[18] However, Bok's glowing discussion of his "warm and memorable reunion" with Ambartsumian met with a sharp response a few months later:

"It is a pity," astronomers Leo Goldberg and Tom Gehrels protested in a letter to *Sky and Telescope*, that a man as politically powerful and scientifically prestigious in the Soviet Union as Ambartsumian has to our knowledge never lifted a finger to aid his unfortunate colleagues. On the contrary, in numerous statements and interviews which have been published . . . he has assailed Soviet dissidents in general and Orlov, a former member of the Armenian Academy of Sciences, in particular.

He has also castigated foreign scientists who have tried to assist their colleagues who are persecuted in the Soviet Union. . . . He was, of course, one of the 40 members of the USSR Academy of Sciences who signed a letter condemning Sakharov nearly ten years ago, and presided over a recent meeting of the Armenian Academy of Sciences during which we have reason to believe Orlov was expelled from membership.[19]

Stung by this letter, Bok stepped up his correspondence with Ambartsumian and Evald Mustel, chairman of the astronomical council for the Soviet Academy of Sciences, asking them to use their influence to help free two Soviet dissident scientists. One of them, a refusnik named Leonid Ozernoy, was a young Jewish astronomer trying to emigrate to Israel or the United States. "If favorable action were forthcoming before Christmas and the New Year," Bok wrote Mustel, "it would make an especially favorable impression and be taken as proof of the desire of USSR astronomers to retain the warm friendship with U.S. astronomers. It would be a real gesture of mercy, compassion and human kindness. We really should be as kind to each other as we can be.

"I hope that you will pardon my almost sentimental attitude, but these are politically dangerous and difficult times in which the world needs more than ever good will among astronomers."[20]

The other dissident, physicist Yuri Orlov, was a founding member of the Soviet Amnesty International and Helsinki Watch groups. In 1972 he wrote thirteen "Questions to Brezhnev" that resulted in an increasing campaign of harassment. Fired from the Institute of Theoretical and Experimental Physics of the Soviet Academy of Sciences for supporting Andrei Sakharov in 1975, Orlov was arrested in February 1977 for distributing copies of the Helsinki Accords on human rights.[21]

The Orlov case received attention in the West when Orlov was beaten while in a prison camp, suffering severe head injuries.[22] Despite this, the Soviet prosecutor would not qualify him for release because, as he said, Orlov had been convicted of "crimes especially dangerous to the State."

Responding to a suggestion from the National Academy of Sciences, Bok wrote Ambartsumian about his Armenian countryman Orlov:

> As you well know, our National Academy of Sciences (of which I am an active member emeritus) has long had an interest in the fate of dissident USSR scientists who are imprisoned. . . . A week or so ago the Academy sent me the attached copies of articles from the *New York Times* and the *London Times* and asked me if I could obtain any information on the condition of Yuri F. Orlov about whom we talked in your office at the observatory two years ago. Since Orlov was put in prison just following his leaving Erevan, you may well have more information on his condition than most scientists in the USSR or USA. If so, would you give me that information, so that I can pass it on to our National Academy of Sciences.[23]

Ambartsumian had not replied openly to Goldberg and Gehrels' stinging criticism in *Sky and Telescope,* nor did he address the dissident question in a July 1982 letter to Bok. He did write, however, that "it is sufficient to look into the half-century long history of relations between Bok and Ambartsumian in order to see that the origin of their friendship has nothing to do with what Goldberg assumes. . . .

"I remember how excited you were," Ambartsumian went on, "when introducing me to the audience gathered in the conference hall of the Australian Academy of Sciences for my lecture on the activity of nuclei of galaxies (1963). Was your enthusiasm commanded by someone else?

"Thus our guilt is in having very deep common scientific interests and even the disagreements on some scientific problems have solidified our friendship. I hope it cannot be destroyed even by the command of Dr. Goldberg."[24]

Despite the efforts of the world scientific community, Orlov was not freed until 1986. He and American news correspondent Nicholas Daniloff were liberated as part of a U.S.-Soviet trade in which Soviet spy Gennadi Zakharov returned to Moscow.

In January 1982, a few months after his Soviet visit, Bok visited an observatory site at the very cradle of civilization, on Iraq's Mount Korek, east of the Tigris River. Bok was proud of his former student, May Kaftan-Kassim, who was a leading force behind the project. As a young Iraqi student in the early 1950s, she went to Harvard, where Bok was setting up his radio astronomy program, and she had been part of the team that completed the 60-foot Agassiz radio telescope in 1956.

When Kaftan-Kassim returned to Baghdad in the mid-1970s, she quickly turned her enthusiasm toward launching the new observatory in her native country. Together with Hamid Al-Naimiy and other former students of Manchester University's astronomer Zdenek Kopal, Kaftan-Kassim persuaded the Iraqi government to start construction on a 30-meter radio telescope, a 3.5-meter reflector, and a 1.2-meter reflector. As project manager of the operation, Kaftan-Kassim invited several American astronomers, naturally including Bok, to a symposium to celebrate the start of observatory construction in January 1982. Thrilled to be a part of his student's success, Bok flew to Baghdad. He was met not by Kaftan-Kassim, but by a young man in a car.

Puzzled as to where Kaftan-Kassim was, Bok asked the driver when he would be seeing her. The answer was "Dr. Kaftan" (as she was then known) "has gone on a holiday." More insistent prodding by Bok revealed that Kaftan had actually gone back to the United States. By the following morning Bok was concerned and upset. "Your men are in charge," he said to Kopal, who was also in Baghdad for the dedication. "What can they tell us about May Kassim? What do you know about her?"

Kopal's answer, as Bok remembered, was not encouraging. "You might as well get used to it," he smiled. "Kassim is now a non-person." Apparently she had been replaced virtually on the eve of the conference, and had returned to the United States.

Kopal delivered his opening address to an audience of 200 people, including Najil Khalil, head of Iraq's Council of Scientific Research, the minister of education, and other senior government officials, and a bevy of armed guards. Bok seethed as he listened. The opening remarks did not include any mention of his former student. After the addresses were completed, Bok rose.

"Before we continue," he said in a loud voice, "we should recognize that this meeting would never have taken place were it not for my student, May Kassim. She is the one who started this whole project, and her name has not been mentioned. She has now disappeared and I don't know where she is. But I would like to have it go down for the record that many of us love May Kassim. Some of her close friends are in this audience, and realize that her contribution ought to be recognized."

After Bok returned from his trip he quickly learned that Kaftan-Kassim had returned to the United States and was living in Connecticut. Despite his personal sadness, Bok would continue to support the observatory project. "Iraq is trying in one bold step," Bok later wrote, "to build and operate an observatory that will rate with the mightiest. The project deserves to succeed, and anyone active in the worldwide development of astronomy should be prepared to lend a helping hand."[25]

Years later Kopal wrote that "May Kassim's absence from Baghdad in January 1982, was caused by the fact that, without Bok's knowledge, she declined to accept an invitation to come. If she came, she would have been asked questions by the government of fiscal nature, which she would have probably found embarrassing."[26] For whatever its reason, the Iraqi government took a dislike to her, and she wisely left the country.

A few months after his unsettling visit to Iraq, Bok got an invitation to China. Thrilled with the prospect, he told friends that he wanted "to go to China more than anything." As vice-president of the International Astronomical Union and president of the American Astronomical Society, Bok tried to bring China back into the world astronomical community, and he had been bitterly disappointed not to be invited on Goldberg's trip in 1976 (see chapter 14). Bok left Tucson on September 2, 1982, and a few days later was lecturing on "Our Milky Way" to thirty students at Beijing University. A similar pattern would characterize his entire visit: thirty to forty astrophysicists, most of them under age 35, listening to the sentence by sentence simultaneous translation of his lecture.

Bok was touched by the exuberance of his young audiences. Never afraid to interrupt with questions, the students kept him busy for at least two hours each session, an unchanging routine that kept up until he reached the observatory at Shanghai. There he met a totally different group of people, one he found somewhat dour. "To be perfectly frank," he recalled, "their expressions didn't change and they never reacted to jokes like the others did." This Shanghai audience, he later learned, consisted of people who operated China's national time service. "There was no discussion; at the end they clapped about five times, in unison, and walked out like a military formation."

Despite several mild attacks of angina and edema, which swelled his feet and ankles, Bok insisted on climbing to the top of the Great Wall. At its base he gazed upward—the flight of steps seemed interminable, but he was not about to come all this way and not scale China's historic landmark. Working slowly, he climbed 85 irregular, stone-cut steps to the top.

"China has a very special charm," Bok felt, "of making you feel welcome and at home." In Shanghai, he finally had an unedited glimpse of

Chinese life. Unable to get a first-class room there because Prime Minister Thatcher and her entourage were in town on a state visit from England to conclude the treaty in which England would give up control of Hong Kong, he found himself in simpler quarters that looked out on a little alley, across which he could see a shop with some twenty girls embroidering and forty boys sewing blue jeans. "The first morning when I got up," he remembered, "I looked out my window and waved at them. And they all waved back. Later when I returned, they would shout at me from across the alley and wave, and have fun. They were all very cheerful. But the lighting in their room was deplorable, just like you would expect in an old-fashioned sweat shop.

"The feeling I had throughout China," Bok added, "was that the Chinese were proud of their communistic experiment and wanted to make a go of it. I have seen that in no other part of the world, certainly not in Russia, where I saw a large number of drunks; clearly all sorts of emotional things at work. In China, superficially at least, the people were cheerful, happy, having a lot of fun. The boys and girls, while working, were joking and talking all the time. Nobody seemed to be quiet. It was interesting to see that sweat shop in operation for ten days."

The stress of leaving China was dangerous. Even though Bok was in a wheelchair, the rush to the plane gave him an attack of angina so severe that he thought he might not make it to the plane. Several tablets of nitroglycerine helped calm his system, and when he finally boarded he relaxed and felt fine again. But shortly after he returned home he noted that almost any stress would cause an angina attack. When a trip planned for Indonesia with a group of amateur astronomers fell through, the aging astronomer was so upset that he had to take nine nitroglycerine tablets to bring his angina under control.

At the end of 1982 the American Astronomical Society invited Bok to deliver its prestigious Henry Norris Russell lecture during its meeting in Boston the following January. In a moving introduction to the large audience of astronomers from all over the country in January 1983, all Bok's former students were asked to rise. A substantial fraction of the people in the audience stood up—astronomers from Harvard and Australian National Universities, from the University of Arizona, and from other universities where Bok's guest lectures had inspired and influenced generations of astronomers.[27]

Bok quickly secured a new invitation to see a total eclipse of the Sun in the spring of 1983 and to lecture in Indonesia. He was off again. His doctor approved his continued travel but gave him strict instructions on how he should sit on an airplane and even arranged with the airlines to get him a bulkhead seat with extra room so that he could prop up his feet. Bok's own letters to his Indonesian hosts emphasized his need to take a long afternoon nap and follow other precautions. He loved the wheelchair. "I can advise anybody not to fight off a wheelchair for traveling," he noted. "Wheelchair passengers always have the right of way through customs and get treated royally."

Torrential rains pelted Bok's Indonesian hotel the night before the June 11, 1983, eclipse. "I know this will be my last eclipse," he told his friends Jay and Judy Anderson who were on the eclipse trip with him.[28] Late that night the storm moved out and eclipse morning dawned clear. As the last bus to the center of the path of totality left, Bok stayed put; he would miss only about ten seconds of the five-minute total eclipse by foregoing the extra travel to the place where the total phase was longest. As the Moon blocked out more and more of the Sun, he watched the effects of the changing environment around him. "I sat there with my glass of beer and enjoyed it thoroughly. I decided I will not look for shadow bands. I will not look for little crescents between leaves. I will not look for anything. I will not look through a telescope. I'll sit for the whole five minutes and watch." The Moon's shadow rushed closer and closer, darkening the sky rapidly. Suddenly the full strength of the lunar shadow enveloped him. Bok looked up to see a vanished Sun replaced by a crown of light. The Sun's outer atmosphere or corona looks different at each eclipse; this time it appeared almost circular around the darkened Sun. As he enjoyed the thrilling event through an almost completely clear sky, he remembered back to a bicycle trip he took to Norway many years earlier. It had been cloudy that day so long ago, and all his scientific preparations yielded nothing. This time, with an eclipse just to enjoy, the weather was beautifully clear.

For Bok, however, the highlight of this trip was not the eclipse at all, but a simple dance of some Indonesian children that filled him with emotion. Bart was entranced by the children. As he watched, his mind went back to a childhood memory of an Indonesian orchestra he heard in Holland on a long-gone Sunday afternoon. He recalled his mother's words: "Sit quietly, Barty, and listen carefully. The Indonesians are going to play now, and you can hear the sounds that are their culture. They are not ours; they are theirs."

Suddenly the dance was over, and someone asked Bart to thank the children on behalf of the eclipse watchers. Slowly he stood up, walked toward the front of the room and looked directly at the children. He told them of his distant memory that had returned so clearly as if time had stood still. Now it was the children's turn to sit entranced, with tears in their eyes. "It is through dances and through music," Bart concluded, "that the Indonesians and the Dutch have formed an unbreakable bond."

Last Trip

Bart returned from Indonesia feeling healthy and upbeat. He was already making plans for his next trip, a symposium on the two small nearby galaxies known as the Magellanic Clouds. Although he had not paid too much attention to the clouds in his later years, he had presided over a Magellanic Cloud symposium in his last year in Australia.[29] "Did you know that I was on top of the heap on the Magellanic Clouds in 1966?" he once asked, saying the same words that he used to describe his riding a bicycle at age three.

The 1983 symposium was set for early September in Tübingen, West Germany. His way would be paid by the European Southern Observatory in return for two weeks of lectures at their headquarters at Garching, near Munich. In addition, Bok would attend a conference in Strasbourg, France, on statistical astronomy and visit the Vatican and Heidelberg Observatories. Finally he would revisit his birthplace in Holland. There was also a tentative invitation to come to Peru in early 1984.

It was during his last two years of life that Bart Bok and I worked steadily on collecting material for this biography. When he was not traveling, we met at his home for an hour or two each week, usually over drinks. "You can't do a biography if you don't drink, David. Boswell did Johnson's in a tavern. So you have a choice. Wine or sherry." After he returned home from Indonesia, these interviews became much more intense. He asked that we meet twice as often, and our sessions lasted longer than before. One day he talked about death, challenging it with his usual vigor: "If I have a heart attack I will thank the dear Lord for giving me one at the right time. My heart is getting bigger, so that ought to happen pretty soon.

"Death is not a frightening thing," he added. "When it comes, I will have a feeling that I have lived a full life. I don't know what comes next but I have no fear for it, but I do hope that it comes as quickly as it did for Priscilla."[30]

And at the end of each interview, Bart would come to the front door to wave as I drove off. After our interview on August 1, 1983, we went out for a Mexican dinner and then returned to his house. As usual he saw me to the door. "Don't forget to watch me wave goodbye at you," he said. "It's what I always do." As I turned the corner I looked back and saw him still smiling, still standing at the door.

The next afternoon Bart telephoned to thank me for the dinner and to ask when I thought the biography would be completed. We talked about his plans to attend the Magellanic Clouds symposium. But as the conversation ended he grew sad. "Poor Bart Bok is not very organized these days," he said. "I just called to say goodbye."

On August 5, 1983, Bart Jan Bok was looking forward to a happy weekend and had put champagne on ice in anticipation of a friend's visit. He was about to get into his car to meet her at the airport. But just as he had wished, death came swiftly that Friday afternoon. As his heart finally gave out, he collapsed in his dining room.

That weekend his family and friends gathered at his home, and soon after the University of Arizona had a memorial service, one to which he doubtlessly would have objected. One month later the Symposium on Structure and Evolution of the Magellanic Clouds began in Tübingen. Bok would have enjoyed the breadth and depth of material presented in almost ninety papers over four days. But he would really have appreciated that the volume of printed papers was dedicated to his memory, with a full page portrait at the front of the book.[31] More than ever, he was on top of the heap on the Magellanic Clouds.

"When you are in an observatory at three o'clock in the morning," he loved to say, "stop your photograph. Stop your photometer. Walk away from the telescope. Walk down the stairs. Walk out the front door. Now walk twenty paces—no more, no less. Then stop—and look up at the sky—just to make sure you are making bloody sense."

Notes

Preface

1. Adapted from the introduction to D. H. Levy, "Bart Bok at 75," *Astronomy* 10 (1982), 24–28.

1. Beginnings

1. Kirschhoff's three laws stated that: (1) An incandescent solid, liquid, or dense gas emits radiation at all wavelengths. (2) Radiation from a glowing rarefied gas is emitted at discrete wavelengths, as bright lines on a dark background. (3) Radiation from a continuous source passing through a comparatively cool gas is absorbed at discrete wavelengths, as dark lines on a bright background. The dark lines correspond in wavelength to the bright lines that the gas is capable of emitting.

In summary, an incandescent solid, liquid, or dense gas emits radiation at all wavelengths, but a diffuse gas emits radiation only at particular wavelengths, forming a line spectrum.

2. B. J. Bok, "The Bigger and Better Milky Way." Lecture to Montreal Centre of the Royal Astronomical Society of Canada, March 1982.

3. A. Bailey, *The Light in Holland* (New York: Knopf, 1970), 118.

4. Bok's family was blessed with good health. Both his parents died from cancer after long lives, his mother in 1945 and his father in 1954. Bart's birthplace is now a national monument, the result of a coincidence that had nothing to do with the Bok family. His uncle was in charge of restoration of old buildings in the Netherlands, and the house in which Bart was born had been used long ago as a packing house for the Dutch East India Company. Although several such

buildings still stood, by the 1930s they had become old and dangerous, and the government wished to tear down all but two of them. Bart's uncle had the option of choosing which ones. Since Bart's family home had the good fortune of being in a central location, it was an obvious choice for preservation.

2. Leiden University

1. A. S. Eddington, *The Internal Constitution of the Stars* (Cambridge: Cambridge University Press, 1926). An edition in German was published in 1927.

2. A. V. Douglas, *The Life of Arthur Stanley Eddington* (London: Thomas Nelson and Sons, 1956), 88.

3. B. J. Bok, interview, July 20, 1983.

4. A collaborator with Bohr in the theory of the atom, in 1937 Kramers would introduce his Nobel Prize winning concept of charge conjugation, in which it is asserted that each particle is replaced by an antiparticle; positive charges are replaced by negative ones and vice-versa (e.g., protons with antiprotons, electrons with positrons). It is a philosophically important discovery since it portrays a symmetrical world; by reversing the charges, events still occur the same way. For a background discussion on charge conjugation, see Isaac Asimov, *The Left Hand of the Electron* (New York: Doubleday, 1972). See also Max Dresden's biography, *H. A. Kramers: Between Tradition and Revolution* (New York: Springer-Verlag, 1987).

5. D. DeVorkin, *Interview with Dr. Bart J. Bok* (New York: American Institute of Physics, 1979), 14–16.

6. B. J. Bok and P. F. Bok, *The Milky Way*, 5th ed. (Cambridge: Harvard University Press, 1981), 157. Unless otherwise noted, references to *The Milky Way* are to the fifth edition.

7. Ibid., 163.

8. A *parsec*, for parallax-second, is a unit of measure of distance based on making two measurements of a star from opposite sides of the Earth's orbit. A parsec is equal to 3.3 light years.

9. Bok and Bok, *Milky Way*, 155.

10. DeVorkin, 36.

11. Ibid.

12. Bok and Bok, *Milky Way*, 159.

13. The function is plotted as a graph, with absolute magnitudes against the numbers of stars in the cube. Magnitudes are a measure of star brightnesses; apparent magnitudes are the brightnesses of stars as we see them. Absolute magnitudes are a way of showing the magnitude of all stars if they were at a single distance, 10 parsecs or 33 light years, from us. The concept of absolute magnitudes allows us to make direct comparisons of stars without having to worry about

different distances, giving an understanding of the actual energy outputs, the luminosities, of stars.

For a good discussion of luminosity functions, see Bok and Bok, *Milky Way*, 102–6.

14. B. J. Bok, "On the Systematic Error in the Proper Motions of Boss' System," *Bulletin of the Astronomical Institute of the Netherlands* 5 (1928): 1.

15. Astrophysicist Otto Struve (1897–1963) came from a family rich in astronomical tradition, including five observatory directors. His contributions prompted much of our early understanding about dark matter in the galaxy, rapidly rotating stars, and close binary stars. See "Otto Struve," *Sky and Telescope* 25 (1963), 247.

16. O. Struve, "On the Calcium Clouds," *Popular Astronomy* 34 (1926): 12.

17. B. J. Bok, "On the Oscillating Ca+ lines in O and B Stars," *Bulletin of the Astronomical Institute of the Netherlands* 4 (1927): 12. A spectrum of a star is a representation of its light divided into component colors. O and B are types of stars that are part of the system of classifying stars according to spectral types O, B, A, F, G, K, M, R, N, and S. If the observation is conducted in a particular manner, the resulting display shows bands of light traversed by dark lines known as absorption lines. A discussion on spectral classification can be found in Bok and Bok, *Milky Way*, 61–70.

18. *Popular Astronomy* 36, no. 9 (November 1928): 511.

19. The instrument was later named the Priscilla Fairfield Bok telescope in her honor.

20. J. H. Oort, "An Introduction," *Mercury* 13 (1984): 34.

3. Harlow Shapley

1. Mildred Shapley Matthews, interview, December 12, 1990.

2. H. Shapley, *Through Rugged Ways to the Stars* (New York: Charles Scribner's Sons, 1969), 17.

3. Founded by George Ellery Hale in the early years of the twentieth century, Mount Wilson Observatory quickly became one of the world's premier astronomical institutions. Located in the mountains near Pasadena, California, the observatory consists of three solar telescopes, and a 60-inch and a 100-inch reflector.

4. M. Shapley Matthews, interview.

5. Shapley, *Through Rugged Ways*, 58.

6. D. Levy, *Observing Variable Stars: A Guide for the Beginner* (Cambridge: Cambridge University Press, 1989).

7. See H. Leavitt, "Periods of 25 Variable Stars in the Small Magellanic Cloud," and H. Shapley, "On the Nature and Cause of Cepheid Variation in the Magellanic Cloud," both in *Harvard College Observatory Circular*, no. 173

(1912), and H. Shapley, "On the Nature and Cause of Cepheid Variation," *Astrophysical Journal* 40 (1914), 105–22. These seminal papers are excerpted in Harlow Shapley's *Source Book in Astronomy 1900–1950* (Cambridge, Mass.: Harvard University Press, 1960). In addition, "Discovery of the Period-Magnitude Relation" appears on 186–89 and "The Pulsation Hypothesis" follows on 190–97.

8. Proper motion is a measure of a star's angular motion through space. Stars that are closer to us tend to have larger proper motions.

9. M. Shapley Matthews, interview.

10. Ibid.

11. S. I. Bailey, *The History and Work of Harvard Observatory, 1839 to 1927: An Outline of the Origin, Development, and Researches of the Astronomical Observatory of Harvard College together with Brief Biographies of its Leading Members* (New York: McGraw-Hill Book Company, for the Observatory, 1931).

12. M. Shapley Matthews, interview.

13. B. Z. Jones and L. G. Boyd, *The Harvard College Observatory 1839–1919* (Cambridge, Mass.: Harvard University Press, Belknap Press, 1971), 189.

14. A description of Upton's beautiful 1896 atlas is found in George Lovi's "Uranography Yesterday and Today," in W. Tirion et al., *Uranometria 2000.0* (Richmond, Va.: Willmann-Bell, 1987), xxxvi–xxxvii.

15. Jones and Boyd, *Harvard College Observatory*, 193.

16. This account of the *Pinafore* story is adapted from Jones and Boyd, *Harvard College Observatory*, 189–92, and *Popular Astronomy* 38, no. 3 (March 1930): 125–27.

17. Jones and Boyd, *Harvard College Observatory*, 191.

18. *Popular Astronomy* 38, no. 3 (March 1930): 125–27.

19. K. Haramundanis, ed., *Cecilia Payne-Gaposchkin: An Autobiography and other Recollections* (Cambridge: Cambridge University Press, 1984), 208.

20. B. J. Bok, interview.

21. M. Shapley Matthews, interview.

22. Jones and Boyd, *Harvard College Observatory*, 388. In 1899 Mrs. Williamina Paton Fleming became curator of astronomical photographs (the highest position to that time given to a woman at Harvard) and directed the work, which was done almost entirely by the women assistants at the observatory, practically until her death in 1911.

23. Among many other major contributions, Hoffleit produced several editions of the Yale University Observatory *Catalogue of Bright Stars* (3d ed.: New Haven, 1964). For many years she was director of the Maria Mitchell Observatory, where her summer program for young students developed a national reputation.

24. M. Shapley Matthews, interview.

4. "Miscellaneous Nonsense Vaguely Related to Eta Carinae"

1. B. J. Bok, "The Spectrum of Eta Carinae," *Popular Astronomy* 38 (1930): 399–400.

2. B. J. Bok, *The Distribution of the Stars in Space* (Chicago: University of Chicago Press, 1937).

3. Haramundanis, ed., *Cecilia Payne-Gaposchkin*, 157.

4. A planetary nebula is a sphere of stellar material surrounding a star. Resulting from a release of material, either gradually or explosively, from the star's outer atmosphere, these nebulae are common objects, many of which can be seen through small telescopes. See E. A. Milne, "Thermodynamics of the Stars," *Handbuch der Astrophysik III* (Berlin: J. Springer, 1930), 65–255 (ch. 2).

5. Interview of Bok by DeVorkin.

6. Levy, *Observing Variable Stars*, 170.

7. The broader emission lines represent light that comes from the nebulous shell surrounding the star after its outburst.

8. Levy, 171.

9. J. A. Graham, C. M. Wade, and R. M. Price, "Bart J. Bok: A Memoir," *Biographical Memoirs of the National Academy of Sciences* 64 (forthcoming).

10. B. J. Bok, *A Study of the Eta Carinae Region*. Harvard College Observatory Reprint, no. 77, 1932.

11. This comment was found inadvertently by the author during a search of Harvard photographic plates.

12. *Sky and Telescope* 20, no. 2 (August 1960): 76.

13. M. Shapley Matthews, interview, December 12, 1990.

14. Haramundanis, *Cecilia Payne-Gaposchkin*, 208.

15. H. Shapley, *Beyond the Observatory* (New York: Charles Scribner's Sons, 1967), 139.

16. B. J. Bok, "Harlow Shapley: Cosmographer and Humanitarian," *Sky and Telescope* 44, no. 6 (1972): 357.

17. A. Hoag, interview, November 1, 1983.

18. P. Millman and D. Sabatini, personal communication.

19. Concert Notes, 30.

20. B. J. Bok, interview, July 2, 1982.

21. B. J. Bok, "Harlow Shapley," *Biographical Memoirs of the National Academy of Sciences* 49 (1978): 241–91.

5. Astronomy and Astropolitics

1. The Hertzsprung-Russell diagram is discussed in several places in Bok and Bok's *Milky Way*, notably 95–96. See also D. DeVorkin, "Stellar Evolution and

the Origin of the Hertzsprung-Russell Diagram" in *The General History of Astronomy*, vol 4 of *Astrophysics and Twentieth-Century Astronomy to 1950: Part A*, ed. O. Gingerich (London: Cambridge University Press, 1984), 90–108.

2. Astronomers have tried to keep on top of misplaced credit problems for generations. One of the more famous examples is that of Bode's Law, which proposes a formula for describing distances from the Sun to each of the planets. Although Titius discovered the numerical relation, Bode popularized it. Even though it properly is the Titius-Bode Law, it is still commonly known as Bode's Law.

3. B. J. Bok, interview, July 31, 1982.

4. E. Hubble, *The Realm of the Nebulae* (New Haven: Yale University Press, 1936). Repr. New York: Dover, 1958. Galaxy distribution discussion is on p. 69.

5. H. Shapley, *Galaxies* (Philadelphia: The Blakiston Company, 1943).

6. *Harvard Bulletin* 889 (1932); see also *Harvard Reprints* no. 90 (1933).

7. A revised edition of the *Shapley-Ames Catalogue of Galaxies* was published as recently as 1987.

8. C. W. Tombaugh, "The Great Perseus-Andromeda Stratum of Extra-Galactic Nebulae and Certain Clusters of Nebulae Therein as Observed at the Lowell Observatory," *Publications of the Astronomical Society of the Pacific* 49, 291 (1937): 259.

9. C. W. Tombaugh, interview, July 9, 1988.

10. D. H. Levy, *Clyde Tombaugh: Discoverer of Planet Pluto* (Tucson: University of Arizona Press, 1991), 113.

11. H. Shapley and A. Ames, *A Survey of the External Galaxies Brighter than the Thirteenth Magnitude* (Cambridge: Annals of the Astronomical Observatory of Harvard College, 1932).

12. K. Haramundanis, *Cecilia Payne-Gaposchkin*, 189–90.

13. B. J. Bok, "The Stability of Moving Clusters," *Harvard College Observatory Circular* no. 384 (1934).

14. Ambartsumian had studied how very large star clusters can lose the stars that had lower masses. Ambartsumian concluded that these stars escape with more than their expected share of energy, with a resulting tendency of the cluster to lose its cohesion and eventually disintegrate. As these stars escape, the entire cluster would tend to contract.

15. Bok and Bok, *Milky Way*, 125–27.

16. B. J. Bok, *The Distribution of the Stars in Space* (Chicago: University of Chicago Press, 1937).

17. Ibid., 87.

18. Ibid., vii.

19. The stellar count research would lead Bok into a number of directions after the book appeared. One involved Bok and Donald MacRae, one of his students who later went on to become a prominent Canadian astronomer. The paper

appeared in 1938 in the unlikely *Annals of the Academy of Science of New York,* and pushed star count and luminosity function analyses to new limits. By 1938, this research had become especially interesting because telescopes were getting bigger and star counts were going to ever higher magnitudes.

20. In addition to the public forum, the observatory papers, including some by Bok, were published in 1937 in a special issue of the *Harvard Annals,* an important volume that contains several seminal investigations dealing with galactic structure that were in progress at Harvard at the time. Cf. B. J. Bok and W. F. Swann, "Photovisual Magnitudes for the Selected Areas at Delta = +75 Degrees," *Harvard College Observatory Tercentenary Papers,* no. 18, *Harvard Annals* 105 (1937): 371–81.

21. D. Hoffleit, "Meghnad Saha Dies," *Sky and Telescope* 15, no. 7 (1956): 306.

22. Saha had many papers published in *Philosophical Magazine and Journal of Science.* One of the first was in vol. 33, sixth series (1917): 256–61; two others were "On the Fundamental Law of Electrical Action," vol. 37, sixth series (1919): 347–71, and "On the Physical Properties of Elements at High Temperatures," vol. 46, sixth series (1923): 534–43. By the third paper he was applying his work to stellar spectra.

23. G. Reber, "Cosmic Static," *Astrophysical Journal* 91 (1940): 621–24.

6. Waves of War

1. Peter J. Kuznick, *Beyond the Laboratory: Scientists as Political Activists in 1930s America* (Chicago: University of Chicago Press, 1987), 5.

2. B. J. Bok, Discussion, *Science* 100 (1944): 217–18.

3. General Notes, *Popular Astronomy* 46 (1938): 351–52.

4. B. J. Bok, "Report on Astronomy," *Popular Astronomy* 47 (1939): 356–72.

5. Ibid.

6. In 1940 that article was translated into Chinese for the China Association for Science and Technology by Dr. Li Jing. During Bok's 1982 trip to China his hosts gave him a copy of the translation.

7. Kuznick, *Beyond the Laboratory,* 103.

8. Ibid., 239.

9. D. H. Menzel, "The Telescope," *Sky and Telescope* 1, no. 1 (1941): 7.

10. L. J. Robinson, "How S&T Came to Be," *Sky and Telescope* 82, no. 5 (1991): 472.

11. M. Lockwood, "The Sky," *Sky and Telescope* 1, no. 1 (1941): 7.

12. B. J. Bok, "The Exchange of Astronomical Publications during the War," *Popular Astronomy* 49 (January 1941): 57–58.

13. Bok and Bok, *Milky Way,* 177.

14. References include interviews and B. J. Bok, "Uco Van Wijk" (obituary notice), *Quarterly Journal of the Royal Astronomical Society* 8, no. 4 (1967): 386.

15. M. C. Meyer and W. L. Sherman, *The Course of Mexican History* (New York: Oxford University Press, 1979), 603–4.

16. B. J. Bok, "Mexico's New National Observatory," *Sky and Telescope* 1, no. 2 (1941): 3–4.

17. "New Mexican Observatory Dedicated," *Sky and Telescope* 1, no. 5 (1942): 13.

18. See B. J. Bok, "Tonanzintla Revisited," *Sky and Telescope* 4, no. 6 (1945): cover, 3–5.

19. Robert E. Sherwood, *Roosevelt and Hopkins: An Intimate History* (New York: Harper & Brothers, 1948), 226.

20. Levy, *Clyde Tombaugh*, 119–22.

21. B. J. Bok, *Navigation in Emergencies* (Washington: United States Coast Guard, 1942).

22. F. Wright, interview, July 9, 1984.

7. Putting the S in UNESCO

1. B. J. Bok, "UNESCO: A Work in Progress," *Physics Today* 2, no. 7 (1949): 16.

2. B. J. Bok and I. Amdur, Letter, *New York Times*, Sept. 2, 1945.

3. B. J. Bok, "Science and the Maintenance of Peace," *Science* 109 (1949): 131.

4. W. Laves and C. Thomson, *UNESCO: Purpose, Progress, Prospects* (Bloomington: Indiana University Press, 1957), 28.

5. Preamble, *Constitution of the United Nations Educational, Scientific and Cultural Organization.* Adopted in London on November 16, 1945.

6. B. J. Bok, "The First National UNESCO Conference," *American Scientist* 35 (1947): 372.

7. Kuznick, *Beyond the Laboratory*, 248.

8. Ibid.

9. H. S. Truman, speech to the American Association for the Advancement of Science, September 13, 1948, in *The Private Papers of Harry S. Truman*, ed. R. H. Ferrell (New York: Harper & Row, 1980), 149.

8. Darkness and Brightness in the Milky Way

1. B. J. Bok and P. F. Bok, *The Milky Way*, 1st ed. (Philadelphia: Blakiston, 1941), 1.

2. Ibid.

3. D. Brouwer, "Harvard Books on Astronomy," *American Scientist* 30, no. 2 (1942): 159.

4. Ibid., 162.

5. B. J. Bok, *Distribution of the Stars in Space,* 124.

6. B. J. Bok, *Study of the Eta Carinae Region.*

7. B. J. Bok and E. F. Reilly, "Small Dark Nebulae," *Astrophysical Journal* 105 (1947): 255.

8. See "The Horsehead Nebula: A Bok Globule in the Making?" *Sky and Telescope* 69 (1985): 12; "Bok Globules and Star Birth," *Sky and Telescope* 71 (1986): 147; and "Bart Bok was Right," *Sky and Telescope* 81 (1991): 485–86.

9. W. Baade to B. J. Bok, March 25, 1947.

10. B. J. Bok to W. Baade, April 7, 1947.

11. W. Baade to B. J. Bok, April 21, 1947.

12. "Thousands of Suspected Globules," *Sky and Telescope* 15, no. 4 (1956): 170.

13. F. Hoyle, *The Black Cloud* (New York: Signet, 1959), 16. Two and a half degrees arc roughly equivalent to five full Moon diameters.

14. Ibid, 18.

15. Ibid., 108.

16. Thanks to a large donation from Agassiz, Shapley and Bok arranged to change the name of the observatory's Oak Ridge Station. It has since been changed back.

17. F. Wright, interview, July 9, 1984.

18. G. Merton, "Comets," *Monthly Notices of the Royal Astronomical Society* 110 (1950): 175.

19. Comet information from S. K. Vsekhsvyatskii, *Physical Characteristics of Comets* (Jerusalem: Israel Program for Scientific Translations, for the National Aeronautics and Space Administration, 1964), 539; also G. W. Kronk, *Comets: A Descriptive Catalog* (Hillside, N. J.: Enslow, 1984), 148–49.

20. Jones and Boyd, *Harvard College Observatory,* 270.

21. Ibid., 246–48.

22. "In Focus," *Sky and Telescope* 9, no. 6 (1950): cover, 130, 133.

23. A. Hoag to D. Levy, March 1991.

24. W. Baade to B. J. Bok, December 21, 1950.

25. B. J. Bok, "Perspective on South Africa," *Harper's Magazine,* July 1952, 52.

26. Ibid., 59.

27. Ibid., 58.

28. Ibid., 59.

9. Harvard Twilight

1. H. Shapley, *Through Rugged Ways to the Stars*, 151.

2. *New York Times*, Nov. 5, 1946.

3. This story was prepared from interviews of Bok and others, as well as from Shapley's *Through Rugged Ways to the Stars*, 150–54.

4. *New York Times*, Nov. 15, 1946.

5. Ibid.

6. *New York Times*, Nov. 16, 1946.

7. *New York Times*, Mar. 16, 1947.

8. H. Shapley, *Through Rugged Ways*, 157. Although Shapley discusses in this book public statements McCarthy made about him, he does not mention the Senate hearings with their list of his 37 memberships in subversive organizations.

9. Sen. J. McCarthy, State Department Employee Loyalty Investigation, *Hearings before a Subcommittee of the Committee on Foreign Relations* (Senate Subcommittee on S. Res. 231), 81st Cong., 2d sess., *Senate Committee Hearings*, vol. 946, no. 2, 125, March 1950.

10. Ibid., 126.

11. Ibid., 127. McCarthy dated Shapley's participation in the anti-Rankin group from a *New York Times* article printed a few months *before* the director's HUAC appearance.

12. F. L. Whipple, interview, August 1, 1983.

13. B. J. Bok and F. L. Whipple, "Preliminary Observations of Nova Monocerotis," *Publications of the American Astronomical Society* 10 (1939): 32.

14. W. G. Hoyt, *Planets X and Pluto* (Tucson: University of Arizona Press, 1980), 205.

15. F. L. Whipple, *The Mystery of Comets* (Washington: Smithsonian Institution Press, 1985), 145, 146–47.

16. Whipple published his theory in two papers. "A Comet Model. I. The Acceleration of Comet Encke," *Astrophysical Journal* 111 (1950): 375–94, explains how the changing orbit of Periodic Comet Encke can be explained by a comet nucleus structure consisting of meteoric material through which frozen gases sublimate, producing gas emissions that accelerate the comet. The second paper is "Physical Relations for Comets and Meteors," *Astrophysical Journal* 113 (1951): 464–74.

17. J. Piaget, "The Right to Education in the Modern World," *UNESCO: Freedom and Culture* (New York: Columbia University Press, 1951), 69–119.

18. B. J. Bok, "Freedom and Science," *UNESCO: Freedom and Culture*, 233.

19. Ibid., 242.

20. Ibid., 244.

21. Ibid., 245.

22. Ibid., 245.

23. Ibid., 246.

24. Ibid., 247.

25. H. Shapley, "Harvard Observatory Director Appointed," *Sky and Telescope* 13, no. 5 (1954): 143.

26. Ibid., 143, 149.

27. L. Goldberg, "Donald Howard Menzel," *Sky and Telescope* 53, no. 4 (1977): 249.

28. Ibid., 250.

29. O. Gingerich, "The Discovery of the Spiral Arms of the Milky Way," *Proceedings of the IAU Symposium 106* (July 1983), Center for Astrophysics Preprint Series, no. 1847, 3.

30. Ibid.

31. W. Baade to B. J. Bok, February 8, 1949.

32. "Spiral Arms of the Galaxy," *Sky and Telescope* 11, no. 6 (1952): 138–39. See also W. Morgan, S. Sharpless, and D. Osterbrock, "Structure in the Neighborhood of the Sun," *Astronomical Journal* 57 (1952): 3.

33. "Astronomical Highlights of 1952" (American Astronomers' Report), *Sky and Telescope* 12, no. 2 (1952): 45. Shapley's leading highlight is "1. Tentative detection of the spiral arms of the galaxy by W. W. Morgan and other Yerkes Observatory astronomers, and by B. J. Bok and his Harvard collaborators for the southern sky."

34. O. Struve, "Galactic Exploration by Radio," *Sky and Telescope* 11, no. 9 (1952): 215.

35. B. J. Bok, "Radio Studies of Interstellar Hydrogen," *Sky and Telescope* 13, no. 12 (1954): 408.

36. John Bok, interview, August 1984.

37. D. Hoffleit, "Harvard Radio Telescope," *Sky and Telescope* 12, no. 3 (1953): 74.

38. F. L. Whipple, personal communication, June 27, 1991.

39. D. S. Heeschen, "Harvard's New Radio Telescope," *Sky and Telescope* 15, no. 9 (1956): 388.

40. B. J. Bok to Arthur Sutherland, Law School of Harvard University, cc. Dean McGeorge Bundy, Feb. 23, 1954. The material for the subcommittee story was gleaned from this letter as well as from interviews.

41. B. J. Bok, interview, December 13, 1982. Bok added that his memory might not be accurate; and indeed his written letter does not show that Bok said anything about Bibles.

42. B. J. Bok to Arthur Sutherland.

43. Ibid.

44. "The Artificial Satellite" (American Astronomers' Report), *Sky and Telescope* 15, no. 3 (1956): 112.

45. F. Whipple, personal communication, June 27, 1991.

46. J. A. Graham, C. M. Wade, R. M. Price, "Bart J. Bok—A Memoir," *Biographical Memoirs of the National Academy of Sciences*, 64.

47. A. A. Hoag, interview, November 1, 1983.

48. C. Sawyer to D. Levy, September 10, 1991.

10. The Australian Years

1. *Sky and Telescope* 15, no. 8 (1956): 339.

2. S. Cockburn and D. Ellyard, *Oliphant: The Life and Times of Sir Mark Oliphant* (Adelaide: Axiom Books, 1981), 177.

3. O. J. Eggen, "The Australian Commonwealth Observatory," *Sky and Telescope* 15, no. 8 (1956): 340.

4. Ibid., 342–43.

5. F. Kerr, "Australia's 210–foot Radio Telescope Project," *Sky and Telescope* 18, no. 12 (1959): 666–68.

6. S. C. B. Gascoigne, "Australian Astronomy since the Second World War," in R. W. Home, *Australian Science in the Making* (Sydney: Australian Academy of Science and Cambridge University Press, 1988), 358–59.

7. Ibid., 359.

8. S. C. B. Gascoigne, "Bart Bok at Mount Stromlo," *Mercury* 13, no. 2 (1984): 45.

9. Ibid.

10. Ibid., 46.

11. B. J. Bok, "Mount Stromlo Observatory," *Hemisphere* 10, no. 3 (1966): 6. See also B. J. Bok, "Annual Report for the Year 1960" (Canberra: Australian National University, Mount Stromlo Observatory, 1961), 3.

12. Gascoigne, "Bart Bok at Mount Stromlo," 46.

13. Cockburn and Ellyard, *Oliphant*, 212.

14. J. Nehru, *Toward Freedom: The Autobiography of Jawaharlal Nehru* (Boston: Beacon Press, 1967), 439. "Pandit" is Hindu for learned man or teacher.

15. T. Buckley, personal communication, May 18, 1992.

16. Soviet astronomers G. G. Getmanzev, K. S. Stankevitch, and V. S. Troitsky found a 91.6 cm signature of heavy hydrogen or deuterium. B. J. Bok, "Jodrell Bank Symposium on Radio Astronomy," *Sky and Telescope* 15, no. 1 (1955): 22.

17. O. Struve, "Galactic Co-ordinates," *Sky and Telescope* 17, no. 12 (1958): 617.

18. J. Glaspey to D. Levy, August 19, 1991.

19. B. J. Bok, *The Astronomer's Universe* (London: Cambridge University Press, 1958), 66–67.

20. B. J. Bok, "The Spiral Structure of our Galaxy," letter to *The Observatory* 79 (1959): 58–62.

21. B. J. Bok, "The Arms of the Galaxy," *Scientific American* 201, no. 6 (1959): 92–104.

22. However, Bok later noted R. Humphreys' finding that these Cepheids were too few in number to be reliable tracers. Cf. Bok and Bok, *Milky Way*, 300.

23. Bok, "The Arms of the Galaxy." Bok used this *Scientific American* piece to speculate on the origin of arms; if an arm were surrounded by magnetic fields, it might move outward as a unit. As it moved farther from the galactic center it would slow down. Bok proposed that the outermost arms move outward at a rate of some three thousand light years per galactic rotation of 200 million years.

24. B. J. Bok, "An International Discussion of Milky Way Research," *Sky and Telescope* 26 (1963): 6.

25. *Sky and Telescope* 82 (1991): 11.

26. L. Rudaux and G. de Vaucouleurs, *Larousse Encyclopedia of Astronomy* (New York: Prometheus Press, 1959), 391–92.

27. B. J. Bok, "The Interstellar Medium," *Sky and Telescope* 22, no. 2 (1961): 89.

28. Ibid., 90.

29. B. J. Bok and P. F. Bok, "A Photoelectric Sequence of Magnitudes and Colors for Selected Area 141," *Astronomical Journal* 56 (1951): 35.

30. B. J. Bok and P. F. Bok, "Four Standard Sequences in the Southern Hemisphere," *Monthly Notices of the Royal Astronomical Society* 121, no. 6 (1960): 531.

31. The work resulted in two papers; the first was B. J. Bok, P. F. Bok, and J. M. Basinski, "Colour-Magnitude Arrays for Two Associations in the Large Magellanic Cloud," *Monthly Notices of the Royal Astronomical Society* 123 (1961): 487–96. The second was B. J. Bok and P. F. Bok, "Integrated Magnitudes and Colours of Young Associations in the Large Magellanic Cloud," *Monthly Notices of the Royal Astronomical Society* 124 (1962): 435–44. These papers appeared also as *Mount Stromlo Observatory Reprints* nos. 51 and 67.

32. Bok and Bok, "Integrated Magnitudes and Colours of Young Associations in the Large Magellanic Cloud," 435, 436. This paper was also one of the first to use the colour-magnitude indicators $(B-V)_0$ and $(U-B)_0$ to make their selection of groupings of stars more precise. These technical results were obtained by measuring stars using three color filters, ultraviolet (U), Blue (B) and a filter designed to imitate the scotopic response of the human eye (V), and then subtracting these measurements from similar ones made on comparison stars.

33. Gascoigne, "Bart Bok at Mount Stromlo," 46.

34. B. J. Bok, "Education for Women: Forgotten Part of our Work Force," *Canberra Times*, January 15, 1964.

11. The Anglo-Australian Observatory

1. S. C. B. Gascoigne, K. M. Proust, and M. O. Robins, *The Creation of the Anglo-Australian Observatory* (Sydney: Cambridge University Press, 1990), 49.

2. M. Oliphant to B. Robinson, April 28, 1983.

3. Gascoigne et al., *Anglo-Australian Observatory*, 50.

4. Bok, "Mount Stromlo Observatory," 4.

5. B. J. Bok, "The Search for New Observatory Sites in Australia," *Journal of the Royal Astronomical Society of Canada* 54, no. 6 (1960): 258. Also available as Mount Stromlo Observatory Reprint no. 33.

6. Ibid., 261.

7. Ibid., 262.

8. Gascoigne et al., *Anglo-Australian Observatory*, 52.

9. Ibid., 51.

10. Ibid., 52.

11. Two excellent sources for the history of the Anglo-Australian telescope are, from the Australian side, Gascoigne et al., *The Creation of the Anglo-Australian Observatory*, and from the British side, A. C. B. Lovell, "The Early History of the Anglo-Australian 150-inch Telescope (AAT)," *Quarterly Journal, Royal Astronomical Society*, 26, no. 4 (1985): 393–455.

12. Lovell, "Early History of Anglo-Australian Telescope," 399.

13. Ibid., 395.

14. The flower garden proposal atop Mt. Kosciusko actually had come from the Academy's Flora and Fauna Committee, which intended to study the possibilities of major biological projects. Gascoigne et al., *Anglo-Australian Observatory*, 361–62.

15. He addressed ANZAAS's Section A (Mathematics, Physics, and Astronomy). R. MacLeod, ed., *The Commonwealth of Science: ANZAAS and the Scientific Enterprise in Australia 1888–1988* (Melbourne: Oxford University Press, 1988), 377.

16. B. J. Bok, "The Future of Astronomy in Australia," *Australian Journal of Science* 25 (1963): 285. The address was delivered on August 21, 1962 in Sydney. Bok notes at the beginning of the published version of his address that "some of my conjectures regarding the Academy's report . . . were in error and I have therefore rewritten parts of Section 4" (281). It is this section which is used in the text; the original address might have been even more potent.

17. Ibid., 286.

18. Ibid., 286.

19. Ibid.

20. Gascoigne et. al., *Anglo-Australian Observatory*, 31.

21. A photograph of the King of Thailand appearing at Stromlo in 1962 appears in *Hemisphere* 10, no. 3 (1966): 7.

22. "Bart," Menzies laughed later in an informal conversation with Bok, "I looked magnificent that day. All these robes and honors—I looked in the mirror and said 'Bob, you have never looked more splendid!'"

23. D. N. Phipps, Introduction to Bok lecture, October 26, 1978. In retrospect, Gascoigne argued that Cherry should not be overly criticized. He was president of an academy that was less than ten years old, one that still lacked the experience to influence the government effectively. In a later letter, Cherry opined that "the Academy is well aware of the astronomers' case, and is sympathetic to it; but it is also aware of desirable projects in other branches of science. In my view Australia can afford to pursue the lot, without significant scientific competition" (Gascoigne et al., 32).

24. Lovell, "Early History of Anglo-Australian Telescope," 407.

25. *Hansard Parliamentary Debates*, Session 1962–63. First Session of the Twenty-Fourth parliament (Third Period). New series, vol. H. of R. (1963): 161, 580.

26. Ibid., 160.

27. Ibid.

28. Ibid., April 10, 1963, 580.

29. K. Crowley, ed. A *New History of Australia* (Melbourne: William Heineman, 1974), 456.

30. *Hansard*, 581.

31. Ibid., 582.

32. Ibid.

33. Ibid., 587.

34. Gascoigne et al., *Anglo-Australian Observatory*, 52.

35. Programme, Opening of Siding Spring Observatory, Australian National University, April 5, 1965.

36. Gascoigne et al., *Anglo-Australian Observatory*, 52.

37. Cockburn and Ellyard, *Oliphant*, 256.

38. Gascoigne, "Bart Bok at Mount Stromlo," 46.

39. Lovell, "Early History of the Anglo-Australian Telescope," 393.

40. T. M. Cherry to B. J. Bok, April 30, 1965, in Lovell, "Early History of the Anglo-Australian Telescope," 413.

41. B. J. Bok to Sir Mark Oliphant, August 12, 1965.

42. Sir Mark Oliphant to B. J. Bok, October 21, 1974.

12. Of Birds and Presidents

1. T. Buckely, personal communication, May 18, 1992.
2. B. J. Bok, "World's Astronomers Meet in Moscow," *Sky and Telescope* 18, no. 1 (1958): 8–9.
3. Ibid., 7.
4. R. M. Price, personal communication, June 14, 1991.
5. P. L. Brown, *Comets, Meteorites, and Men* (London: Robert Hale and Company, 1973), 91.
6. *Canberra Times*, March 15, 1966.
7. The White House, telegram to B. J. Bok, May 17, 1968.
8. The White House, telefax to Professor and Mrs. B. J. Bok, undated.
9. White House dinner menu, May 27, 1968.
10. B. J. Bok to President Johnson, May 29, 1968.
11. *Coonabarabran Times*, Oct. 19, 1978. Also *Northwest Magazine, Barraba Gazette*.
12. Gascoigne, "Bart Bok at Mount Stromlo," 47.

13. Arizona

1. *Tucson Daily Citizen*, June 18, 1964.
2. L. C. Peltier, *Starlight Nights: The Adventures of a Star-Gazer* (New York: Harper and Row, 1965), 183.
3. A. B. Meinel to D. Levy, August 4, 1991.
4. T. Gehrels, interview, July 26, 1991.
5. Ibid.
6. Meinel to Levy, August 4, 1991.
7. B. J. Bok to Flamingo Motel, May 25, 1964.
8. B. J. Bok to A. B. Meinel, April 13, 1964.
9. B. J. Bok to A. B. Meinel, 21 January 1964.
10. A. B. Meinel to B. J. Bok, March 19, 1964.
11. H. D. Rhodes to B. J. Bok, Dec. 28, 1964.
12. J. Glaspey to D. Levy, August 19, 1991.
13. *Tucson Daily Citizen*, April 28, 1970.
14. T. Gehrels, interview.
15. Glaspey to Levy, August 19, 1991.
16. Ibid.
17. R. E. White, interview, July 29, 1991.
18. D. L. Crawford, interview, Aug. 5, 1991.
19. B. J. Bok to Sir Mark Oliphant, August 12, 1965.
20. R. L. Hilliard, *The Steward Observatory 90-inch Reflector.* University of

Arizona, dedication booklet, June 23, 1969. Regarding the geometry of the dome, Hilliard writes (p. 3) that it "represents the intersection of a horizontal quarter cylinder with a vertical cylinder 52 feet in diameter. The biparting dome shutters lie on the surface of the horizontal quarter cylinder."

21. M. Tuve, telegram to B. J. Bok, March 11, 1966.

22. J. A. Hynek and J. R. Dunlap, "Image Orthicon Astronomy," *Sky and Telescope* 28, no. 3 (1964): 126.

23. M. F. Walker, "Image-Tube Observations at Cerro Tololo," *Sky and Telescope* 40, no. 3 (1970): 132.

24. R. E. White, interview.

25. B. J. Bok to Dean Bowen C. Dees, February 12, 1968.

26. *Arizona Wildcat*, April 25, 1968.

27. Ibid.

28. B. J. Bok to B.C. Dees, May 16, 1969.

29. R. Weymann to D. Levy, August 7, 1991.

30. B. J. Bok, "Steward Observatory and the Department of Astronomy, University of Arizona," *Bulletin of the American Astronomical Society* 2, no. 1 (1970): 135–44.

31. J. Greenstein, "Bart Jan Bok," in B. T. Lynds, ed., *Dark Nebulae, Globules, and Protostars* (Tucson: University of Arizona Press, 1971), v.

32. B. J. Bok, C. S. Cordwell, and R. H. Cromwell, "Globules," in Lynds, ed., *Dark Nebulae, Globules, and Protostars*, 54.

33. Ibid., 52. There are other situations where the birth of new stars could take place, the best known of which is the outburst of a supernova. As the shock waves from the outburst push outward, they pass through thick concentrations of interstellar gas, creating an environment where star formation can occur.

34. Ibid., 37, 47.

35. B. J. Bok and P. F. Bok, "Photometric Standards for the Southern Hemisphere," *Astronomical Journal* 74 (1969): 1125ff.

36. J. H. Piddington, "The Density-Wave Theory of Galactic Spirals," *Astrophysical Journal* 179, no. 3 (1973): 763.

37. B. J. Bok, "Comments on the Piddington Paper," unpublished, December 15, 1972. A circular letter to "all who are interested in the spiral structure of our galaxy."

38. B. J. Bok, "The Spiral Structure of Our Galaxy—I," *Sky and Telescope* 38, no. 6 (1969): 395.

39. B. J. Bok, "Summary and Outlook," a paper presented at the conclusion of the Symposium on The Spiral Structure of our Galaxy, Basel University, September 4, 1969.

40. B. J. Bok, "A Brief Memorandum about the Life and Career of Priscilla Fairfield Bok: 1896–1975" *Mira Newsletter* 3, nos. 1–2 (1980): 6.

41. J. Glaspey to D. Levy, August 19, 1991.

42. J. Hall, "Bok Opposed to Reducing Scientific Ties with Chile," *Tucson Daily Citizen*, December 30, 1970.

43. *Chicago Daily Tribune*, January 22, 1932; January 24, 1932; January 26, 1932.

44. The Winnie Judd story was summarized by Brent Whiting, *Arizona Republic*, Jan. 19, 1991.

45. B. J. Bok to Governor J. Williams, June 1971.

46. J. Williams to B. J. Bok, June 30, 1971.

47. B. Whiting, *Arizona Republic*.

14. A Far and Radiant Resting Place

1. B. J. Bok, interview, July 14, 1983.

2. J. Sherry, interview, February 8, 1986.

3. R. D. Gehrz and E. P. Ney, "The Core of Eta Carinae," *Sky and Telescope* 44, no. 1 (1972): 5.

4. E. Gaviola, "Eta Carinae. I: The Nebulosity," *Astrophysical Journal* 111 (1950): 408 and fig. 1.

5. Gehrz and Ney, "Core of Eta Carinae," 5.

6. *Sky and Telescope* 45, no. 4 (1973): 207.

7. The term *H II region* was first popularized by Bengt Strömgren as a region of ionized hydrogen gas in space. An H I region, involving un-ionized hydrogen, consists of cold, dark, interstellar gas. See his "On the Density Distribution and Chemical Composition of the Interstellar Gas," *Astrophysical Journal* 108 (1948): 244. (At about 10,000 Kelvin, H II regions are far hotter than the 100 Kelvin H I regions.) Stewart Sharpless first suggested the use of "H II region" over "emission nebula" for regions like the Carinae and Orion nebulae: "An H II region is an entity defined not only in terms of the ionized gas but also in terms of the hot stars which are responsible for the ionization" ("A Catalogue of H II Regions," *Astrophysical Journal* Supplement 4 [1959]: 257).

8. B. J. Bok, "The Bigger and Better Milky Way."

9. Bok and Bok, "Integrated Magnitudes and Colours of Young Associations in the Large Magellanic Cloud." Cf. chap. 10, nn. 29, 30.

10. P. F. Bok and C. D. Boyd, "Proper Motions of Forty Three Cluster-Type Variables," *Harvard Bulletin* 893 (1933). See chap. 3, n. 8.

11. Arlene and Clifford Newman, personal communication.

12. P. F. Bok to B. J. Bok in Paris, August 28, 1971.

13. P. F. Bok, Australia, to B. J. Bok, Paris, Sept. 3, 1971.

14. J. M. Greenberg and H. C. van de Hulst, *Interstellar Dust and Related Topics* (Dordrecht and Boston: D. Reidel, 1973). Although Bok did not offer a

paper, S. Tapia's presentation on "The U, B, V, R, and I Extinctions in Four Areas of the Southern Coalsack" (44–51) extends a research project Bok began in 1971 to undertake a star count program in this dark nebula, and announces the presence of several globules there.

15. Bok, "Brief Memorandum about Priscilla Fairfield Bok," 5.

16. J. Sherry, interview, February 8, 1986.

17. Bart Bok, handwritten note, no addressee, no date other than July 1974.

18. R. Weymann to B. J. Bok, October 28; this letter had no year, but since it discussed Bok's resignation from the IAU Vice-Presidency it was likely 1973.

19. Earlier Dietz articles were reprinted in 1968 in an undated booklet called *A Science Editor Visits the University of Arizona*.

20. R. E. White, interview, July 29, 1991.

21. Concert program, The Arizona Chamber Orchestra, October 16, 1975.

22. B. J. Bok to Dean R. L. Hull, College of Fine Arts, University of Arizona, December 11, 1975.

23. R. L. Hull to B. J. Bok, December 17, 1975.

24. Form for donation of body for educational and research purposes, University of Arizona Medical Center, December 29, 1967.

25. R. Weymann, personal communication, August 7, 1991.

26. The words are taken from Bart Bok's own copy of the *Appalachian Spring* album: *Great American Ballets*, vol. 2. Aaron Copland, *Rodeo (Four Dance Episodes) & Appalachian Spring (Suite)*, Robert Irving conducting the Concert Arts Orchestra, Seraphim records.

27. B. J. Bok, *A Memorial Bench for Priscilla Fairfield Bok (1896–1975)*, privately printed announcement by Bok, May 14, 1976.

15. From Astrology to Valentine's Night

1. I. Velikovsky, *Worlds in Collision* (New York: Doubleday, 1950). As a student, University of North Carolina astronomer Gerald Cecil came up with the "Veli-unlikli" quip.

2. B. J. Bok and M. W. Mayall, "Scientists Look at Astrology," *The Scientific Monthly* 52 (1941): 233.

3. B. J. Bok, "A Critical Look at Astrology," *The Humanist* 35, no. 5 (1975): 6. Article later reprinted in *Objections to Astrology* (Buffalo, N. Y.: Prometheus Books, 1975).

4. G. M. Hopkins, *The Sermons and Devotional Writings of Gerard Manley Hopkins*, ed. C. Devlin, S. J. (London: Oxford University Press, 1959), 264.

5. D. T. Regan, *For the Record: From Wall Street to Washington* (San Diego: Harcourt Brace Jovanovich, 1988), 73.

6. Bok, "Scientists Look at Astrology," 233–35.

7. Ibid., 242.

8. Ibid., 244.

9. The story was constructed from interviews with Bok, with assistance from S. O'Marr, *My World of Astrology* (New York: Fleet Publishing, 1965).

10. R. Dilworth, "Bok Calls Astrology Scientifically Empty," *Arizona Daily Wildcat*, February 2, 1971.

11. B. T. Lynds to D. Levy, September 7, 1991.

12. Ibid.

13. E. Maggio, "Astrology attacked by Dr. Bok," *Arizona Daily Star*, December 30, 1970.

14. "Objections to Astrology," *The Humanist* 35, no. 5 (1975): 5–6.

15. R. Revelle to P. Kurtz, July 2, 1975.

16. G. E. Uhlenbeck to P. Kurtz, July 7, 1975.

17. *Objections to Astrology*, 10.

18. B. J. Bok, "A Critical Look at Astrology," 6.

19. Ibid., 8.

20. Ibid., 9.

21. *Boston Globe*, Sept 3, 1975.

22. *The Humanist* 35 (1975): 20–27.

23. *People*, Sept. 22, 1975, 16.

24. G. F. Will, "'Must' theory of scientists draws notice," *Journal World*, September 19, 1975.

25. P. Horn, News Line: "Scientists Look to the Stars, And Find Them False," *Psychology Today* 9, no. 9 (1976): 23.

26. Mary Ann Van Sickle to T. George Harris, Editor in Chief, *Psychology Today*, February 13 (Friday), 1976.

27. B. J. Bok, "Debunking Astrology," *Physics Today* 30 (1977): 83.

28. *TWA Ambassador*, inside back cover, December 1975, enclosed with J. Eddy to B. J. Bok, Jan. 5, 1976.

29. B. T. Lynds, personal communication, August 6, 1991.

30. So delighted was Bart with this friendship that it was one of the first things he discussed with me, on January 4, 1980.

31. "Have you *ever* seen a profile like that?"

32. B. J. Bok to R. D. Brown and J. R. Philip, September 23, 1977.

33. L. Goldberg, "American Astronomers Visit China—I," *Sky and Telescope* 56, no. 4 (1978): 280.

34. The ten formed a formidable, well-chosen group: Victor Blanco (Cerro-Tololo Interamerican Observatory), E. Margaret Burbidge (University of California at San Diego), Leo Goldberg, chairman (Kitt Peak National Observatory), David S. Heeschen (National Radio Astronomy Observatory), George H. Herbig

(Lick Observatory), Allan R. Sandage (Hale Observatories), Martin Schwarz-
schild (Princeton University), Nathan Sivin (University of Pennsylvania), Harlan
J. Smith (University of Texas), and Charles H. Towns (University of California
at Berkeley). *Sky and Telescope* 56, no. 4 (1978): 279.

35. To preserve her privacy, I have chosen to use a pseudonym.

36. M. Crawford, interview, September 1, 1990; also M. Shapley Matthews,
interview, December 12, 1990.

37. Announcement of Selby Lecture, CSIRO, Division of Radiophysics,
H. C. Minnett, chief.

38. D. McGee, Announcement for Bok lectures in Sydney, October 1978.

39. D. N. Phipps, Introduction to Bok lecture, October 26, 1978.

40. B. J. Bok, [IAU symposium comments on star formation in the Magellanic Clouds] in T. de Jong and A. Maeder, *Star Formation* (Dordrecht and Boston: D. Reidel, 1977), 22–23; "Globules and Star Formation," *The Moon and
the Planets* 19 (1978): 153–56.

41. B. J. Bok, M. E. Sim, and T. G. Hawarden, "A Conspicuous Globule in
the Southern Coalsack," *Nature* 266 (1977): 145–47.

42. B. J. Bok, "Dark Nebulae, Globules, and Protostars" (Bruce Medal Lecture), *Publications of the Astronomical Society of the Pacific* 89 (1977): 597–611.
Bok dedicated this article "to the memory of my wonderful wife, Priscilla Fairfield Bok."

43. B. J. Bok, "The Universe Today," in *Man's Place in the Universe* (Tucson:
College of Liberal Arts, University of Arizona, 1977), 94–139.

44. B. J. Bok, "The Star Clouds of Magellan," *Natural History* 88 (1979): 86–
91.

45. B. J. Bok, "Harlow Shapley," *Biographical Memoirs, National Academy of
Sciences* 49 (1978): 241–91.

46. *The Sydney Morning Herald*, Oct. 19, 1978.

16. Last Years

1. K. Johnson to D. Levy, June 3, 1991.

2. An interesting historical account of this early work is in L. Kühn's *The
Milky Way: The Structure and Development of our Star System* (New York: John
Wiley and Sons, 1982), 17–19.

3. B. J. Bok and P. F. Bok, *The Milky Way*, 3d ed. (Cambridge, Mass.: Harvard
University Press, 1956), 239.

4. The different values come from S. Newcomb, *Astronomy for Everybody*
(1902; rpt. New York: Doubleday, 1932), 309–10; B. J. Bok, *Distribution of the
Stars in Space*, xiii; Bok and Bok, *Milky Way*, 1st ed. (1941), 91; 3rd ed. (1956),
119; 4th ed. (1974), 118; 5th ed. (1981), 152.

5. Bok and Bok, *Milky Way*, 3rd ed., 248.

6. Bok and Bok, *Milky Way*, 4th ed., 243.

7. B. M. Tinsley, "Theoretical Overview: Interactions Among the Galaxy's Components," in W. B. Burton, *The Large-Scale Characteristics of the Galaxy*, International Astronomical Union Symposium no. 84 (Boston: D. Reidel, 1979), 431. See also Bok and Bok, *Milky Way*, 5th ed., 170–72.

8. Ibid.

9. Advertising circular for "The Big and Beautiful Milky Way," October 10, 1978, University of Tasmania.

10. D. P. Clemens, J. L. Yun, and M. H. Heyer, "Bok Globules and Small Molecular Clouds: Deep *IRAS* Photometry and ^{12}CO Spectroscopy," *Astrophysical Journal Supplement Series* 75 (1991): 877–904.

11. B. J. Bok, "Discussion on the Teaching of Astronomy," *Transactions of the International Astronomical Union* 12B (1966): 635.

12. Ibid., 636.

13. Ibid.

14. B. J. Bok to S. D. Sinvhai, Bangalore, Mar. 14, 1980.

15. B. J. Bok, draft of editorial intended for *Bulletin of the Astronomical Society of India*, April 10, 1980, Bombay. The published version appeared with only stylistic changes; e.g. "all is not well" was replaced with "However, everything in Indian Astronomy is not as it should be." *Bulletin of the Astronomical Society of India* 8, no. 1 (1980): 3–4.

16. B. J. Bok to K. D. Abhyankar, July 28, 1980.

17. B. J. Bok to M. C. Pande, July 28, 1980.

18. B. J. Bok, "Reflections: Solar Eclipse '81," *Sky and Telescope* 62, no. 4 (1981): 322–23.

19. L. Goldberg and T. Gehrels, "Reply to Bok," letter, *Sky and Telescope* 63, no. 5 (1982): 445.

20. B. J. Bok to E. R. Mustel, November 18, 1982.

21. Orlov describes his experiences in *Dangerous Thoughts: Memoirs of a Russian Life*, trans. T. P. Whitney (New York: Morrow, 1986).

22. "Dissident in Soviet Union is Hurt in a Camp," *New York Times* June 9, 1983.

23. B. J. Bok to V. A. Ambartsumian, July 19, 1983.

24. V. A. Ambartsumian to B. J. Bok, July 21, 1982; quoted by permission of Bok.

25. B. J. Bok, "Iraq's New National Observatory," *Sky and Telescope* 63, No. 7 (1982): 35.

26. Z. Kopal, personal communication, February 1992.

27. B. J. Bok, "Some Current Trends in Milky Way Research," *Astrophysical Journal* 273, no. 2 (1983): 411–20. Bok's Russell lecture was published in *Astro-*

physical Journal two months after his death, followed by a succinct obituary (p. 420) that reflected his career in these two sentences: "Bart J. Bok: Died 1983 August 5, ending a career as researcher, director of several observatories, teacher, and supervisor of many graduate theses. Dr. Bok stimulated many of the early researchers in radio astronomy, and has been a pioneer in and coordinator of galactic structure studies."

28. J. and J. Anderson, personal communication, July 10, 1991.

29. B. J. Bok, "Magellanic Clouds," *Annual Review of Astronomy and Astrophysics* 4 (1966): 95–144.

30. B. J. Bok, interview, Fall 1982 (a few weeks after his China trip).

31. S. van den Bergh and K. S. de Boer, *Structure and Evolution of the Magellanic Clouds*, International Astronomical Union Symposium no. 108 (Boston: D. Reidel, 1984), x. The story about "making bloody sense" is courtesy E. J. Maggio.

The Writings of
Bart and Priscilla Bok

This bibliography is based on a partial list provided by Bart Bok. I have tried to make it as complete as possible, and I thank Arthur A. Hoag for providing a record of Priscilla Bok's writings.

Works by Bart J. Bok

1927

"On the Oscillating Ca+ Lines in O and B Stars." *Bulletin of the Astronomical Institute of the Netherlands* 4:9–12.

1928

"On the Systematic Error in the Proper Motions of Boss' System." *Bulletin of the Astronomical Institute of the Netherlands* 5:1–8.

And van Rhijn, P. J., and W. J. Klein-Wassink. *The Proper Motions of 2292 Stars Derived from Plates Taken at the Radcliffe Observatory.* Publication of the Kapteyn Astronomical Laboratory, no. 42.

1929

And van Rhijn, P. J. *Photovisual Magnitudes for the Selected Area at Declination +75°, Derived from Plates Taken at the Leander McCormick Observatory by H. L. Alden and P. van de Kamp.* Publication of the Kapteyn Astronomical Laboratory, no. 44.

1930

"Note on Galactic Rotation." *Harvard College Observatory Bulletin*, no. 876, 8–14.

"The Spectrum of Eta Carinae." *Popular Astronomy* 38:399–400.

1931

The Analysis of Star Counts. Harvard College Observatory Circular, no. 371.

The Secular Parallaxes of the Stars of Different Apparent Magnitude and Galactic Latitude. Publication of the Kapteyn Astronomical Laboratory, no. 45.

1932

A *Study of the Eta Carinae Region.* Harvard College Observatory Reprint, no. 77. [This is the published version of Bok's dissertation.]

1934

"The Apparent Clustering of External Galaxies." *Harvard College Observatory Bulletin*, no. 895, 1–8. Reprinted in *Nature*, 133:578.

The Stability of Moving Clusters. Harvard College Observatory Circular, no. 384.

1935

The Percentage of Dwarfs among the Faint G and K Stars in High Galactic Latitudes. Harvard College Observatory Circular, no. 400.

1936

"Galactic Dynamics and the Cosmic Time-scale." *The Observatory* 59:76–84.

1937

The Distribution of the Stars in Space. Chicago: University of Chicago Press.

And Lindsay, E. M. "Investigations of Galactic Structure, I: Counts of Stars with Apparent Photographic Magnitudes Brighter Than 13.5 in the Southern Hemisphere." *Harvard College Observatory Annals* 105:255–95.

And McCuskey, S. W. "First List of Objective Prism Velocities (fields in Taurus and Cygnus)." *Harvard College Observatory Annals* 105:327–55.

And Swann, W. F. "Photovisual Magnitudes for the Selected Areas at Declination +75°." *Harvard College Observatory Annals* 105:371–81.

1938

"Current Milky Way Problems." *Scientific Monthly* 46:397–415.

"Star Counts." *Transactions of the International Astronomical Union* 6:282–83.

And Lindsay, E. M. "Note on the Stellar Distribution in the Vicinity of a Southern Galactic Window." *Proceedings of the National Academy of Sciences* 24:4–9.

1939

"Galactic Density Gradients." *Astrophysical Journal* 90:249–70.

"Report on Astronomy." *Popular Astronomy* 47:356–72. Translated into Chinese by Dr. Li Hen and published by the Science Society of China, Shanghai, 1940.

And Whipple, F. L. "Preliminary Observations of Nova Monocerotis" (Abstract). *Publications of the American Astronomical Society* 10:32.

1940

And MacRae, D. A. "Tests of R. W. Wood's Bi-prism Grating" (Abstract). *Publications of the American Astronomical Society* 10:60.

And Rendall, J. M. "The Milky Way in Monoceros" (Abstract). *Publications of the American Astronomical Society* 10:45.

1941

"The Exchange of Astronomical Publications during the War." *Popular Astronomy* 49 (January): 57–58.

"Galactic Problems" (Abstract). *Publications of the American Astronomical Society* 10:220.

"Mexico's New National Observatory." *Sky and Telescope* 1, no. 2:3–4.

And Bok, Priscilla F. *The Milky Way.* 1st ed. Philadelphia: Blakiston Co.

And MacRae, D. A. "The Stellar Distribution in High and Intermediate Latitudes." *Annals of the New York Academy of Sciences* 42:219–58.

And Mayall, M. W. "Scientists Look at Astrology." *Scientific Monthly* 52:233–44.

1942

Navigation in Emergencies. Washington, D.C.: United States Coast Guard.

"A Search for Comparatively Unobscured Fields in Low Galactic Latitudes." *Publications of the American Astronomical Society* 10:246–47.

1943

"Recent Progress in Astrophysics: Galactic Research in Holland during 1942." *Astrophysical Journal* 98:235–39.

"Stars and Nebulae." In American Association of Scientific Workers, Boston-Cambridge Branch, *Science from Shipboard: A Simple Manual of Information and Instruction for Those who Cross the Seas in Ships to Fight for Freedom.* Washington, D.C.: Science Service.

1944

"The Milky Way." *Popular Astronomy* 52:261–318. Reprinted, Harvard College Observatory Reprint, no. 260.

And Wright, F. W. *Basic Marine Navigation*. Boston: Houghton Mifflin.

1945

"An Adventure in Galactic Research." *Popular Astronomy* 53:340–46.

"Galactic Structure in Puppis and Vela" (Abstract). *Astronomical Journal* 51:121.

"Tonantzintla Revisited." *Sky and Telescope* 4, no. 6:3–5.

And Amdur, I. Letter, *New York Times*, September 2.

And Bok, P. F. *The Milky Way*. 2d ed. Philadelphia: Blakiston.

And Rendall-Arons, J. M. "The Milky Way in Monoceros." *Astrophysical Journal* 101:280–99.

And Wright, F. W. "The Stellar Distribution for Two Southern Fields." *Astrophysical Journal* 101:300–13.

1946

"Red Magnitudes in Harvard Standard Region C5." *Harvard College Observatory Bulletin*, no. 918, 19–22.

"Science in UNESCO." *Scientific Monthly* 63:327–32.

"The Time-scale of the Universe." *Monthly Notices of the Royal Astronomical Society* 106:61–75.

1947

"The First National UNESCO Conference." *American Scientist* 35:371–76.

And Reilly, E. F. "Small Dark Nebulae." *Astrophysical Journal* 105:255–57. [First discussion of what later became known as Bok Globules.]

1948

The Center of the Galaxy. Astronomical Society of the Pacific Leaflet, no. 230.

"Dimensions and Masses of Dark Nebulae." *Harvard Observatory Monograph*, no. 7, 53ff. (Centennial Symposia, December 1946).

"Maelkevejens Centrum." *Nordisk Astronomisk Tidskrift* (Copenhagen), 117ff.

"UNESCO and the Physical Sciences." *Bulletin of the Atomic Scientists* 4:343ff.

And Boutelle, B. D. and M. Olmsted. "Space Reddening and Density Gradients for the Anti-center" (Abstract). *Astronomical Journal* 53:197.

1949

"Science and the Maintenance of Peace." *Science* 109:131–37.

"UNESCO: A Work in Progress." *Physics Today* 2, no. 7:16–17, 28–32.

And Olmsted, M. "Colors of Four Faint Cepheids in Cygnus." *Harvard College Observatory Bulletin*, no. 919, 1–6. Abstract in *Astronomical Journal* 54 (1949): 123.

And Olmsted, M. and B. D. Boutelle. "The Milky Way at the Junction of Gemini, Monoceros and Orion." *Astrophysical Journal* 110:21–39. Reprinted, Harvard College Observatory Reprint, no. 331.

1950

"The Milky Way." *Scientific American* 182, no. 2:30–39.

"The Southern Milky Way." *Monthly Notes of the Astronomical Society of Southern Africa* 9:43ff.

And Olmsted, M. "The Use of the Schmidt Telescope in Stellar Photometry." *Popular Astronomy* 58:257–67.

1951

"The Cloud Structure of the Interstellar Absorbing Medium." *Monthly Notes of the Astronomical Society of Southern Africa* 10:51ff.

"The Depths of the Milky Way." *Popular Astronomy* 59:501–11.

"Dynamics and Evolution of Star Clusters." *Sky and Telescope* 10:211, 213, 239–40.

"Freedom and Science." In *UNESCO: Freedom and Culture*, 229–66. New York: Columbia University Press.

"Irregularities in the Galactic Absorbing Layer." *Harvard College Observatory Bulletin*, no. 920, 1–5.

"A Photoelectric Sequence of Magnitudes and Colors for Selected Area 141" (Abstract). *Astronomical Journal* 56:35.

"Progress of Photoelectric Work at the Boyden Station, Sept. 1950–May 1951." *Monthly Notes of the Astronomical Society of Southern Africa* 10:39ff.

And Cillié, G. "The Photoelectric Light Curve of TW Ceti." *Harvard College Observatory Bulletin*, no. 920, 29–31.

1952

"Perspective on South Africa." *Harper's Magazine*, July 1952, 51–59.

"The Southern Sky." *Scientific American* 187, no. 1:46–57.

"Spiral Arms of the Galaxy." *Sky and Telescope* 11:138–39.

"Studies of the Southern Milky Way." *Proceedings of the American Philosophical Society* 96:540–55.

And van Wijk, U. "Photoelectric Colors of B stars in Five Regions of the Southern Milky Way." *Astronomical Journal* 57:213–22. Reprinted, Harvard College Observatory Reprint, no. 45 (2d ser.). Abstract in *Astronomical Journal* 56 (1952): 122.

1953

"Three Weeks of Symposia, I and II." *Sky and Telescope* 31:12–14, 45–49.

And Bester, M. J., and C. M. Wade. "De sudlesse Spiralarm unserer Milchstrasse." *Physicalische Blatten* 9:24ff.

And Bester, M. J., and C. M. Wade. "A Search of Southern H-Emission Regions" (Abstract). *Astronomical Journal* 58:36.

1954

"Astronomical Problems Connected with the 21-cm Line." *Journal of Geophysical Research* 59:192ff.

"The New Radio Astronomy." *The American Scholar* 23:449–58.

"Radio Studies of Interstellar Hydrogen." *Sky and Telescope* 13:408–12.

And Connolly, J. K. "Star Counts for the Section of the Milky Way Between Galactic Longitudes 160° and 173°." *Astronomical Journal* 59:384–87.

And Ewen, H. I. "Research of the 21-cm Radiation at Agassiz Station" (Abstract). *Astronomical Journal* 59:318.

1955

"Conditions for Photoelectric Research at the Boyden and Agassiz Stations of Harvard Observatory" (Abstract). *Astronomical Journal* 60:29–30.

"Gas and Dust in Interstellar Clouds." *Astronomical Journal* 60:146–48.

"Jodrell Bank Symposium on Radio Astronomy." *Sky and Telescope* 15:21–27.

"New Science of Radio Astronomy." *Scientific Monthly* 80:333–45.

"Photographic Studies of Southern Emission Nebulae." *International Astronomical Union Symposium*, no. 2, 27–28.

"The Relative Concentration of Interstellar Hydrogen and Cosmic Dust." *Mémoires de la Société Royale des Sciences de Liège* (4th ser.) 15:480–95.

"Science in International Cooperation." *Science* 121:843–47.

"Seeing as a Factor in the Selection of a Site for a Photoelectric Observatory" (Abstract). *Astronomical Journal* 60:32.

"Size and Type of Telescope for a Photoelectric Observatory" (Abstract). *Astronomical Journal* 60:31.

And Bester, M. J., and C. M. Wade. "Catalog of H II Regions in the Milky Way for Longitudes 250°–355°" *Proceedings of the American Academy of Arts and Sciences (Daedalus)* 86:9ff.

And Kourganoff, V. "The Committee for the Distribution of Astronomical Literature and the Astronomical News Letters." In A. Beer, ed., *Vistas in Astronomy*, vol. 1, 22–25. New York: Pergamon Press.

And Lawrence, R. S., and T. K. Menon. "Radio Observations (21-cm) of Dense Dark Nebulae." *Publications of the Astronomical Society of the Pacific* 67:108–12.

And Wade, C. M. "Associations of OB Stars and H II Regions in the Southern Hemisphere." *Publications of the Astronomical Society of the Pacific* 67:103–7.

And Wade, C. M. "A Preliminary Classification System for H-Emission Nebulae." *International Astronomical Union Symposium*, no. 2, 35–36.

Foreword, R. Wyler and G. Ames, *The Gro Hen Book of Astronomy* (New York: Simon and Schuster).

1956

"The George R. Agassiz Radio Telescope of Harvard Observatory." *Nature* 178:232–34.

"Mount Stromlo Observatory." *Southern Stars* 17:44ff.

"Milky Way Structure in Sagittarius and Carina: A Study in Contrasts." In *Vistas in Astronomy*, vol. 2, 1522–38. New York: Pergamon Press.

"Palomar-Schmidt Star Counts for Two Heavily Obscured Fields." *Astronomical Journal* 61:309–16. Reprinted, Harvard College Observatory Reprint, no. 87 (1956), 2d ser.

"21-cm Astrophysics." In *Het Voetspoor van Kapteyn*.

"Virginia Conference on the Cosmic Distance Scale." *Sky and Telescope* 15:345–48.

1957

And Bok, Priscilla F. *The Milky Way*. 3d ed. Cambridge, Mass: Harvard University Press.

1958

The Astronomer's Universe. Cambridge: Cambridge University Press; Melbourne: Melbourne University Press.

"Exploring the Southern Skies." *Hemisphere* 10:2ff.

"The Paris Symposium on Radio Astronomy." *Sky and Telescope* 17:620–23.

"World's Astronomers Meet in Moscow." *Sky and Telescope* 18:7–11.

And Bok, P. F. "Four Photoelectric Sequences for the Southern Hemisphere" (Abstract). *Astronomical Journal* 63:303.

1959

"The Arms of the Galaxy." *Scientific American* 201, no. 6:92–104.

"The Spiral Structure of our Galaxy" (Letter). *The Observatory* 79:58–62.

And Basinski, J. M., and K. Gottlieb. "Optical Identification of Southern Radio Sources." In *Paris Symposium on Radio Astronomy* (IAU Symposium, no. 9), 514–22. Stanford: Stanford University Press.

1960

"Concerning Protostars." In *Source Book in Astronomy 1900–1950*, edited by H. Shapley, 300–15. Cambridge, Mass.: Harvard University Press.

"The Observational Basis for Stellar Evolution." In *From Nucleus to Universe: A Course of Selected Lectures in Physics and Astronomy*, ed. S. Butler and H. Messel. Sydney: University of Sydney, Shakespeare Head Press.

"The Search for New Observatory Sites in Australia." *Journal of the Royal Astronomical Society of Canada* 54, no. 6:257–68. Reprinted, Mount Stromlo Observatory Reprint, no. 33 (1960).

"Trends in Astronomical Research for Australia." *Australian Journal of Science* 22.

"Two Famous Dutch Astronomers." *Sky and Telescope* 20:74–76.

"Wolf's Method of Measuring Dark Nebulae." In *Source Book in Astronomy, 1900–1950*, ed. H. Shapley, 285–88. Cambridge, Mass.: Harvard University Press.

And Bok, P. F. "Four Standard Sequences in the Southern Hemisphere." *Monthly Notices of the Royal Astronomical Society* 121:531–42.

1961

"The Interstellar Medium." *Sky and Telescope* 22, no. 2:86–91.

"The Southern Milky Way." *Proceedings of the Royal Institution of Great Britain* 38:552–74. Reprinted, Mount Stromlo Observatory Reprint, no. 45.

And Bok, P. F., and J. M. Basinski. "Colour-Magnitude Arrays for Two Associations in the Large Magellanic Cloud." *Monthly Notices of the Royal Astronomical Society* 123:487–96. Abstract in *Astronomical Journal* 66:279. Reprinted, Mount Stromlo Observatory Reprint, no. 51.

1962

"Problems of Stellar Evolution." *Australian Mathematics Teacher* 18:25ff.

And Bok, P. F. "Integrated Magnitudes and Colours of Young Associations in the Large Magellanic Cloud." *Monthly Notices of the Royal Astronomical Society* 124:435–44. Reprinted, Mount Stromlo Observatory Reprint, no. 67.

1963
"The Future of Astronomy in Australia." *Australian Journal of Science* 25:281–87. [Contains his controversial address regarding the Australian Academy of Sciences.]
"How Space Research May Benefit Astronomy." *Australian Science Teachers Journal* 9:4ff.
"An International Discussion of Milky Way Research." *Sky and Telescope* 26:4–7.
"Our Expanding Universe." Donovan Memorial Trust Lecture. *Proceedings of the Royal Society of Victoria* 76:29ff.
"A Proposed British Commonwealth Southern Observatory." *Australian Journal of Science* 26:6ff.
And Bok, P. F., and J. A. Graham. "The Distance of a Group of Early Type Stars in Norma." *Publications of the Astronomical Society of the Pacific* 75:514–19.

1964
"Astronomer Looks at Science Education." *Australian Science Teachers Journal* 10:29–31, 33–35, 37–39.
"Education for Women: Forgotten Part of our Work Force." *Canberra Times,* January 15, 1964.
"Galactic and Extragalactic Structure." Tata Institute of Fundamental Research (Bombay). London: Published for the Tata Institute by Oxford University Press.
"The Large Cloud of Magellan." *Scientific American* 210, no. 1:32–41.
"An Outline of the Spiral Structure of the Southern Milky Way (220° <1" <335°)." In *IAU/URSI Symposium,* no. 20, 147–55. Canberra: Australian Academy of Sciences.
Siding Spring Observatory. Pamphlet. Sydney: Land Printing House.
"A Young Assocation in the Large Magellanic Cloud." In *IAU/URSI Symposium,* no. 20, 335–42. Canberra: Australian Academy of Sciences.
And Basinski, J. M. "Stellar Distribution Near the South Galactic Pole." *Mount Stromlo Memoir,* no. 16; vol. 4, no. 1.
And Gollnow, H., J. V. Hindman, and M. Mowat. "Radial Velocities Associated with Selected Emission Nebulae in the Small Magellanic Cloud." *Australian Journal of Physics* 17:404–8.

1965

"Astronomy in the Southern Hemisphere." In the yearbook *Science and Humanity 1965*. Moscow: Znaniya Publishing House.

"Closing remarks." In *Symposium on the Magellanic Clouds*, ed. J. Hindman and B. Westerlund, 93–95. Fyshwick, A.C.T., Australia: Union Offset Co., for Mount Stromlo Observatory.

"The Future of Galactic Research." Pawsey Memorial Lecture. *Australian Physicist* 2:79ff.

"The Future of Galactic Research." *Journal of the Astronomical Society of Victoria* 18:62ff.

"Shapley's Researches on the Magellanic Clouds." *Publications of the Astronomical Society of the Pacific* 77:416–21. Reprinted, Sproul Observatory Reprint, no. 150.

"Siding Spring Observatory." *Australian Physicist* 2:102ff.

"The Structure and Dynamics of our Galactic System." Report for IAU Commission 33. *Transactions of the International Astronomical Union* 12A:521–55.

And Bok, P. F., and J. M. Basinski. "Comparative Colour-magnitude Arrays for NGC 1929-37 and Surrounding Areas." In *Symposium on the Magellanic Clouds*, 52–61. Mount Stromlo Observatory.

And Miller, M. J. "The Yale-Columbia Telescope at Mount Stromlo." *Southern Stars* 21:54ff.

1966

"Discussion on the Teaching of Astronomy." *Transactions of the International Astronomical Union* 12B:635–37.

"Graduate Training in Astronomy" (Letter). *Science* 154:590–92.

"Magellanic Clouds." *Annual Review of Astronomy and Astrophysics* 4:95–144.

"Mount Stromlo Observatory." *Hemisphere* 10, no. 3 (1966): 2–8.

"Otto Struve Memorial Symposium." *Sky and Telescope* 32:68–71.

"Radio Astronomy and the Galactic System." *Sky and Telescope* 32:271–74, 341–43.

Review of *Galactic Structure*, Blaauw and Schmidt, eds. *Sky and Telescope* 31:357–61.

"The Search for Faint-Blue Stars." In *International Astronomical Union Symposium*, no. 24, 228–30.

"Stellar Distribution at High Galactic Latitudes." *Transactions of the International Astronomical Union* 12B:435–36.

"Summary, Problems and Outlook." Concluding lecture, Hertsprung Memorial Symposium, Flagstaff, Arizona, 1964. In *Vistas in Astronomy*, ed. A. Beer, vol. 8, 221–27. New York: Pergamon Press.

And Basinski, J. M., and P. F. Bok. "A Color-Magnitude Array for a Dense Region of the Small Magellanic Cloud" (Abstract). *Publications of the Astronomical Society of the Pacific* 78:439–40.

And Bok, P. F., and J. A. Graham. "A Photometric Study of the I Scorpii Association." *Monthly Notices of the Royal Astronomical Society* 131:247–52.

And Kidd, C., and P. Routcliffe. "Photometric Observations of Supergiants in the Large Magellanic Cloud." *Publications of the Astronomical Society of the Pacific* 78:333–36.

1967

And Bok, P. F., and J. M. Basinski. "A Colour-Magnitude Array for a Region in the Core of the Small Magellanic Cloud." *Monthly Notices of the Royal Astronomical Society* 137:55–67.

"The Spiral Structure of Our Galaxy." *American Scientist* 55:375–99.

"Uco Van Wijk" (obituary notice). *Quarterly Journal of the Royal Astronomical Society* 8, no. 4 (1967): 386.

1968

"Some Trends in Galactic Research." *Publications of the Astronomical Society of the Pacific* 80:501–30.

And Gollnow, H., and M. Mowat. "Radial Velocities of OB Stars in Puppis and Norma." *The Observatory* 87:250–52.

1969

"The Magellanic Clouds." *Journal of the Royal Astronomical Society of Canada* 63:105–24.

"Report on Red Emulsion Eastman Kodak Special 098-01." *American Astronomical Society Photobulletin* 1:8–9.

"The Spiral Structure of Our Galaxy: I." *Sky and Telescope* 38:392–95.

And Bok, P. F. "Photometric Standards for the Southern Hemisphere." *Astronomical Journal* 74:1125–30. Erratum for article in *Astronomical Journal* 75 (1970): 665.

1970

Americana Encyclopedia Annual. Entries for Cosmic Rays, Gravitational Waves, High Resolution by Radio, Interstellar Matter, Pulsars, Radio Positions, Spiral Structure, and Ultraviolet Astronomy.

"Basic Problems on the Structure and Dynamics of Our Galaxy." In *Galactic Astronomy*, vol. 1., ed. Hong-Yee Chiu and A. Muriel, 1–120. New York: Gordon & Breach.

"The Spiral Structure of Our Galaxy: II." *Sky and Telescope* 39:21–25.

"Steward Observatory and the Department of Astronomy, University of Arizona." *Bulletin of the American Astronomical Society* 2, no. 1:135–44.

"Summary and Outlook." In *The Spiral Structure of Our Galaxy*, ed. W. Becker and G. Contopoulos, chap. 85, 457–73. Dordrecht and Boston: D. Reidel.

And Hine, A., and E. Miller. "A Progress Report on the Carina Spiral Feature." In *The Spiral Structure of Our Galaxy*, chap. 44, 246ff.

1971

"The Gum Nebula." *Sky and Telescope* 42:64–69. (Report on the symposium held at Goddard Space Flight Center, Maryland.)

"Harlow Shapley, Cosmographer." *The American Scholar* 40:470ff.

"Observational Evidence for Galactic Spiral Structure." In *Highlights of Astronomy*, ed. C. de Jager, 68–87. Dordrecht and Boston: D. Reidel.

And Cordwell, C. S., and R. H. Cromwell. "Globules." In *Dark Nebulae, Globules, and Protostars*, ed. B. T. Lynds, chap. 4, 33–56. Tucson: University of Arizona Press.

1972

"Annual Review of Astronomy." In *Encyclopedia Americana Annual*.

"The Birth of Stars." *Scientific American* 227, no. 2:49–61.

"Comments on the Piddington Paper." Unpublished ms., December 15, 1972. A circular letter to "all who are interested in the spiral structure of our galaxy."

"Harlow Shapley: Cosmographer and Humanitarian." *Sky and Telescope* 44:354–57.

"Het ontstaan van sterren en planeten." *Intermediair* 16:1ff.

"Updating Galactic Spiral Structure." *American Scientist* 60:708–22.

And Abell, G., R. E. Berendzen, E. W. Miller, D. W. Goldsmith, H. M. Gurin, J. D. Trasco, and D. J. van Blerkom. *Guidelines for Employment Opportunities in Astronomy*. Tucson: University of Arizona Multilith Bureau.

And Bok, P. F., and E. W. Miller. "Photometric Standards for the Southern Hemisphere: II." *Astronomical Journal* 77:733–44. Erratum for article in *Astronomical Journal* 78 (1973): 1021. Also special printing, Steward Observatory, 1971.

1973

"The Appearance of the Gum Nebula." In *The Gum Nebula and Related Problems*, ed. S. Maran, J. Brandt, and T. Stecher, 148–51. Washington: National Aeronautics and Space Administration.

"New Problems in Astrometry." *Sky and Telescope* 46:291–94.

President's Report. Tucson: University of Arizona Multilith Bureau. [A presidential address delivered on December 4, 1973 at the Tucson meeting of the American Astronomical Society.]

The State of Astronomy. Tucson: University of Arizona Multilith Bureau. [A presidential address delivered on January 10, 973 at the Las Cruces meeting of the American Astronomical Society.]

Compiled with Argue, A. N., and E. W. Miller. *A Catalogue of Photometric Sequences*. Tucson: University of Arizona Multilith Bureau.

Compiled with Argue, A. N., and E. W. Miller. *Supplement: A Catalogue of Photometric Sequences*. Tucson: University of Arizona Multilith Bureau.

And Cordwell, C. S. "A Study of Dark Nebulae." In *Molecules in the Galactic Environment*, ed. M. A. Gordon and L. E. Snyder, chap. 3, 53–91. New York: Wiley & Sons.

1974

"Probing Our Galaxy." In *Focus on the Stars*, ed. H. Messel and S. T. Butler, chaps. 1–4. Sydney: Shakespeare Head Press.

And Bok, P. F. *The Milky Way*. 4th ed. Cambridge, Mass.: Harvard University Press.

And McCarthy, C. C. "Optical Data for Selected Barnard Objects." *Astronomical Journal* 79:42–44.

1975

"A Critical Look at Astrology." *The Humanist* 35, no, 5:6ff. Reprinted in *Objections to Astrology*.

"Harlow Shapley and the Discovery of the Center of Our Galaxy." In *Copernican Volume of the National Academy of Sciences*. Cambridge, Mass.: M. I. T. Press.

And Jerome, L. *Objections to Astrology*. Buffalo: Prometheus Books.

1976

A *Memorial Bench for Priscilla Fairfield Bok (1896-1975)*. Privately printed announcement, May 14, 1976.

1977

IAU Symposium Comments on Star Formation in the Magellanic Clouds. In *Star Formation*, ed. T. de Jong and A. Maeder, 22–23. Dordrecht and Boston: D. Reidel.

"Dark Nebulae, Globules, and Protostars." Bruce Medal Lecture. *Publications of the Astronomical Society of the Pacific* 89:597–611.

"Debunking Astrology" (Letter). *Physics Today* 30, no. 1:83–84.

"Globules and Dark Nebulae" (Discussion). *The Observatory* 97:42–43.

"The Universe Today." In *Man's Place in the Universe*, ed. D. W. Corson, 94–139. Tucson: University of Arizona Press.

And Sim, M. E., and T. G. Hawarden. "A Conspicuous Globule in the Southern Coalsack." *Nature* 266:145–47.

1978

"Globules and Star Formation." *The Moon and the Planets* 19:153–55.

"Harlow Shapley." *Biographical Memoirs of the National Academy of Sciences* 49:241–91.

"Star Formation in or Very Close to a Southern Globule." *Publications of the Astronomical Society of the Pacific* 90:489.

1979

"The Promise of the Space Telescope." *Congressional Record*, vol. 125, pt. 11 (1979), 13504–6.

"Two Star Clouds of Magellan." *Natural History* 88, no. 6:86–91.

1980

"A Brief Memorandum about the Life and Career of Priscilla Fairfield Bok: 1896–1975." *Mira Newsletter* 3, nos. 1–2:2–6.

"The First Five Years of Jan Oort at Leiden, 1924–1929." In *Oort and the Universe*, ed. H. van Woerden, W. Brouw, and H. C. van de Hulst, 55–58. Dordrecht and Boston: D. Reidel.

Guest editorial, *Bulletin of the Astronomical Society of India* 8, no. 1:3–4.

1981

"Early Phases of Star Formation." *Sky and Telescope* 61:284–93.

"The Milky Way Galaxy." *Scientific American* 244, no. 3:92–120. Reprinted in Paul Hodge, ed., *The Universe of Galaxies*. New York: W. H. Freeman, 1981; and in T. Ferris, ed., *World Treasury of Physics, Astronomy, and Mathematics*. New York: Little, Brown and Co., 1991, 299–321.

"Reflections: Solar Eclipse '81." *Sky and Telescope* 62:322–23.

And Bok, P. F. *The Milky Way.* 5th ed. Cambridge, Mass.: Harvard University Press.

1982

"Disturbing News." Letter. *Arizona Daily Star,* November 2. A whimsical comment to a Nov. 2 *Star* article about the disappearance of natural gas in Arizona.

"Iraq's New National Observatory." *Sky and Telescope* 63:33–35.

1983

"Some Current Trends in Milky Way Research." Russell Lecture. *Astrophysical Journal* 273, pt. 1: 411–20.

1984

"A Bigger and Better Milky Way Galaxy." *Astronomy* 12:6–22.

Works by Priscilla Fairfield Bok

1916

"Observations of Sunspots at Boston University." *Popular Astronomy* 24:474.

1919

And Crawford, R. T., and Edith E. Cummings. "Elements and Ephemeris of Comet d 1919 (Finlay-Sasake)." *Lick Observatory Bulletin*, vol. 10, no. 325: 55. Reprinted, *Harvard College Observatory Bulletin*, no. 702.

And Cummings, E. E. "The Color Curve of the 12-inch Equatorial of the Lick Observatory." *Publications of the Astronomical Society of the Pacific* 31:25–33.

1920

And Cummings, E. E. "Further Note on the Color Curve of the 12-inch Equatorial of the Lick Observatory." *Publications of the Astronomical Society of the Pacific* 32:67.

1924

The Relation of Hydrogen Line Widths to Absolute Magnitude for Class A Stars. Harvard Observatory Circular, no. 264.

1925

And Prof. Losh. "Orbit of Shajn's Comet." *Harvard College Observatory Bulletin*, no. 818, 4.

1926
"Proper Motion of a Red Dwarf." *Harvard College Observatory Bulletin*, no. 834,
7.

1927
"Proper Motion of NGC 6231." *Harvard College Observatory Bulletin*, no. 843,
2–3.

1928
Proper Motions of 217 Southern M Stars. Harvard College Observatory Circular,
no. 322.

1933
And Boyd, C. D. "Proper Motions of Forty Three Cluster Type Variables." *Harvard College Observatory Bulletin*, no. 893, 1–6. [First reference to Priscilla
Fairfield Bok.]

1941
"A. J. Cannon." *Popular Astronomy* 49:282ff; *Publications of the Astronomical
Society of the Pacific* 53:168–70; Harvard College Observatory Reprint, no.
226.
And Bok, B. J. *The Milky Way*. 1st ed. Philadelphia: Blakiston.

1945
And Bok, B. J. *The Milky Way*. 2d ed. Philadelphia: Blakiston.

1951
And Bok, B. J. "A Photoelectric Sequence of Magnitudes and Colors for Selected
Area 141" (Abstract). *Astronomical Journal* 56:35.

1957
And Bok, B. J. *The Milky Way*. 3d. ed. Cambridge, Mass.: Harvard University
Press.

1958
And Bok, B. J. "Four Photoelectric Sequences in the Southern Hemisphere"
(Abstract). *Astronomical Journal* 63:303.

1960
And Bok, B. J. "Four Standard Sequences for the Southern Hemisphere."
Monthly Notices of the Royal Astronomical Society 121:531–42.

1961
And Bok, B. J., and J. M. Basinski. "Colour-Magnitude Arrays for Two Associations in the Large Magellanic Cloud." *Monthly Notices of the Royal Astronomical Society* 123:487–96. Abstract in *Astronomical Journal* 66:279. Reprinted, Mount Stromlo Observatory Reprint, no. 51.

1962
And Bok, B. J. "Integrated Magnitudes and Colours of Young Associations in the
Large Magellanic Cloud." *Monthly Notices of the Royal Astronomical Society*
124:435–44. Reprinted, Mount Stromlo Observatory Reprint, no. 67.

1963
And Bok, B. J., and J. A. Graham. "The Distance of a Group of Early Type Stars
in Norma." *Publications of the Astronomical Society of the Pacific* 75:514–19.

1965
And Bok, B. J., and J. M. Basinski. "Comparative Colour-Magnitude Arrays for
NGC 1929–37 and Surrounding Areas." In *Symposium on the Magellanic
Clouds*, 52–61. Mount Stromlo Observatory.

1966
And Basinski, J. M., and B. J. Bok. "A Color-Magnitude Array for a Dense Region of the Small Magellanic Cloud" (Abstract). *Publications of the Astronomical Society of the Pacific* 78:439–40.
And Bok, B. J., and J. A. Graham. "A Photometric Study of the I Scorpii Association." *Monthly Notices of the Royal Astronomical Society* 131:247–52.

1967
And Basinski, J. M., and B. J. Bok. "A Colour-Magnitude Array for a Region in
the Core of the Small Magellanic Cloud." *Monthly Notices of the Royal Astronomical Society* 137:55–67.

1969
And Bok, B. J. "Photometric Standards for the Southern Hemisphere." *Astronomical Journal* 74:1125–30. Erratum for article in *Astronomical Journal* 75
(1970): 665.

1972
And Bok, B J., and E. W. Miller. "Photometric Standards for the Southern
Hemisphere: II." *Astronomical Journal* 77:733–44. Erratum for article in *As-

tronomical Journal 78 (1973): 1021. Also special printing, Steward Observatory, 1971.

1974

And Bok, B. J. *The Milky Way.* 4th ed. Cambridge, Mass.: Harvard University Press.

1981

And Bok, B. J. *The Milky Way.* 5th ed. Cambridge, Mass.: Harvard University Press.

Bibliography

Asimov, I. *The Left Hand of the Electron.* New York: Doubleday, 1972.

Astronomical Society of the Pacific. *Mercury* 14 (1984). Bart J. Bok Memorial Issue. Edited by A. Fraknoi.

Bailey, S. I. *The History and Work of Harvard Observatory, 1839 to 1927: An Outline of the Origin, Development, and Researches of the Astronomical Observatory of Harvard College together with Brief Biographies of its Leading Members.* New York: McGraw-Hill Book Company, for the Observatory, 1931.

Brouwer, D. "Harvard Books on Astronomy." *American Scientist* 30, no. 2 (1942): 159–62.

Brown, P. L. *Comets, Meteorites, and Men.* London: Robert Hale and Company, 1973.

Cockburn, S., and D. Ellyard. *Oliphant: The Life and Times of Sir Mark Oliphant.* Adelaide: Axiom Books, 1981.

Constitution of the United Nations Educational, Scientific and Cultural Organization (Preamble). Adopted in London on November 16, 1945.

DeVorkin, D. *Interview with Dr. Bart J. Bok.* New York: American Institute of Physics, 1979.

Dilworth, R. "Bok Calls Astrology Scientifically Empty." *Arizona Daily Wildcat,* February 2, 1971.

Douglas, A. V. *The Life of Arthur Stanley Eddington.* London: Thomas Nelson and Sons, 1956.

Eddington, A. S. *The Internal Constitution of the Stars.* Cambridge: Cambridge University Press, 1926.

Eggen, O. J. "The Australian Commonwealth Observatory." *Sky and Telescope* 15, no. 8 (1956): 340–43.

Gascoigne, S. C. B. "Australian Astronomy since the Second World War." In *Australian Science in the Making*, ed. R. W. Home, 345–73. Sydney: Australian Academy of Science and Cambridge University Press, 1988.

———. "Bart Bok at Mount Stromlo." *Mercury* 13, no. 2 (1984): 45–47.

Gascoigne, S. C. B., K. M. Proust, and M. O. Robins. *The Creation of the Anglo-Australian Observatory*. Sydney: Cambridge University Press, 1990.

Gaviola, E. "Eta Carinae, I: The Nebulosity." *Astrophysical Journal* 111 (1950): 408–13.

Gehrz, R. D. and E. P. Ney. "The Core of Eta Carinae." *Sky and Telescope* 44, no. 1 (1972): 4–5.

Gingerich, O. "The Discovery of the Spiral Arms of the Milky Way." *Proceedings of the IAU Symposium*, no. 106. July 1983. Reprinted, Center for Astrophysics Preprint Series, no. 1847, 3.

Goldberg, L. "Donald Howard Menzel." *Sky and Telescope* 53, no. 4 (1977): 249.

Graham, J. A., C. M. Wade, and R. M. Price. "Bart J. Bok: A Memoir." *Biographical Memoirs of the National Academy of Sciences*, no. 64, forthcoming.

Greenberg, J. M., and H. C. van de Hulst. *Interstellar Dust and Related Topics*. Dordrecht and Boston: D. Reidel, 1973.

Greenstein, J. "Bart Jan Bok." In *Dark Nebulae, Globules, and Protostars*, edited by B. T. Lynds, v–viii. Tucson: University of Arizona Press, 1971.

Hall, J. "Bok Opposed to Reducing Scientific Ties with Chile." *Tucson Daily Citizen*, December 30, 1970.

Haramundanis, K. *Cecilia Payne-Gaposchkin: An Autobiography and Other Recollections*. Cambridge: Cambridge University Press, 1984.

Heeschen, D. S. "Harvard's New Radio Telescope." *Sky and Telescope* 15, no. 9 (1956): 388–90.

Hilliard, R. L. *The Steward Observatory 90-inch Reflector*. University of Arizona, dedication booklet, June 23, 1969.

Hoffleit, D. *Catalogue of Bright Stars*. 3d ed. New Haven: Yale University Press, 1964.

———. "Harvard Radio Telescope." *Sky and Telescope* 12, no. 3 (1953): 74.

Hopkins, G. M. *The Sermons and Devotional Writings of Gerard Manley Hopkins*. Edited by C. Devlin, S. J. London: Oxford University Press, 1959.

Horn, P. "Scientists Look to the Stars, and Find Them False." *Psychology Today* 9, no. 9 (1976): 23–24.

Hoyle, F. *The Black Cloud.* New York: Signet, 1959.

Hoyt, W. G. *Planets X and Pluto.* Tucson: University of Arizona Press, 1980.

Hubble, E. *The Realm of the Nebulae.* New Haven: Yale University Press, 1936. Reprinted, New York: Dover, 1958.

Hynek, J. A., and Dunlap, J. R. "Image Orthicon Astronomy." *Sky and Telescope* 28, no. 3 (1964): 126–30.

Jones, B. J., and L. G. Boyd. *The Harvard College Observatory: The First Four Directorships, 1839–1919.* Cambridge, Mass.: Belknap Press, 1971.

Kerr, F. "Australia's 210-foot Radio Telescope Project." *Sky and Telescope* 18, no. 12 (1959): 666–68.

Kronk, G. W. *Comets: A Descriptive Catalog.* Hillside, N. J.: Enslow, 1984.

Kühn, L. *The Milky Way: The Structure and Development of Our Star System.* New York: John Wiley and Sons, 1982.

Kuznick, P. J. *Beyond the Laboratory: Scientists as Political Activists in 1930s America.* Chicago: University of Chicago Press, 1987.

Goldberg, L. "American Astronomers Visit China, I." *Sky and Telescope* 56, no. 4 (1978): 279–82.

Goldberg, L., and T. Gehrels. "Reply to Bok" (letter). *Sky and Telescope* 63, no. 5 (1982): 445.

Laves, W., and C. Thomson. *UNESCO: Purpose, Progress, Prospects.* Bloomington: Indiana University Press, 1957.

Leavitt, H. *Periods of 25 Variable Stars in the Small Magellanic Cloud.* Harvard College Observatory Circular, no. 173 (1912).

Levy, D. H. "Bok Thoughts." *Journal of the Royal Astronomical Society of Canada* 78 (1984): 8–9.

———. *Clyde Tombaugh: Discoverer of Planet Pluto.* Tucson: University of Arizona Press, 1991.

———. *Observing Variable Stars: A Guide for the Beginner.* Cambridge: Cambridge University Press, 1989.

Lockwood, M. "The Sky." *Sky and Telescope* 1, no. 1 (1941): 7.

Lovell, A. C. B. "The Early History of the Anglo-Australian 150-inch Telescope (AAT)." *Quarterly Journal, Royal Astronomical Society* 26, no. 4 (1985): 393–455.

Lovi, G. "Uranography Yesterday and Today." In *Uranometria 2000.0,* ed. W. Tirion et al., xxxvi–xxxvii. Richmond, Va.: Willmann-Bell, 1987.

MacLeod, R. ed., *The Commonwealth of Science: ANZAAS and the Scientific Enterprise in Australia 1888–1988.* Melbourne: Oxford University Press, 1988.

Maggio, E. "Astrology attacked by Dr. Bok." *Arizona Daily Star,* December 30, 1970.

McCarthy, Sen. J. "State Department Employee Loyalty Investigation." *Hearings before a Subcommittee of the Committee on Foreign Relations.* (Senate Subcommittee on S. Res. 231.) 81st Cong. 2d sess. Senate Committee Hearings, vol. 946, no. 2:125–128, 1870.

Menzel, D. H. "The Telescope." *Sky and Telescope* 1, no. 1 (1941): 7.

Merton, G. "Comets." *Monthly Notices of the Royal Astronomical Society* 110 (1950): 173–78.

Meyer, M. C. and W. L. Sherman. *The Course of Mexican History.* New York: Oxford University Press, 1979.

Morgan, W., S. Sharpless, and D. Osterbrock, "Structure in the Neighborhood of the Sun," *Astronomical Journal* 57 (1952): 3. [This and a report in *Sky and Telescope* were the only formal announcements that our galaxy had been discovered to be a spiral galaxy.]

Nehru, J. *Toward Freedom: The Autobiography of Jawaharlal Nehru.* Boston: Beacon Press, 1967.

Orlov, Y. *Dangerous Thoughts: Memoirs of a Russian Life.* Translated by T. P. Whitney. New York: Morrow, 1986.

Peltier, L. C. *Starlight Nights: The Adventures of a Star-Gazer.* New York: Harper and Row, 1965.

Piaget, J. "The Right to Education in the Modern World." In *UNESCO: Freedom and Culture,* 69–119. New York: Columbia University Press, 1951.

Piddington, J. H. "The Density-Wave Theory of Galactic Spirals." *Astrophysical Journal* 179, no. 3 (1973): 755–70.

Reber, G. "Cosmic Static." *Astrophysical Journal* 91 (1940): 621–24.

Regan, D. T. *For the Record: From Wall Street to Washington.* San Diego: Harcourt Brace Jovanovich, 1988.

Robinson, L. J, "How S&T Came to Be." *Sky and Telescope,* 82, no. 5 (1991): 472–76.

Rudaux, L. and G. de Vaucouleurs. *Larousse Encyclopedia of Astronomy.* New York: Prometheus Books, 1959.

Shapley, H. "Astronomical Highlights of 1952." *Sky and Telescope* 12, no. 2 (1952): 45.

———. *Beyond the Observatory.* New York: Charles Scribner's sons, 1967.

———. *Galaxies.* Philadelphia: Blakiston, 1943.

———. "Harvard Observatory Director Appointed." *Sky and Telescope* 13, no. 5 (1954): 143.

————. "On the Nature and Cause of Cepheid Variation." *Astrophysical Journal* 40 (1914): 105–22.

————, ed. *Source Book in Astronomy 1900–1950*. Cambridge, Mass.: Harvard University Press, 1960.

————. *Through Rugged Ways to the Stars*. New York: Scribner's, 1969.

Shapley, H., and A. Ames. *A Survey of the External Galaxies Brighter than the Thirteenth Magnitude*. Cambridge, Mass.: Annals of the Astronomical Observatory of Harvard College, 1932.

Sherwood, R. E. *Roosevelt and Hopkins: An Intimate History*. New York: Harper & Brothers, 1948.

Strömgren, Bengt. "On the Density Distribution and Chemical Composition of the Interstellar Gas." *Astrophysical Journal* 108 (1948): 242–75.

Struve, O. "Galactic Co-ordinates." *Sky and Telescope* 17, no. 12 (1958): 611–14, 617.

————. "Galactic Exploration by Radio." *Sky and Telescope* 11, no. 9 (1952): 214–17.

————. "On the Calcium Clouds." *Popular Astronomy* 33 (1925): 639–53 and 34 (1926): 1–14.

Tinsley, B. M. "Theoretical Overview: Interactions Among the Galaxy's Components." In *The Large-Scale Characteristics of the Galaxy*, ed. W. B. Burton, 431ff. International Astronomical Union Symposium, no. 84. Dordrecht and Boston: D. Reidel, 1979.

Tombaugh, C. "The Great Perseus-Andromeda Stratum of Extra-Galactic Nebulae and Certain Clusters of Nebulae Therein as Observed at the Lowell Observatory." *Publications of the Astronomical Society of the Pacific* 49 (1937): 259ff.

Truman, Harry S. *The Private Papers of Harry S. Truman*. Edited by R. H. Ferrell. New York: Harper & Row, 1980.

TWA Ambassador. Advertisement inside back cover, December 1975, in letter from J. Eddy to B. J. Bok, January 5, 1976.

van den Bergh, S., and K. S. de Boer. *Structure and Evolution of the Magellanic Clouds*. International Astronomical Union Symposium, no. 108. Boston: D. Reidel, 1984.

Velikovsky, I. *Worlds in Collision*. New York: Doubleday, 1950.

Vsekhsvyatskii, S. K. *Physical Characteristics of Comets*. Jerusalem: Israel Program for Scientific Translations, for the National Aeronautics and Space Administration, 1964.

Walker, M. F. "Image-Tube Observations at Cerro Tololo." *Sky and Telescope* 40, no. 3 (1970): 132–38.

Whipple, F. L. *The Mystery of Comets.* Washington: Smithsonian Institution Press, 1985.

White, Raymond E. "Bart J. Bok: A Personal Memoir from a 'Grandson.'" *Sky and Telescope* 66 (1983): 303–6.

Will, G. F. "'Must' Theory of Scientists Draws Notice." *Journal World*, September 19, 1975.

Index

Florence, Arizona, state prison, 138–41
Foelsch, Kuno, 161
France, 50
Franck, James, 6
Freedom and Culture, 80
Frost, Edwin, 44
Fuller, Buckminster, 89

Galaxies, 39
Gale, Henry, 44
Galileo, 96
Gascoigne, S.C.B., 107, 109
Gehrels, Tom, letter to *Sky and Telescope*, 178–79
Genetics, Lamarckian school of, 81
George Russell Agassiz Fellowship, 21
Gerasimovicz, Boris, 90
Germany, 12, 50
Glaspey, John, 103, 127, 128
Globules, Bok, 63–67, 105–6, 135, 171, 176; hydroxyl radical (OII) of, detected, 135
Goldberg, Leo, 167, 168; letter to *Sky and Telescope*, 178–79
Goldwater, Barry, Senator, 176
Gonzales, Ricardo, 25
Gorton, John, 122
Göteberg, 12
Gottleib, Kurt, 100
Graham, Billy, 163
Graham, John, 127
Graham, Martha, 156
Greenbank, WV, 89
Greenstein, Jesse, 135
Greyback, the magpie, 120
Groningen, 3, 13, 15
Gum nebula, 137

Haarlem, 2
Hague, The, 3

Hale, George, 44
Halley, Edmond, 29
Hamburg, 12
Hamlet, castle of, 12
Haro, Guillermo, 171
Harvard Books on Astronomy, The (series), 61
Harvard College Observatory, Building "D", 33, 34
Harvard Observatory parties, 34
Harvard Observatory Philharmonic Orchestra, 34
Harvard Observatory Pinafore, 22ff, 26
Harvill, Richard, 126
Hayden Planetarium, New York, 49
Hayworth, Lee, 130
Heiles, Carl, 135
Heisenberg, Werner, 6
Helsinki Accords on human rights, 179
Helsinki Watch, 179
Hemel en Dampkring, 4, 19
Henry Draper Catalogue, 25
Herbig, George, 65, 171
Herbig-Haro objects, 171
Hercules, 69
Herschel, William, 13–14, 35
Hertzsprung, Ejnar, 7, 10, 38
Hertzsprung-Russell diagram, 37, 38, 82, 191–92
Hiss, Alger, 74
Hitler, Adolf, and astrology, 160, 162
H.M.S. Pinafore (by Gilbert and Sullivan), 22–35
Hoag, Arthur, 68, 94, 127
Hobart, Australia, 108
Hoffleit, Dorrit, 26, 190
Hogg, A. R., 109
Hogg, Helen Sawyer, 24
Holland, 12, 50
Homunculus, of Eta Carinae, 143–44

About the Author

David H. Levy, one of the foremost amateur astronomers in the United States, has discovered eighteen comets, is an expert on variable stars, and has developed astronomy programs for children. His published work includes *Clyde Tombaugh: Discoverer of Pluto* and *The Sky: A User's Guide*, both published in 1991. He writes a column which appears monthly in *Sky and Telescope* magazine, and he lectures frequently around the country. His major awards include the Chant Medal in Canada and the Leslie C. Peltier, G. Bruce Blair, and Amateur Achievement awards in the United States. In 1988 Asteroid 3673 Levy was named in his honor.

BELMONT UNIVERSITY LIBRARY